WOMEN AND RURAL DEVELOPMENT

WOMEN AND RURAL DEVELOPMENT

Dr. Tanuja Trivedi

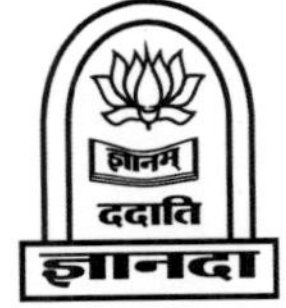

JNANADA PRAKASHAN (P&D)
NEW DELHI

Published by :
JNANADA PRAKASHAN (P&D)
4837/2, 24, Ansari Road, Daryaganj
New Delhi-110002
Phone : 011-23272047
Mobile : 9212137080

Assisted by :
TEXT BOOK PROMOTION SOCIETY OF INDIA
4837/2, 24, Ansari Road, Daryaganj
New Delhi-110002
Phone : 011-23272047
Mobile : 9212137080

Edition: 2016

Women and Rural Development

ISBN: 978-81-7139-332-9

Typesetting by :
Vardhman Computers
New Delhi-110017

Published by Mrs. S. Chowdhary for M/s. Jnanada Prakashan (P&D) Daryaganj, Ansari Road, New Delhi-110 002 and printed at Balaji Offset, Navin Shahdara, Delhi-110032.

PREFACE

The concept of women's empowerment is making deep roots in our country. Gone are the days when Indian women were supposed to see after domestic chores and looks after the upbringing of tiny toddlers. Now, Indian women are not confined to four walls of their homes but spreading their wings like never before. They are marching forward in ever field and making their presence felt in every sphere of life.

Mahatma Gandhi was of the opinion that "India lives in their villages," and it's true even in modern era. Ignoring villages and remotest area means hindrance in the path of our progress and development.

From the period of Vedic age, our women had actively participated in the development and upliftment of rural folk. Their role is applauded and appreciated. Hats off to women's empowerment and awakening that many rural women have emerged in politics, administrative services, scientists, technicians, entertainment, judicial service, and teaching profession.

This book is final product of years of research, field study, face-to-face interaction with rural women in remotest and far-flung areas of our country. We hope that it's informative and entertaining write-ups will delight and guide the readers from the very beginning to the tail end.

CONTENTS

1

EMPOWERMENT OF RURAL WOMEN

Introduction

If NGO employees are advocating behavioural change for self-empowerment such behaviour must also be modelled for successful transmission as suggested in the self-efficacy models of behaviour change. Rural NGOs in India that depend on local population for employees face a limited labour pool who are as likely to be vulnerable to the traditional social pressures and therefore equally marginalised as their clients. This may cause a gap between what the employees may be trained to 'preach' and what they may 'practice' thereby diminishing their effectiveness to motivate change.

This study examines the employees of a successful rural NGO in India that has received accolades for their work in empowerment to establish if the employees actually 'walk the talk'. Using three empowerment instruments, including one developed for this study, we find that employees indeed 'walk the talk' and their index of empowerment is related to their tenure in the NGO. We suggest some policy recommendations based on our findings.

Since the 1990s, women have been identified as key agents of sustainable development and women's equality and empowerment are seen as central to a more holistic approach towards establishing new patterns and processes of development that are sustainable. The World Bank has suggested that empowerment of women should be a key aspect of all social development programmes. Although, a considerable debate on what constitutes empowerment exists, in this chapter we find it useful to rely on Kabeer's definition: "The expansion in people's ability to make strategic life choices in a context where this ability was previously denied to them." For women in India, this suggests empowerment in several realms: personal, familial, economic and political.

Empowerment of Poor Women

Since the 1980s, the Government of India has shown increasing concern for women's issues through a variety of legislation promoting the education and political participation of women. International organisations like the World Bank and United Nations have focussed on women's issues especially the empowerment of poor women in rural areas. In the late 1980s and early 1990s, non-governmental organisations (NGOs) have also taken on an increased role in the area of women's empowerment. NGOs, previously catering to women's health and educational needs, have moved beyond this traditional focus to addressing the underlying causes of deprivations through promoting the economic and social empowerment of women.

There are many challenges that face NGOs who make it their goal to empower women. This chapter addresses one specific challenge that is faced by NGOs located in rural areas that wish to promote women's empowerment. These NGOs have little or no access to skilled social workers. They must often depend on the local population for their employees, employees who may be vulnerable to the similar social pressures and are often equally marginalised as their clients. For rural NGOs to be successful they must attract employees who must at some level be relatively more empowered than the clients. They must have certain credibility to be able to effectively persuade their marginalised clients to alter their ways of thinking on many long-standing traditional issues, such as dowries, child labour, and patriarchal subjugation.

The literature of behaviour change in the health field suggests that self-efficacy is one of the four most commonly cited constructs for behavioural change [1]. Although stated for different purposes and from different perspectives, the literature on self-efficacy can be brought to bear on issues of empowerment. Self-efficacy determines when an individual will undertake new behaviours such as self-empowerment. Low self-efficacy beliefs of women in rural India often stem from the limited and disadvantaged positions women have in society. This makes any behavioural change towards self-empowerment difficult if it merely relies on verbal persuasion. The best way by which self-efficacy is acquired is by combining persuasion with role modelling in a supportive and appreciative environment.

Limitation of Rural NGOs

NGO employees must model empowered behaviours in order to evoke sustained behaviour modification for the empowerment of women they serve. Rural NGOs, who have to often depend on the same local pool for clients and employees, find it difficult to promote empowerment effectively. Despite the training given to employees to promote empowerment among their clients, there may still be a gap between what the employees 'preach' and what they may 'practice' in their own lives. This, in turn, may make them less effective and impede the NGO from achieving its goals.

In this chapter we seek to explore how a relatively small and isolated rural NGO at the foothills of the Himalayas has been successful in the empowerment of rural women living in highly patriarchal and traditional societies.

Background

Chinmaya Rural Training Centre (CRTC) is a successful rural NGO in India that has received accolades for its success in empowering the women of the region and drawing them out of the cycle of dependency. CRTC is located in an impoverished village of Sidhbari, in Himachal Pradesh, nestled in the foothills of the Himalayas. The vast majority of the population is made up of landless poor and unskilled people who have few opportunities for full-time employment. Villagers work the land, owned by a handful of upper caste families. As agricultural activity is seasonal and ceases in the winter months the employees are underemployed. Hence many of them eke out a living through subsistence farming around their homes and are involved in local trade that is generally not profitable. They belong to many of the lower castes and tribes that are categorised by the Indian Government as 'Other Backward Classes' (OBC).[2]

CRTC was the founded by Swami Chinmayananda, a revered Hindu spiritual leader, who chose one of the most depressed areas of the Himachal Pradesh to start a religious centre to practice his beliefs as well as an NGO that would empower local women. Sustainable development of the region, he believed, was only possible if the women were uplifted and could contribute to the success of their family and community. Dr. Kshama Metre, a follower in his religious centre and a practicing pediatrician in New Delhi, took on the leadership of this NGO in 1985.

Starting in relatively small way with a donation of a few sewing machines, Dr. Metre, single-mindedly pursued the vision of empowering the women of the dismal rural area. From this humble beginning, she infused energy and vision to make this organisation into a large well-funded NGO currently serving over 27,000 clients spanning 900 villages offering a variety of programmes that included literacy and health services to sanitation, micro-finance and legal aid.[3] Though women are regarded as the primary focus, by extending their services to include the families of these women where relevant, CRTC ends up serving the entire village community. The effect of empowerment of women creates a powerful influence on the norms, values and finally the laws that govern these communities.

Research Questions

In this chapter we seek to explore how CRTC, a relatively small and isolated rural NGO in the foothills of the Himalayas, has been successful in the empowerment of rural women living in highly patriarchal and traditional societies. The Indian Government as well as CIDA profiles CRTC as a model NGO in the arena of women's empowerment (CIDA, Oct 31, 2000[4]). In particular, we investigate the employees at CRTC, who come from the same villages as the clientele, and examine whether they are significantly different in their levels of empowerment than those they help. Is a gap between the rhetoric and reality of empowerment among the employees? Are employees whose aim is to empower women, empowered themselves? Do they practice what they preach? We seek to uncover the reasons for their success.

Review of Literature

To understand the change, women undergo in becoming empowered we look at two sets of literature: behaviour change and women's empowerment. In the first set of literature we review what leads to successful change, and in the second set of literature we review what is understood as empowerment for women.

Behavioural Change

We first start with a review of the self-efficacy literature and focus on the criteria for successful behaviour change. Bandura suggests that a person's self-expectations determine whether or not certain behaviour will be undertaken, the extent of effort expended by the individual, and whether the individual can persist in the face of challenges encountered. This notion of self-efficacy is mediated by a person's beliefs or expectations about his/her ability to achieve certain tasks effectively or exhibit certain behaviours.

For example, individuals with low self-efficacy regarding their behaviour limit their participation when making difficult behaviour changes and are more likely to give up when faced with obstacles. Their efficacy beliefs about themselves serve as barriers to change, and in this case, their own empowerment. Furthermore, these authors state that self-efficacy is not necessarily an in-born but it and can be acquired and nurtured. This fact makes these concepts particularly relevant to our study. Bandura identifies four ways in which self-efficacy and self-efficacy expectations are acquired: performance accomplishments, vicarious learning, verbal persuasion and physical/affective status.

Performance accomplishments are beliefs that stem from the reactions with which individual accomplishments are greeted. A negative assessment can lower confidence and self-efficacy beliefs; conversely a positive assessment encourages self-efficacy beliefs and the self-efficacy expectations that similar behaviours will be well received in the future. *Vicarious learning* results in beliefs that are acquired by observing modelling behaviours. When the modelling behaviour is undertaken within similar contexts[5] such as gender, economic and social class it presents a realistic option. Thus, one of the most effective strategies for enhancing self-efficacy beliefs and self-efficacy expectations is that modelling behaviour is context specific. It is of little use for a woman of low social class to observe the success of an entrepreneurial woman born to a family of high social standing with access to resources that are unavailable to the poor woman.

Other ways such as '*verbal persuasion*' and '*affective status*[6]' encourage self-efficacy. Persuading women to attempt positive behaviour change and providing a supportive environment in which women can attempt change, further enhances self-efficacy. Changes based on verbal persuasion, affective status and modelling behaviour can lead to significant changes in self-beliefs and self-expectation. These 'personal factors' according to Bandura and Pajares, from an integral part of a triadic relationship necessary for change. They suggest that there is a reciprocal relationship between 'personal factors', 'behaviour' and 'environmental factors', which result in social change.

Changes in personal factors (such as self-efficacy) can affect an individuals' behaviour (willingness to take risks), which can impact on environmental factors (family and society). These relationships are reciprocal and reinforce each other. This suggests that strategies purposefully introduced in order to enhance women's personal factors (self-efficacy) can lead to reinforcing behaviours (such as self assertive behaviour) which in turn can impact and reinforce environmental factors (such as alteration of familial relations). The interaction and reciprocity of the triadic relationship can result in a positive and significant change for women.

Women's Empowerment

Although the notion of women's empowerment has long been legitimised by international development agencies[7], what actually comprises empowerment, and how it is measured, is debated in the development literature. Malhotra, Schuler and Boender, 2002 provide an excellent review of this debate. They review the many ways that empowerment can be measured and suggest that researchers pay attention to the process in which empowerment occurs.

The frequently used Gender Empowerment Measure (GEM) is a composite measure of gender inequality in three key areas: Political participation and decision-making, economic participation and decision-making and power over economic resources. It is an aggregate index for a population and does not measure Empowerment on an individual basis. It is made up of two dimensions: Economic participation and decision-making (measured by the percentage of female administrators and managers, and professional and technical employees), and political participation and decision-making (measured by the percentage of seats in parliament held by women). For our purposes, GEM is limited and does not capture the multidimensional view of women's empowerment. It cannot be assumed that if a development intervention promotes women's empowerment along a particular dimension that empowerment in other areas will necessarily follow. A number of studies have shown that women may be empowered in one area of life while not in others.

While we do not attempt to resolve this debate, we take the position, that women's empowerment can be measured by factors contributing to each of the following: their personal, economic, familial, and political empowerment. We make a point to include household and interfamilial relations as we believe is a central locus of women's disempowerment in India. And by including the political, we posit that women's empowerment measures should include women's participation in systemic transformation by engaging in political action.

Amin, Becker and Bayes split the concept of women's empowerment into three components each measured separately: Inter-spouse consultation index, which seeks to represent the extent to which husbands consult their wives in household affairs; Individual autonomy indices which represents women's self-reported autonomy of physical movement outside the house and in matters of spending money; and the Authority index, which reports on actual decision-making power (which is traditionally in the hands of the patriarch of the family). These indices are similar to those of used by Balk in her 1994 study. Comparable components of empowerment are included in the eight indicators by Hashemi: mobility, economic security, ability to make a small purchases, ability to make larger purchases, involvement in major decisions, relative freedom from domination by the family, political and legal awareness, and involvement in political campaigning and protests.

Several different efforts have been made in recent years to develop comprehensive frameworks delineating the various dimensions along which women can be empowered. We construct four separate components of empowerment in Table 1 that draw from many of the authors mentioned earlier and especially rely on Hashemi (1996) and Amin Becker and Bayes, (1998), as their work seems most relevant for rural women in India.

These measures in Table 1 reflect our belief that to measure women's empowerment more fully and in the broadest sense, it is necessary to add an individualised component representing her political autonomy to the autonomy within the family. Given that the legislation in India reserves special seats for women in elected bodies, even at the village level, an empowerment index for rural women should include her awareness of political issues and participation in the political process.[8]

Methodology

As this chapter seeks to explore how a relatively small and isolated rural NGO in the foothills of the Himalayas has become a model for the development and empowerment of rural disenfranchised women, a few words on the choice of the NGO are appropriate. Using a database from the directorate of NGOs in India[9] we examined several successful women-led NGOs in different parts of India. The criteria for inclusion were that the NGO cater to rural women of lower castes who face traditional gender and class discrimination.

Table 1: Empowerment Measures

Personal Autonomy Index	Generally(1) Occasionally (1/2) Never (0)
Visiting respondents' parental home	
Visiting Hospital	
Visiting village market	
Helping a relative with money	
Setting money aside for respondent's use	
Family Decision Making Index	Wife Alone (1) Joint Decision (1/2) Husband Alone (0)
Children's education in school	
Family planning	
Family day-to-day expenditures	
Going outside of home	
Medical treatment	
Entertaining guests	

(Table contd...)

Buying respondent's traditionally	
Favourite things	
Economic Domestic Consultation Index	Generally(1) Occasionally (1/2) Never (0)
Buying household furniture and utensils	
Purchase of land	
Education/expense of children	
Purchasing Medical treatment of family	
Purchasing women's clothes	
Purchasing children's clothes	
Purchasing daily food	
Political autonomy index	Generally(1) Occasionally (1/2) Never (0)
Voting according to own decision	
Awareness of any political issue	
Participating in any public protest	
Campaigning politically	
Standing for elections	

We also stipulated that the NGO must be a successful grass roots organisation that has the empowerment of women as its mission. It should have received attention for its success both locally and internationally, and whose founder/director had time to meet with us and would allow us to survey the employees. After a limited search, based on telephone calls, we decided to use the Chinmaya Rural Training Centre (CRTC) as it met our criteria, and the Director assured us her cooperation. CRTC has received attention nationally; the Director has been given awards for her work on the empowerment of rural women (Dr. Metre has been featured in *Prophets of New India*, 2004, a book that celebrates heroes who have committed their lives to making a difference. She has been listed as 'The Woman of the Year' in *The Week* magazine, 1993, which annually features a 'Man or Woman of the Year', each of whom has worked to help disadvantaged people and communities) CRTC has also been identified by the Canadian International Development Agency (CIDA) as their 'flagship' NGO that dealt with women's empowerment (CIDA, 2000)[10]. The Centre was identified in 1998 by the NABARD (a Government organisation for agricultural and rural development) as a mother N.G.O. (non-government organisation) for training of N.G.Os.

CRTC empowers women by increasing their ability to contribute to their families' support as well. Concurrently, it undertakes a variety of intervention strategies to attend to the psychological and social well being of women and encourages them to take part in the political process in their villages. CRTC is a successful NGO on a variety of scales. Whether using Korten's 'generational strategies', or Uvin et al's measures of 'scaling up', or Kassam and Handy's (2001) measures of 'vertical integration', CRTC rates high in meeting the goals of women's empowerment.

Research Methods

Ethnographic and survey research was undertaken at CRTC. Face to face interviews were conducted with CRTC's employees, and participant observation of the meetings and activities that took place at CRTC during two weeks in January in 2003 followed by visit in March 2004 to present our findings and tie up some loose ends. We also observed and documented the various programmes at the village level where the women gathered at a prearranged time to participated in a variety of programmes.

To document the levels of empowerment among women in the NGO, we drew our data from the employees who were responsible for the services that were designed to empower the rural village women. At the leadership level we interviewed nearly all of the Supervisors (15/16) of the various programmes. These Supervisors administered the 'Field workers' who went into the villages and worked directly with the village women. We interviewed 32 of the 57 Fieldworkers who assisted the Supervisors. We also chose to interview 25 local women living the area that the NGO served. They represented women who were eligible to be among the Recipients' of the services of the NGO, by the fact they lived in the areas the NGO served.

Although these are potential recipients we call them 'Recipients' for convenience. We chose not to interview current recipients of services, as we wanted to establish a baseline of empowerment among the village women from whom the employees were drawn. As all of the employees lived in the neighbouring villages before seeking employment (and still continue to live in these villages) the findings on the empowerment indices of the 'Recipients' may also be seen to reflect the those of the employees *before* coming to the NGO.

We chose to interview women employees ('Supervisors' and 'Fieldworkers') and eligible women 'Recipients' to ascertain the main research question, of whether the employees were 'walking the talk' and if the employees were significantly different from the recipients. In other words, did the women employees who intervened to help promote the empowerment of women were themselves empowered. We were seeking to establish whether the employees own individual levels of empowerment were significantly different from the recipients of the services. Furthermore, we interviewed individuals at both levels of hierarchies in the organisation to ascertain if all employees had same or differing levels of empowerment.

Opportunistic Sample

We decided to interview half of the 'Fieldworkers'. We ended up with a sample of 32/57 of 'Fieldworkers'. The latter was an opportunistic sample, in that we simply interviewed all the employees who happened to be present in the CRTC headquarters on the days we visited. During the period we visited the NGO, there was a rotation of the 'Fieldworkers' assigned to duties at villages coming in to meet with the 'Supervisors'. We were, thus, able to interview 32 of the 'Fieldworkers'.

The sample of women eligible to be recipients was done by employing two of the NGO employees to visit every third house in the village and identify women who would be likely potential recipients. We were able to get a sample of 25 women who were willing to be interviewed. Two 'Supervisors' helped us fine tune and translate our instrument for the 'Recipients', which included the measures of women's empowerment used for the employees. Additionally, we trained one local woman to undertake the interviews due to their fluency in the language.[11]

To get a better understanding of how the NGO worked, and how the employees were selected and trained, we conducted several interviews conducted with the Director, Dr. Kshama Metre, over the course of two weeks. These interviews ranged from short half an hour discussions to longer two-hour conversations. Dr Metre also invited us to visit the weekly meetings held with all staff so we could observe first hand the training and interactions. We also attended six meetings in the villages held by staff with the clients to observe their interactions as well.

Findings

In this section, we turn to the findings obtained from the interviews. We present our findings as follows: Section A presents general demographic data of all three groups of respondents: 'Supervisors', 'Fieldworkers' and 'Recipients' and examines for any differences in these three groups; Section B presents empowerment levels of all three groups of respondents and a statistical analysis of the data and Section C presents qualitative findings on the NGO-based on interviews with the executive director of the NGO who has run the NGO for the last nineteen years.

Section B: Demographic and Socio-economic Profile

The women in our study are all from the district of Sidhbari, Himachal Pradesh. There is a wide age spread in the total number of respondents (72).[12] They range in age from 21 to 65; most women are married and lived with their husbands and have an average of 2.74 children. Only five women in our study did not live with a spouse, three of the women are divorced and two are widowed. Divorce is not common in the rural areas and the general tradition is to put up with an abusive spouse or a bad marriage.

With reference to caste 89% (64/72) of the women categorise themselves as low caste or 'OBC' (Other Backward Classes). This is a 'catch all' category developed by the Government of India census to include some of the most marginalised caste segments of Indian society. Four of the 'Supervisors' belong to the higher castes, as do two of the 'Fieldworkers' and one from the group of 'Recipients'.

Family structure is relevant to discussion of empowerment. As many of the questions relate to domestic decisions-making to establish empowerment levels family structures can influence the responses. The traditional family structure in India is not a nuclear family, it a joint family.

In this system, when a son marries, he continues to reside with his parents with his wife and their children. The daughter on the other hand goes to her husband's home and lives with his parents, unmarried siblings, and the families of his married brothers. The parents of the husband, in a joint family, tend to hold decision-making authority that often overrides the authority of any of the married sons or their wives. Twenty-nine of the seventy two (40.28%) women in our study live in traditional joint families, whereas the rest lived in a nuclear family setting, which is far less than the norm in Himachal Pradesh of over 50% (Niranjan Sureender & Rao, 1998). The women had an average of 6.13 years of education (The literacy rate in Himachal Pradesh is 77.13% which is much above the national average of 65.38%; Male literacy is 86% and female literacy is 68%.

Alochal Consumption

In this area where alcoholism is rampant, we asked our respondents if they had problems related to alcohol consumption. We find that half of the women (36) suggested that they had experienced problems related to the alcohol consumption by their husbands. This ranged from beatings and the use of household money for alcohol to unemployment. The differences between the groups were striking, in that the least amount of alcoholism was present in the families of 'Fieldworkers', (6/32) and the most in the 'Recipients' (23/25), where as the half the 'Supervisors' experienced alcohol related problems.

We then compared the differences of the means of several socio demographic variables and the means of the empowerment index between the three groups: 'Supervisors', 'Fieldworkers' and 'Recipients', to see if they differed significantly on any of the socio demographic variables and empowerment levels (See Table 2). While they appeared significantly different on the number of all counts with the exception of age, the Scheffe Post Hoc test showed that not all the differences were significant.

TABLE 2

Comparison of Means of Socio-Economic Data and Empowerment Index for 'Supervisors', 'Fieldworkers' and 'Recipients'

Mean	Super-visors	Field-workers	Recipients	ANOVA F Test 3 groups	T-Test for 2 groups S and F Sig 2-tailed
Age	40	38.94	36.64	0.818	0.669
No. of Kids	3	2	3	5.117*	.048*
Income class	1.79	1.65	1.32	5.348*	0.357
Years of Education	10.27	8	1.4	51.380**	.032*
Years in NGO	10.53	6.4	N/a	N/a	.008**
Empowerment Index	21.72	17.47	9.4	37.815**	.007**

* Correlation is significant at the 0.05 level.

** Correlation is significant at the 0.01 level.

Scheffe Post Hoc tests reveals that for the variables Education and Income class there were no significant differences between the 'Supervisors' and 'Fieldworkers', but both groups of employees were significantly different from the 'Recipients'. This is not surprising, as NGO employees need to be literate and have education to be hired as professional employees.

The (income) class variable asked respondents to choose between three classes income: high, middle or low. The results show that respondents only chose either low or middle. This is expected given the poverty level in this area. We find that there were no significant differences between the 'Supervisors' and 'Fieldworkers', but both groups of employees were significantly different from the 'Recipient' group. This may be explained by the fact that NGO employees earn a steady income while the 'Recipient' group do not have a steady income and are dependent on the local economy. Only six of the 'Recipient' group worked outside the home as compared to all the 'Fieldworkers' and 'Supervisors'.

Finally, the Scheffe Post Hoc test shows significant differences between all three groups on the empowerment index. Each group was significantly different from the other. In the next section, we examine this finding closely.

Section B: Empowerment Levels of Respondents

There is a clear downward slide in rates of empower-ment as one descends the ranks of 'Supervisors', 'Fieldworkers' and 'Recipients'. Table 3 gives the individual and aggregate scores on the Empowerment index (E-Index) for the three groups. Comparing the E-index between these groups, we find that it is significantly different between these three groups.[13]

Furthermore, we note as mentioned above, the Scheffe Post Hoc test reveals significant differences in the E-Index between the 'Recipients' and the two employee groups of the NGO. This confirms our initial hypothesis, that NGO employees whose job is to empower the poor and disenfranchised village women do not only resort to rhetoric but also live their own lives significantly differently from that of their clientele. In other words, they 'walk the talk' in their own daily lives.

TABLE 3

Empowerment Indexes for 'Supervisors', 'Fieldworkers' and 'Recipients'

Group	Personal Autonomy Index	Family Decision-Making Index	Economic Consultation Index	Political Autonomy Index	Aggregate E-INDEX
'Supervisors'	5.73	5.27	5.23	5.49	21.72
'Fieldworkers'	4.33	4.33	4.36.	4.45	17.47
'Recipients'	3.02	3.02	2.54	0.82	9.4
All groups	4.17	4.07	3.91	3.41	15.55

As we observed patterns of significant differences in the E-Index between the "Fieldworkers" and "Supervisors" we attempt to uncover the underlying factors that may account for this difference. The literature suggests several factors of influence: age, education, income, and family structure. To this mix we add their 'tenure in the NGO'. We do this as we believe being in contact with the mission and values of the NGO, that promotes the empowerment of women, must affect their daily lives.

Review of the Independent Variables in our Model: Age: Mason, pointed out that a woman's behaviour varies across the stages in the life cycle. As a woman grows older, experience can teach her to stand up for her own rights. As her children grow older and are less dependent on her she can assert herself better without the threat to her children's well being. Also within the traditional family structure, as a woman gets older and her sons get married and her own in-laws grow older and die, the Indian woman is promoted from the comparatively obedient daughter-in-law to the role of a mother-in-law, the one 'who must be obeyed'.

Family Structure: A women's role in household decision-making: control over money matters and other important household matter is a function of the family structure (Malhotra and Mather 1997). Whether a woman lives in a joint family (which includes the mother in law), or where she is a mother in law, or if she lives in nuclear family structure will impact her autonomy. We expect that in a joint family she will have less autonomy than in a nuclear family structure. Of course this may be mitigated by age as discussed above.

Education: It has been argued that one of the indicators of empowerment. Indeed, many of the variables that have traditionally been used as proxies for empowerment, such as education and employment, are better described as "enabling factors" or "sources of empowerment". Empowerment includes cognitive and psychological elements, such as a women's understanding of her condition of subordination and the causes of such conditions. This requires an understanding the self and the cultural and social expectations, which may be enabled by education (Stromquist, 1995) Hence we expect education to be positively linked to the E-Index, as human capital will facilitate empowerment.

Tenure at NGO: If the NGO is providing models of empowerment through its leadership and core values, we expect that association and the length of tenure with the NGO will effect the E- Index positively. Although, education may be an enabling factor as suggested above, experiences (of self and others) allows a woman to see that the lack or autonomy in her life choices not as a given but something that can be changed. We expect that the interventions made by the NGO for women in general give the employees the wherewithal on how changes can be made and the impetus to make further changes in their own lives.

Thus, we expect the E-Index to be a function of age, family structure, income class, education and tenure at the NGO. A bivariate analysis reveals that there are no significant correlations among the independent variables and dependent variable except tenure at the NGO.[14] In order to understand the combined effects of all the conceptualised variables, we use a regression model using the data for 'Fieldworkers' and 'Supervisors' combined, we do not include the 'Recipient' group, as they all have zero years at the NGO. This will provide an estimate of the combined explanatory power of the independent variable on the E-Index.

We use the equation

E = F (A, E, I, F, T) where:

EI = E-Index–dependent variable, an aggregate of four separate indexes

E = Education (years of formal education)

A = Age in years,
C = income class (Dummy variable 0= low income, 1= Middle income),
F = family structure (Dummy variable 0= nuclear, 1= Joint family),
T = years of tenure at the NGO

The regression in Table 4 shows that years in the NGO, and education are two significant explanatory variables. In both, the bivariate analysis and the regression model, the years in the NGO are significant. It is interesting to note that education is only significant in the regression model. This suggests, that education, in and of it self, may not be sufficient to give a woman a high E-Index. It is likely that a woman with higher human capital is more receptive to the experiences of a working in an NGO. Thus, we see the explanatory power of education when combined with longer tenure at the NGO.

TABLE 4

Regression Analysis

Linear Regression Model: Dependent Variable: E-Index	**Unstandardised Coefficients**		**Standardised Coefficients**	**t**	**Sig.**
	B	**Std. Error**	**Beta**		**p**
(Constant)	12.524	4.425		2.831	.007
Woman's highest level of education	.423	.210	0.28	2.020	.050
Income Class	-2.600	1.502	-.231	-1.731	0.091
AGE	4.686E-02	.073	.089	.639	0.526
Family Structure	2.067	1.328	.202	1.556	.127
Years in NGO	.548	.131	.538	4.167	.000

R square = .40
N = 47

What needs further explanation is why the variables such as age, income class, education, and family structure were not significant in the regression model. One explanation may be, that given the poor rural environment from which these women originate; the social traditions and disenfranchisement of women were similar regardless of their education or age. The income variation was also fairly minor, as our qualitative notes showed. The respondents were asked to say whether they were classified themselves between upper, middle or lower income classes. Almost all said "lower class."

On some prodding, those with any regular source of income put themselves in the middle class. What is surprising to us is how many women lived in nuclear families still scored low on the E-Index. However, they lived in fairly close proximity to their in laws and extended families, and we think that this negated the influence of family structure

Section C: Qualitative Analysis

The findings in this section rely on many interviews conducted with the Director, Dr. Shama Metre and attending staff and community meetings over the course of two weeks by both authors. We first report on the challenges encountered by Dr. Meter in hiring employees, the training of local employees and how the NGO functioned.

When Dr. Metre chose to expand her NGO she could not afford to import trained employees from neighbouring cities, for two reasons, the costs were fairly substantial and city folk did not like staying in rural areas for any great length of time. Retention is a major problem given the harsh conditions and lack of amenities. Dr Metre took this challenge and turned it into an opportunity to hire local labour. Trained local labour was not available, so Dr Metre identified some of women clients of her NGO who showed qualities of leadership and worked with them.

Single handedly she counseled this small group of poor and marginalised woman and persuaded them they are entitled to a better life, that acceptance of subjugation is not their *karma*. She also made them aware of their legal and constitutional rights. She brought about what she and many of the employees referred to as '*jagruti*' or awakening. The word '*jagruti*' was often repeated in our intensive personal interviews as that moment of epiphany when the women realised that they did not *have* to accept their low status in society as God given – that they could, and should, fight to better their lot. Over a period of time, she was able to change their lives through personal interventions and guidance.

When these women were self-supporting and had confidence in their own capacity to make change, she recruited them to work for her. Only when she had recruited and trained a handful of them did she start new programmes in the NGO, which hitherto had simply been a paediatric clinic. It was a slow process, but Dr. Metre chose to do this intentionally. Her vision was to use these women to help other women, not only through intervention strategies, but also as role models who would encourage local women to stand up for their rights and take charge of their lives. We noted that in the staff meetings and community meetings these homegrown 'Supervisors' and 'Fieldworkers' were quick to share their own experiences and thus were effective models. They showed village women who came to seek assistance from the NGO that they themselves faced similar circumstances could rise above them.

Stimulating community discussions among women through organised village women's groups (Mahila Mandils)—persuade and encourage women to undertake behaviour changes in a supportive atmosphere where every individual effort is lauded. More importantly, the audience can identify with the leaders as they are of the same class, religion and geographical region and are therefore subjected to similar oppression yet they are living examples of empowerment and have managed to rise above the subjugation. This realistic modelling, in an appreciative and supporting atmosphere as we have suggested, is a powerful from of vicarious learning and more likely to motivate behaviour change especially when combined with persuasion in a supportive and appreciative environment earlier.

Though the modelling of homegrown employees is an effective method of empowering women, many of the employees as well as Dr Meter, credited their success to their firm belief in God. This self-efficacy, grounded in a spiritual conviction, is what they conveyed to their clientele. One supervisor put it this way "It is not your *karma* to be subjugated, rather God expects that you take control of your life and help yourself". This message was reflected in many ways by many of the Supervisors and "Fieldworkers". This spirituality, we were told, acts as social glue among the employees and clientele, connects and engenders trust amongst them and gives support to the overall agenda. This is no means an overtly religious NGO; the spirituality is often an unspoken bond and simply frames the norms and values of the organisation.

Several authors have written on the relevance of spiritual and religious capital, and this idea of promoting behaviour change with the added benefit of such capital is gaining currency (Greive & Bingham, 2001; Fowler , 1997; Strachean, 1982; Whitfield, 1985). Further research with spiritual capital in mind may point to the success of CRTC from another perspective. We suggest that because of the frequency with which it was mentioned, and despite the fact that this is not a religious NGO and the fact that our questionnaire did not elicit any information related to religion or spirituality, this issue may have potential in explaining some of our findings. We are unable to say more given our research did not systematically address this point.

Our in depth interviews allowed us a glimpse into the manner in which the 'Supervisors' had managed to transform their own lives before training to assist other women to bring about similar changes into their lives. Although it is not possible to document all their stories what is indicative from our findings is that all of the women employees who had come to the NGO for assistance, despite their education level, would have scored very low on the E-Index before being employed. We give one story to illustrate many of the stories, all of which have common denominators of subjugation, poverty and helplessness.

Murma used to be a poor helpless woman with four children who was beaten regularly by an alcoholic husband. There was not enough money to buy food or clothing for the children and Murma would eke out a subsistence living by begging and borrowing from neighbours and relative. Lacking education, skills and finance, Murma had resigned herself to a dismal fate until she heard of the CRTC programme.

Skeptical that she would be accepted, she ventured to join a women's group run by the NGO and enrolled her children in a children's programme. Thereafter she received informal help with health and welfare services and some training to make her functionally literate. She later joined a micro credit group and received entrepreneurial training. She was spiritually convinced that she could and should improve her lot and help her other sisters achieve the same enlightenment. Murma was one of the first local women hired to work in the NGO 18 years ago.

Today, she owns a mushroom farm and is economically self-sufficient. She even managed to support her errant husband until he died recently. She is now senior supervisor and has also trained in political leadership. Though, she lost in the elections of the local village council or 'panchayat,' she plans to try again. Murma is now a model of empowerment devoted to helping empower other rural women; she also lobbies for change and liaisons with government.

Conclusion and Policy Implications

CRTC is a rural NGO set in the foothills of the Himalayas is a successful NGO with a goal of empowering the poor rural women. CRTC does not have access to trained employees from cities and had to find local women to nurture, empower and train to be responsible and effective employees. This potential disadvantage turned out to be an advantage. By employing women who come from similar backgrounds as their clientele, CRTC was able to have a staff that was able to not only 'walk the talk' but also serve as credible models of the changes that were possible. The high scores in overall empowerment of the 'Supervisors' and 'Fieldworkers' as compared with the potential 'Recipients' confirm this.

Many stories documented by Pelletier, and our own qualitative findings from the interviews, give credence to the fact that these women were indeed marginalised before coming into contact with the NGO. In fact almost all of the 'Supervisors' had come to the NGO as clients seeking assistance, and today score very high on the Empowerment Index as compared to women from the villages where they live (our 'Recipient' group).

Many of the 'Fieldworkers' were also helped by the NGO (in different ways) before they were employed in their current positions. They now live successfully in the same society and within the same traditions as their clientele. Many had experienced similar abuse and subjugations and yet managed to transcend their oppressions with help from the NGO. Today, they score high on the Empowerment Index as compared to women from the villages where they live (our 'Recipient' group). It would have been ideal to measure the E- Index for a woman before she joined the NGO and some years later, however, it was not possible. Hence, we used the random sample from the village (Recipients) as a comparison group. However the stories and documentation of the village women stands testimony to their powerless before they contacted and later joined the NGO.

Our findings on the E-Index for the three groups ('Supervisors', 'Fieldworkers' and 'Recipients') showed significant differences. The traditional variables did not explain these differences. In the regression analysis between the two groups of employees showed that the only explanatory variables were tenure at the NGO and education. It is interesting to note that although there was no correlation between education and E- Index, combined with Tenure at the NGO, education proved to be an explanatory variable. Education is not correlated to the E-Index in any of the groups nor when the three groups are taken as one whole. This lends further credence to the idea that education is an enabling factor and not a measure of empowerment as argued by Kishor.

Hiring practices of local residents as employees makes the NGO sustainable as its resources as well as clientele are from the same region. The NGO does not have to rely on importing any of its labour from the cities, which is expensive, and often with a high turnover rate. Furthermore, the processes by which the NGOs help empower women are closely identified with the four ways suggested by Bandura in which self-efficacy is acquired. The NGO through its hiring, training and empowering process provides all four modes: performance accomplishments, vicarious learning, verbal persuasion and physical/affective status.

We now turn to policy implications of our findings. Woolcock suggested that by paying greater attention to the mechanisms shaping institutional success we can better delineate factors that contribute to success so that these strategies can be deliberately nurtured. With this in mind we ask what lessons can we draw from the experiences of CRTC that can be applied to other rural NGOs?

Our findings suggest that CRTC did not succeed despite having 'homegrown' local employees but because of them. Because 'Fieldworkers' and 'Supervisors' employed by CRTC were from the same environment as the marginalised women they served and because they had risen out of the circumstances that face many of the clients, they served as credible role models. Many rural NGOs face the predicament of finding trained employees. The experience of CRTC suggest that such employees can be found among the clientele and nurtured and trained to take on positions of responsibility.

The traditionally disadvantaged position of poor rural women is reinforced by low self-efficacy beliefs that prevent them from undertaking difficult behaviour changes and the message of NGOs fall on deaf ears. If they do initiate such changes their low self-efficacy beliefs lead them to give up such changes when they meet with any opposition. However when the message comes from leaders who act as realistic models of empowerment the poor and marginalised women are convinced that they can also transform their lives.

If modelling by local employees are seen as one of the most effective ways of empowering subjugated women, then rural NGOs should adopt policies that deliberately target, as employees, some of the poorest and marginalised women from the areas that they wish to serve. These women should be carefully nurtured and helped to overcome traditional barriers and, once they are empowered, they should be trained as 'Supervisors' and 'Fieldworkers' to run an integrated gamut of services that address and enable the various aspects of the lives of the women they hope to serve. This also results in a management style that is grounded in the reality of the experiences lived by the employees and clientele alike. The regular staff meetings is a venue where time is set aside to celebrate the efforts of those trying to change their own lives and that of others. This practice shares indigenous practices with others and nurtures an environment, which allows risk taking.

Further research is necessary on the spiritual underpinnings we found at CRTC. If the spiritual capital enhanced the behaviours we found, this would give faith based NGOs an edge in working with marginalised women. Perhaps, an explicitly shared vision and common values may provide the 'spiritual' capital in the case of secular NGOs. Although, we are not certain how spiritual capital plays out, our results indicate a strong likelihood that 'indigenous' capital provided by local employees will enhance the process of empowerment for women.

NOTES AND REFERENCES

1. Literature review from "Evaluating Primary Care Behavioural Counseling Interventions: An Evidence-based Approach" By Evelyn P. Whitlock, M.D., M.P.H.A, C. Tracy Orleans, Ph.D.b, Nola Pender, R.N., Ph.D., FAANc, Janet Allan, R.N., Ph.D., C.S.d *Am J Prev Med* 2002; 22 (4): 267-84.
2. No firm definition exists for this classification, although it is commonly used and refers to people are identified by their low social position in the traditional caste hierarchy of Hindu society.
3. The main building where CRTC has its offices is a hub of activity where women meet up with other women and attend lectures, puppet shows and sing songs, all conveying the mantra of "you can do it too!" An aura of prayer and spirituality permeates these gatherings and the religious songs are often performed for strength and guidance in meeting goals.
4. Dr. Mètre received the prestigious Ojaswini Award in 2000 for excellence in her field of service (Chinmaya Yuv Kendra Magazine, 2002).
5. In India, where this research is based, we include caste as a determinant of class for successful modelling behaviours.
6. 'Affective status' suggests that people learn best in a supportive environment, people do not easily learn in high stress situations, such as criticism.
7. *Women Key to Effective Development (December 6, 2001)* World Bank Press) *Engendering Development Through Gender Equality in Rights, Resources, and Voice* is a Policy Research Report by the World Bank.
8. Although there are many success stories of women's participation, there is a widespread abuse of this legislation. Often in rural

villages, close examinations of the local Panchayats (elected governing village councils) reveal that men govern behind the women who 'front' so as to comply with this legislation. A spouse or other male family member has put the woman's name forward, and used it to as a front for their own political participation (REFS White, 1992; Goetz and Sen Gupta, 1994))

9. Pre-1996 from the Directory of Organisations working on Gender Issues, and post-1996 organisations from telephone directories and word of mouth.

10. To highlight the successes of the NGOs dealing with women's empowerment, CRTC founder and director Dr. Shama Metre, was chosen as keynote speaker and asked to share her experiences in participatory development in rural areas at a conference on Development in Ottawa organised by CIDA on International Cooperation Days (June 18-20, 2001).

11. Many respondents spoke Pahadi (a local dialect similar to Punjabi) which is understood without great difficulty to Punjabi speakers.

12. This number includes 15 "Supervisors", 32 Field workers and 25 eligible recipients.

13. Using the ANOVA, we get the F statistic 37.815 significant at $p<.001$.

14. Using the T-test for Family structure ($t=1.29$) and Income class ($t=.62$) these are e not significant, $p>.05$. For Years of Tenure at the NGO, Age and Education, only Years of Tenure at the NGO is significant at $p<.01$ (Pearson correlation =0.556 at $p<.01$).

2

EMPOWERMENT OF RURAL WOMEN THROUGH THE PANCHAYAT SYSTEM

Background

India's children and families are fed, clothed and sheltered by the labour of women. Its water and firewood are gathered by the hands of women. Its family farms and rural economy are productive because of women's work. Yet, when men are asked, they say women do nothing at all. Because of women's low social status, their work goes unacknowledged, unvalued and unsupported. Women carry a triple burden. They make indispensable contributions in all areas of rural life and economic activity, particularly in household maintenance, agriculture, and incomegenerating activities.

Woman's role in the conservative patriarchal society of Bihar, is determined more by men, tradition and livelihood patterns. As in the other patriarchal societies, these influences have restricted her role largely to home, hearth, child rearing and those farming activities which have a basis in gender rather than equity.

In the decade of 1980s, a number of developments particularly the movements and struggles during the emergency and post-emergency periods led to more debates on women issues and renewed activity in favour of women. These included an increased focus on women in development in 6th and 7th five year plans. The National Perspective Plan (NPP) for women and the alternative perspective plan offered by the women's movement. The National Front government of V.P. Singh introduced another constitutional 72nd amendment bill in 1990, including in it not less than 1/3rd reservation for women in membership at all levels. In 1991, the Bill was reintroduced in the Parliament by the Congress government which finally became the 73rd amendment of the Constitution, providing reservations for women in rural local self governing bodies.

In December 1992 Indian Parliament passed a new amendment to the Indian Constitution to revive and revitalize the Panchayati Raj—the rural local self government in India. It has mandated representation of at least 33% women through election, thus, legitimised entry of women in a critical mass in the mainstream politics at the grass root level in the whole country and has created political space for women across caste and class. It is a major step for inclusive politics and addressing as it does their continued political marginality it has a potential of changing the existing gender relations.

Women have always and almost everywhere been on the fringe of political and social power. Like other states Bihar is no exception and continues to have marginal representation of its women in political institutions. In our lower house of National Parliament women representatives have increased from 14 (i.e. less than 3%) in 1952 to 43 in 1998 and 47 in the next election. The similar situation continues in the States despite our having had a woman PM and women CMs. Has the formal change brought by the institutional intervention of reservations adequately addressed women's marginality or has it only led to their numerically expanded presence? Has the numerical presence transformed these structures made them more receptive to women's needs and concerns or has patriarchy already succeeded in defeating the intentions of the amendment?

Right to Information

According to the Department of Rural Development, as a result of Panchayat elections in all the states, there are about 3.4 million elected representatives at all levels of Panchayat. Out of this, an overwhelming majority are new entrants, particularly from the weaker sections of society i.e. SC/ST and women. It is necessary to evolve a comprehensive policy of right to information to women Panchayat workers. A strong role for women in political decision-making is the key to the development and implementation of a meaningful state policy for women. The poor participation of women in political decision making is both the cause and effect of gender inequality. Their persistent marginalisation from development processes, demonstrate the urgent need to strengthen their role in political decision-making.

Women Panchayat members' role their own perception of it is quite limited. They think their job is only to inform the Mukhiya about the various needs of their own wards village. More often than not, these are petty constructions/repair/maintenance jobs. That they have any role or say in the implementation phase is not widely shared by them. Their concern is narrowed down to their own village and possibility of larger collaboration for tackling wider issues like water or vegetable cooperative is rarely considered. Block officials are still exercising many of the functions which actually belong to women Panchayat functionaries; Bureaucracy seems reluctant to give up the privileges, on one pretext or the other. There is a widespread agreement that women's influence in the political process remains at the fringes. As women have entered political structures, some doubts and dilemmas have also surfaced. For instance:

- The "genuineness" of women's participation, as compared to "proxy" participation, has become a matter of concern;

- The issue of prerequisites necessary to make women participate has become an imperative that must be addressed;
- They cannot make a more substantive difference unless they are empowered.

If patriarchy is at the root of this situation, will the system not defeat the intentions of the amendment? There are issues of power, authority, hierarchy and control which bring up the essentiality of change in power structures and gender relations, if we hope to see transformed and transformative politics. It was with this endeavour in mind that the idea for empowering the women Panchayat workers through the establishment of an interactive FORUM of Women Panchayat Representatives was conceived. The activities designed for the FORUM (PWPC) would help to develop strategies to empower the women as leaders.

Objective of the FORUM (PWPC)

- To provide a platform to the Women PRIs to share their real life experience as leaders;
- How do they perceive 50% reservation for women in Panchayat elections?
- To create awareness among the women leaders regarding their roles and responsibilities as PRIs;
- To create awareness of Right to Information;
- To create awareness of Education;
- Role as a stakeholder in Gender Budgeting
- To create awareness among the women leaders regarding Migration, Trafficking and HIV/AIDS;
- To analyse the impact of women's participation in Panchayati Raj—A phenomena of their hypervisibility or invisibility?

The compilation of recommendations in the FORUM based on past and future expectations of women Panchayat representatives would serve as a Charter of elected women representatives for the dos and don'ts in the Panchayati Raj system, thus bringing the agenda of women panchayat workers into public policy making.

The Issues Discussed

It was also felt that panchayats in general and the women panchayat representatives in particular will have an important role to play in terms of livelihood in the age of globalisation. Essential services like health and education can be more effectively delivered, provided panchayat members become empowered.

Now that the new Bihar Government has announced 50% reservation for women PRI candidates, will this formal change brought by the institutional intervention adequately address women's marginality, or will it only lead to their numerically expanded presence? Will the numerical presence transform these structures and make them more receptive to women's needs and concerns, or will patriarchy succeed in defeating the intentions of the amendment?

Seeking answers to these crucial questions, the Members of Equity Foundation decided to bring out a CHARTER of Women Panchayat Representatives in the first meeting of FORUM. The matters discussed before the formulation of charter: The FORUM will bring together the various stakeholders to share experiences and evolve a collective strategy for addressing the role of women in grass root politics. Finally, Charter of Demands of elected women representatives was brought out in the first meeting of the FORUM on the 7th day of July.

1. Training

- The present training system and facilities for elected members is totally inadequate. Therefore, the State

Government must immediately allocatead equatere sources for conducting capacity building programmes for the elected representives and functionaries of PRIs. The training programme should include topics like roles and responsibilities of local body representatives (which should include information about present day system, local body elections, and legal competencies of various tiers).

- Setup Panchayat Training Centres for women atleast one in each division, to strengthen the capacity building of women representatives within a year of their election. Local body representatives should be given knowledge about procedures, session conducting skills and agenda preparation for meetings.
- Try to make them capable to attend the meetings more effectively. Make them capable to handle the technical details of the panchayat administration, how different tiers function and their relationship with government.
- Refresher courses be organised atleast once every year. Training programmes for women panchayat members should aim at continuous skill upgradation including internet access to enable them to handle panchayat work with competence and efficiency.
- Provide literacy training under special crash programmes for illiterate women Panchayat members.
- Water Literacy Programme should be implemented in every village on the issue of water conservation and its proper management.

2. Facilitate exchange programmes for panchayat women representatives inside and outside the State.
3. Remove Gender inequality and discrimination in education sector. Gram Panchayats should be given the power to depute the suitable young persons on voluntary basis to work in those schools where there is short age of teachers.

4. Gender Sensitisation of Stakeholders
    - Introduce regular gender sensitive reorientation programmes for the MPs, MLAs, Civil Society and bureaucrats about the funds, functions and functionaries of the Panchayats.
    - Ensure that due consideration is given by authorities at all levels to the proposals of the Gram Sabha, particularly those relating to issues of women and children.
5. Facilitate formation of women's associations at different levels to act as pressure groups on all fronts–community education, better law enforcement and deterrent punishment (female foeticide or trafficking of girl children, domestic rape or harassment at workplace, domestic violence).
6. Law and order
    - Ensure that State Government opens a 'toll free help line' for panchayat women at the state and district levels to attend to emergent needs (adverse or otherwise) of elected women functionaries of PRIs interms of police assistance, information dissemination, legal assistance, counselling, etc., with a view to strengthen women's participation in local governance. The State level helplines should also act as a resource centre.
    - Provide for stringent laws to deal with those committing violence against women candidates during and after elections.
    - The State Government should hold Lok Adalat (monthly) to resolve legal problems at the Panchayat level.
    - All women's police stations should be established or posting of a Mahila (female) officer in every Thana should be ensured.
    - Provide right to land and housing in joint names of spouses and for single, deserted, Dalit, tribal, widowed and battered women, and for those rendered homeless in caste/communal riots and due to displacement.

- Strictly implement the law regarding equal wages for women.
- We demand that the Government should develop schemes for constituting electric crematoriums in every Panchayat so as to eradicate the existing castes crimination even in burial grounds.

7. Incentive

- We urge the Government of Bihar that, Instead of giving allowances and honorarium to the Panchayat Representatives, the Government should make anamendment to the Bihar Panchayats Act, ensuring salaries to them, as that of the Kerala and Karnataka Panchayats Act.

8. Ensure Responsibility

- All Centrally Sponsored Schemes and State development programmes in Bihar must be brought under the Local Government Institutions for the implemention.
- Ensure that the government provides funds for celebrating women's empowerment day at the state and district levels. For demarcating powers between different tiers of PRIs, the State Government should take necessary administrative steps for making of "activity mapping" exercise into concrete reality based on principle of subsidiarity.
- Right to collect professional tax, entertainment tax and toll tax should be endowed with village Panchayats and Municipalities

9. Strengthening the Accounting & Audit System/Social Audit of the Panchayats:

Considering the resolve of the State Government to devolve untied funds to the Panchayats, there is a need to strengthen accounting and auditing, and most important social audit at the Panchayat level. Thus, we urge the State Government to provide powers to Gram Sabha with regard to the approval of development projects, beneficiary selection and social audit. The findings of social audit should be acted upon:

- Awareness about schemes and programmes and the role of PRIs and other departments in those schemes.
- Principles of transparency, accountability and community participation with a view to improving service delivery and setting service delivery standards.
- Participatory planning and monitoring, including greater involvement over planning and monitoring the activities of the local bureaucracy.
- Internal committee dynamics, and in particular ensuring effective participation of women, SC and STR epresentatives.

10. In order to solve the serious problem of poor infrastructure of Panchayats in the State, adequate infrastructure including own building and IT infrastructure should be made available to all the village panchayats. It is matter of great concern that even after the allocation of funds by the Government of India through the Ministry of Information and Technology for computerisation of all the Panchayats in the State. The progress has not been satisfactory in creation of e-panchayats till date.
11. The institution of ombudsman to address grievances and check irregularities must be taken up immediately as in case of Kerala.
12. The State should undertake to develop a new administrative operating system for the Panchayats based upon the devolution of functions, funds and functionaries and for which it should develop the following manuals for the Panchayats:
    - Budget Manual
    - Accounts Manual
    - Audit Manual

- Procurement Manual
- Office Management System
- Management Manuals for transferred institutions
- Public Works execution Manual
- Fiscal Responsibility Legislation for the PRIs.

13. Performance audit should be done to review the actual performance, physical and financial, vis à vis the annual targets and identify the constraints in achieving the target.
    - Creating Competition amongst the Panchayats With a view to promoting healthy competition amongst the Panchayats the State Government will consider to identify 'beacon' Panchayats and awarding 'Swaraj' Trophies to them, for excellence in performance at all levels. A Committee comprising the Panchayat members, Members of Legislative Assemblies and Councils and experts from other walks of life will be set up to identify and institutionalise the best practices developed by the Panchayats.
    - Give awards for outstanding performance by women representatives at all levels of the panchayats in the state.

14. Information
    - Provisions of accurate information regarding HIV/AIDS, its treatment, care, training of health care providers at all levels required.
    - Doctors, functional testing equipment and ambulances must be made available in all PHCs. Ensure counselling and help lines to enable people to live positively despite graveillness.
    - Construction of Safe and hygienic Delivery rooms in every Panchayat.
    - A Library Cum Information Centre should be established in every village so as to provide opportunities for dissemination of information about development schemes

alongwith necessary information and knowledge pertinent to the common life of people is made possible. This should be linked to egovernance.

- Implementation and creation of favourable environment and seeking of desired cooperation for programme like Sarva Shiksha Abhiyan, IGP National Rural Employment Guarantee Scheme, and Right to information etc. meant for livelihood supports such as Old Age Pension, widow Pension and social welfare programmes as well.

15. Construction of Panchayat Bhavan.
16. Ban Alcoholism.
17. Panchayat *Prahari* should be for medine very village to check migration.
18. Women's special buses should be introduced.
19. And finally ensure equality and efficiency in Gender Budgeting why?

Women's empowerment is not a new concept. Yet, in the midst of huge allocations of outlays and revenues, the government very often loses sight of this priority that has been established for women's issues.The outcome of many new programmes that were started in the last plan to benefit women, are not known, such as the NRHM and Sarva Shiksha Abhiyan. Despite heavy budgetary provisions, the quality of ICDS centres is very deplorable and in so me are as centres have also failed to deliver. The allowance and pensions for widowed women neverr each them and their own child renturn them out of their houses.

When officials are questioned, the explanation that is given is very little resources and limited budget or the money was not released by the ministry or circular or permission was not given in time. The mindset towards gender is not sensitive, While drawing up the budget, it is important to realise that the allocations for women are not mere numbers they are the lives of women, of girls who do not go to school or those pregnant mothers who died enroute to hospital, due to lack of transport. Therefore, there should be a proper mechanism to keep vigil on the flow of benefits to women from the schemes and plans so that the funds reach those for whom they are meant.

Even today, there are no separate chapter for women and children in the State plan. Gender issues are always covered under the category of social welfare such as health nutrition, education and labour. Thus, while preparing the budget women's need should be made visible. Women's exploitation, proximity to health care and CHCs must be taken into consideration while building roads and infrastructure. There is a growing awareness that women are left out of the developmental process.

There is acompelling need to take steps to ensure a fair allocation of government budgetary resources to women. Gender inequity has to be removed from the budget making process and it should be made inclusive.

Utilisation of Resources

For implementation of the plan, gender sensitive budgetary provisions, proper, efficient and effective utilisation of allocated resources, crucial role of elected women representatives is felt. But they are unaware of their financial powers (Implementation of budget and relevance of gender sensitive budgeting). Very few *Mukhiyas* (Head) have undertaken significant initiative in various developmental projects in their village, such as improving roads, the local school, investing in clean running water, in public and private sanitation projects and in pensions for widows. They have no participation in allocation of Panchayat budget. The issues, often ignored by men, range from health and sanitation to campaigns against alcoholism and domestic violence. At the first decade of this new millennium, many of the entrenched social evils that have persisted for thousands of years will begin to change if women panchayat representatives are made aware of gender sensitive budget.

We need to push Government to adopt these demands of women in spirit and in letter within laws and policies. Likewise, we need to press Government to ensure enabling conditions for all women PRIs in Bihar to attain equality of status as well as equal access to services as part of their basic human rights. Today, we dedicate this Charter to all women living in Bihar. With grief, we remember the women candidates or their family members who have needlessly died due to violence. We raise our voices against these denials of rights as violations of women's human rights. In salute to all women survivors of individual and structural violence, we pledge to fight discrimination, oppression and marginalisation and to move towards peace and justice and empowerment.

NOTES AND REFERENCES

Crook, Isabel, Lu Dongxiao, Lisa Stearns, 1995. "A conversation with Wu Qing," in *A Rising Public Voice: Women in Politics Worldwide,* Alida Brill (ed.). NY: Feminist Press. pp 41-57.

Edwards, Louise, & Mina Roces, eds., 2000. *Women in Asia: Tradition, Modernity and Globalisation.* Ann Arbor: U. of Michigan Press.

Florini, Ann H. (ed.) 2000. *The Third Force: the Rise of Transnational Civil Society.* Washington, DC: Carnegie Endowment for International Peace.

Fraser, Arvonne & Irene Tinker, editors, forthcoming. *Networking for Change: Women and International Development.* New York: Feminist Press.

Ganguly-Scrase, Ruchira, 2000. "Diversity and the status of women: the Indian experience," in *Women in Asia: Tradition, Modernity and Globalisation,* Louise Edwards and Mina Roces, editors. Ann Arbor: U. of Michigan Press, pp. 85-111.

Jayawardena, Kumari, 1995. *The White Woman's Other Burden.* London: Routledge.

—, 1986. *Feminism and Nationalism in the Third World.*

Kabeer, Naila, 1994. *Reversed Realities: Gender Hierarchies in Development Thought.* London: Verso.

Lee, In-ho. 1995. "Work, education, and women's gains: the Korean experience," in *The Politics of Women's Education: Perspectives from Asia, Africa, and Latin America,* Jill Conway and Susan Bourque, editors. Ann Arbor: U. of Michigan Press. pp. 77-104.

Loutfi, Martha Fetherolf (ed.) 2001. *Women, Gender and Work: What is Equality and How do we get it?* Geneva: ILO.

Moser, Caroline O. N., 1993. *Gender Planning and Development: Theory, Practice and Training.* London: Routledge.

Nussbaum, Martha & Jonathan Glover, eds. 1995. *Women, Culture and Development: A Study of Human Capabilities.* New York: Oxford University, Press.

Sen, Amartya, 1999. *Development as Freedom.* New York: Anchor Books.

Shiva, Vandana, 2001. "Golden rise and neem: biopatents and the appropriation of women's environmental knowledge," *Women's Studies Quarterly,* special issues on Earthwork" *Women and Environments,* 29/172:12-23.

Silliman, G. Sidney & Lela G. Noble, 1997. *Non-Governmental Organizations in the Philippines: Civil Society and the State.* Honolulu:U of Hawaii Press.

Sizoo, Edith (ed.) 1997. *Women's Lifeworlds: women's narratives on shapting their realities.* London: Routledge.

Tinker, Irene (ed.) 1990. *Persistent Inequalities: Women and World Development.* New York : Oxford University Press.

Tinker, Irene, & Gale Summerfield, eds. 1999. *Women's Rights to House and Land: China, Laos, Vietnam.* Boulder CO: Lynne Rienner.

Todd, Helen. 1996. *Women at the Center: Grameen Bank Borrowers After One Decade.* Boulder CO: Westview.

UN 2000. *Human Development Report, 2000.* NYC: UNDP.

3

RURAL WOMEN AND PANCHAYATS

The Millennium Development Goals (MDGs) have also highlighted the various issues concerning. The goals include the eradication of extreme hunger and poverty, universal primary education, gender equality, empowerment for women, reduction of child mortality, improvement of maternal health, combating HIV/AIDS, malaria and other diseases as well as ensuring environmental sustainability and developing a global partnership for development. All these goals assume additional significance once it is realised that women suffer a lot of deprivation due to lack of achieving the above goals. As for example, it is well known that majority of the poor in the world are found among women, the percentage of illiteracy among the women is higher than those of men, and access to primary health care is always denied to large percentage of women so on so forth.

Realising the above picture, various governments have been taking various measures to improve the conditions of women. Indian government is no exception. Along with various measures such as providing micro-credit to women, the government has also amended the Constitution in 1993 in which the local government institutions have been given a new lease of life to plan and execute the local development planning in which not less than one-third seats have been reserved for women. The local government institutions are known as panchayats or village councils in India. According to 73rd Constitution Amendment Act, 1993, the panchayats have been given tenure of five years, an election and a finance commission, 29 subjects to plan and execute and a wide, based participation at the grassroots level. Interestingly, the 29 subjects given to panchayats include eradicating the poverty to providing primary education as well as the other aspects of well-being of the villagers. In other words, the panchayats have been involved in the task of fulfilling the MDG in a participatory manner. It is our contention that being in the panchayats the women themselves have been involved in the task of the local development(in turn fulfilling the MDG) in a big way and have assumed the role of leadership in Asia in spite of being the beginners in the political process.

In order to test the above hypothesis, the following steps will be followed. First, some of the government initiatives including that of panchayats and the structure of those institutions will be discussed followed by a discussion on the impact of the panchayats on the lives of villagers. After that, the impact of panchayats on women such as social mobilisation etc. as well as the quality of participation will be taken up. After that some of the factors affecting the quality of participation will be high lighted. A summing up will follow in the last section.

Government Initiatives and Pancahayati Raj Institutions

After Independence, the government of India did take various initiatives to improve the status of women in India. The government initiatives can be characterised as 'Women in Development' 'Gender and Development' and finally 'Rights – based development'.

The details of these approaches have been discussed by many. (Human Development in South Asia 2001; Mohanty and Mahajan 2004). Suffice to say here that the government of India passed a piece of progressive legislation in 1993 to enable the presence of a 'critical mass' of women in the decentralised decision making process. The above enabling measure can be characterised as the facilitator of 'rights based approach' to women's empowerment. These would address some of the deprivations which face Asian women in general and Indian women in particular. In the next section, some of the features of the panchayats will be discussed.

The Constitution (Seventy-third Amendment Act) was originally initiated by the late Rajiv Gandhi as Sixty-fourth Amendment but got defeated in the Parliament. It was passed after the death of Rajiv Gandhi during the tenure of Narasimha Rao. Since the Act was a landmark in the history of the local government or Panchayati Raj system, it is worthwhile to narrate some of the salient features of the above Act. First of all, the new Panchayati Raj system has a three tier system namely, village panchayat, block panchayat and district panchayat.

The size of population in an area determines the size of each tier. In each tenure about 600 District panchayats, 5912 Block panchayats and 2,31630 gram panchayats are formed in which around three million elected representatives interact. The most important feature of the Act from the women's perspective is the reservation of at least one-third of total seats for women both at the functionaries and membership level.

Another hallmark of the above Act is the importance given to the gram sabha or the village assembly, having adults of the panchayat as its members. The panchayats act as an executive body and the gram sabha acts as the watchdog to which the panchayats would be accountable. Panchayats have a separate Finance Commission as well as an Election Commission (Mathew 2000). Twenty-nine subjects ranging from agriculture access to primary education, and poverty alleviation have been devolved to the panchayats. Needless to say that the panchayats have been given the tasks of planning, implementing and monitoring those subjects which form the core of millennium development goals.

Almost all the schemes meant for poverty alleviation directly such as Swarnajayanti Gram Swarozgar Yojana (SGSY), Gram Samridhi Yojana etc. are routed through the panchayats, though money is subject to sanction from the Central Government.

At present, the Employment Guarantee Scheme (EGS) providing 100 days of work to whoever seeks for it has been routed through the panchayats. The main chunk of the panchayat income is utilised on infrastructure (construction of small irrigation structures, source of drinking water, roads, repairing of community buildings etc.), and implementing the welfare schemes (old age and widow pension and maternity benefits). In principle, the panchayat has complete flexibility in allocating these funds (Chattopadhyay and Dublo 2004).

For the first time, incidentally, the Eleventh Finance Commission (meant for allocating finances to local bodies in different states) has devoted one complete chapter for panchayat's finance. It has recommended an amount of 80,000 million rupees ($1=45 Rupees) for all the panchayats in the country. This amount is meant for five years! Even though it is highly inadequate and fulfils only a fraction of the requirements, it is worthwhile to note that the Commission gives due emphasis on the index of decentralisation. Incidentally, the amount of money given to each village panchayat varies from state to state. For example, in West Bengal, a gram panchayat gets on an average 1.5 million rupees per year but in a state like Rajasthan, it used to get only 60 thousand rupees in the first tenure. In Kerala on the other hand, panchayats were given 35 to 40 per cent of the plan funds to work with. In terms of the financial resources, it amounted to 1025,000 rupees excluding the grant from the central government in one year only. Interestingly, the new government at the centre has been reiterating the importance of panchayati raj institutions in furthering the rural development. The government has set up a separate panchayati raj ministry and so far eight consultative meetings have been organised by the ministry to discuss various aspects of the system with a view to make it more efficient than before.

At the same time, it is worth mentioning that the real fiscal decentralisation in terms of deciding to spend money their own way and augmenting local revenue is yet to be with the panchayati raj institutions. The study conducted by the World Bank showed that none but only two states in Kerala and to some extent, Karnataka have devolved the financial and administrative power to the panchayats.

Impact of the Panchayats on the Lives of Villagers

The first and foremost impact of the above Act has been the widening and strengthening the base of participatory democracy. Because of reservation a large number of women has been elected particularly from the lower socioeconomic strata. Further, at least 90 per cent of the ward members are from low socioeconomic background and those of higher categories are from the high caste/class. Almost all the states have conducted elections at the panchayat level. Some states have conducted the elections for the second time. About three million elected representatives have been elected to these political institutions of which about one million are women as mentioned above. The most significant impact of the legislation has been to bring five million women to active politics within a span of ten years (Buch 2000).

We are interested to know the impact of the large number of women emerging at the level of grass roots politics which will be taken up at a later stage. The arithmetic of the five million women can be explained in the following manner. First of all, in each tenure one million women get elected. Secondly for each seat two to three women on an average contest the election. Thus, all together five to six million women participate in the political process. Yet another impact of the PRIs is the reduction of poverty ratio from 38 per cent to 26 per cent and a slight increase in the rate of urbanisation by 2 per cent between 1991 and 2001.

At least, a major part of these results can be explained by the implementation of schemes meant for poverty alleviation through panchayats. It is interesting to note that within a span of two years, between 1999 and 2001, about 35793 million rupees were allocated, out of which 72 per cent was utilised. About 2.4 million Swarozgaries (self-earners) were assisted of which 44 per cent are women. By the way, the government has a policy to allocate at least 30 per cent of the total amount of money available for any scheme for women.

This forms a significant portion of a total sum of 97650 million rupees, which were allocated for rural development, rural employment and poverty alleviation programmes for the financial year 2001-02. Unfortunately, the total allocation of financial resources to rural development is not restricted through panchayats, but the schemes routed through these institutions are better targeted, as is pointed out a little later.There are debates regarding the role of decentralisation in reducing the incidence of poverty in a particular area. Johnson, who has reviewed the existing literature on the subject, is of the opinion that there is a weak relationship between decentralisation and the reduction in poverty.

Johnson also cites other studies to show that the panchayats provide space for marginalised sections of the people to articulate their needs. Further, it is also observed that the panchayats decisions are not restricted to class. On the other hand, other experts have shown that the panchayats were responsible for reducing the poverty ratio in India by targeting the delivery of services in a more focussed manner. (Bardhan and Mukherjee 2004).

The authors have done extensive empirical research in West Bengal. They have pointed out that panchayats in West Bengal have targeted land reforms, delivery of agricultural mini-kits, initiating employment programmes and access to credit - all of which have led to poverty alleviation. They have analysed the performance of 89 villages and the time period extends to twenty years. Of course, they agree with the above author in so far as inequality of assets and lack decentralisation is concerned but they also conclude that if the political party in power feels vulnerable at the state level then the anti-poverty programmes are targeted in an efficient manner. The literature on decentralisation and development outcomes is more or less silent regarding the gender. However, if one clubs women with the poor the same analysis as above will be applicable.

Impact of Panchayats on Women

The impact of panchayats on women's lives have been tremendous, and varied. In fact, the entry to the panchayats has been described by some as a beginning of a 'silent revolution'. These institutions have influenced social, political and economic lives of the village women in more than one ways as will be seen below.

The sources of data are:

(a) A longitudinal study of 235 elected women representatives in panchayats in 22 panchayats spread over three districts of Orissa—an eastern state of India keeping different locales in mind, with an objective of monitoring and capacity building for leadership roles. The study was conducted for four years. Close monitoring of their performance in the panchayats, and capacity building and other related activities were taken up at the village level. The project spanned five years. It was taken up by the Institute of Social Sciences, New Delhi.

(b) A survey was conducted among more than 800 Elected Women Representatives (EWRs) from fourteen states who had come to attend an annual programme to celebrate the Women's Political Empowerment Day to New Delhi. A written questionnaire was fielded among the EWRs to know their views about various issues. In addition, various micro-studies which have been conducted in different parts of India have also been cited.

Institutional Impact: Engendering Development

According to various micro-studies including our own observations from the field, about 80-90 per cent women attend the panchayat meetings regularly. Given their sheer numbers, one might conclude that democracy has become more participatory than before, at least at the grassroots level. This argument is strengthened by the fact that the socioeconomic background of these women showed that majority of them come from the lower income group, particularly in the case of membership at the village panchayat level. As for example, about eighty five per cent of the EWRs who came to the above programme were from village panchayats and most of them belonged either to Scheduled Caste or Scheduled Tribes or Other Backward Castes—all three castes are at the bottom of the caste hierarchy. So far, they have been excluded from the decision-making process. Asked about whether they attended gram sabha or village assembly or not—which is mandatory for the panchayats members—about seventy per cent of them said that they participated the meeting regularly. In so far as the effective participation of these women is concerned, it is noticed that if they get outside support in terms of NGO intervention, women's groups, or any other social or political movement, the women become relatively more vocal. Their knowledge about the functioning of the panchayats increases.

Again, the EWRs were asked as to what kind of activities they have taken up during their tenure, they pointed out that ensuring safe drinking water, air distribution of ration, looking after the village sanitation, etc. have been their main priority. Related to the above issue (the impact on the institutional standards) is the question of the 'proxy women'.

Let us define the term called proxy women. It is alleged that since many of the women are first timers and are illiterate they depend on their men folk for conducting the panchayat activities. In other words, the women follow their men folk without understanding the implications. Hence, they are termed as 'proxy' women.

There are several issues involved here. First of all, the husbands or other male relatives shield them from the panchayat Secretary, and block development officers if they try to harass the women. In fact, some of the state governments (Uttar Pradesh and Rajasthan) have passed a rule that the women elected representatives should be accompanied by their male relatives to the panchayats. This is because in some cases, the secretaries of the panchayats, and male colleagues tried to implicate inexperienced women by asking them to sign blank cheques. Some of the women chiefs went to jails because of those acts. In many cases, no-confidence motions were passed in the panchayats, against the women chiefs on false charges.

Again, even if they depend on their husbands, the power relation between husband and wife has already changed because of reservations, particularly because the husband gets a chance to come to the public sphere because of the wife, and in the process the character of patriarchy gets altered. As a result, in many low-income families the husband—wife relationship has not soured. On the other hand, the husband supports the wife and also helps her in her domestic work. Even the other members of the family including the mother-in-law and sister-in-law help her to complete domestic chores. The community leaders of the same caste also support the women candidates.

Besides, those who argue that the women coming to panchayats are all 'proxy' women forget to analyse their socio-economic background. Many of the women, even in places like Northern India, are recruited from the white-collar background. Since they are educated and know about the working of the official system they will not remain silent in the panchayat meetings. The same critics assume that all the men who work on behalf of women are corrupt and want to grab power. But in reality, it may not be true.

Finally, the 'proxy' women syndrome is seen only in the first one or two years of the tenure. Gradually, the women become independent, as studies conducted in Karnataka show. In the process, they come to know about many modern institutions like courts, block development office, agriculture and other offices, the existence of various officials and some times about the Prime Minister, Chief Ministers and other ministers.

Women not only take up issues relating to basic needs, such as, drinking water, availability of doctors and teachers in the villages, which are dear to them, but also general developmental activities, for example, augmenting the income of the panchayats and generating irrigation facilities for the paddy field. The micro-study conducted by the Institute of Social Sciences referred to earlier also shows that not only are the schemes better targetted but also the knowledge about different largesse such as widow and old age pensions, availability of free rice spreads fast among the women because of the presence of women in the panchayats. The women of the neighbourhood act as the 'watchdog' in compelling the elected women to deliver at least some goods. Women of the villages can easily approach the women elected members and can get subsidised rice at any time.

Micro-studies conducted in various parts of the country reveal that given a chance the elected women representatives try to engender the developmental activities. For example, in her study on twelve all women panchayats, Datta pointed out that elected women representatives gave more priority to such programmes, which were 'need based' and 'sustainable'.

Thus, we see that, contrary to the popular criticism, the standard of the political institutions at the grassroots level has not been lowered as a result of women's reservations and on the other hand the development process has been engendered to some extent.

Social Mobilisation

Involvement of three million women in grass roots politics by itself has created an expansion of public space as well as that of private space for the women. In the public space, they have been allowed to attend the panchayat meetings along with other male colleagues, address gram sabha (village assembly), go to government offices to meet the Block Development Officer and other Line Department personnel. In addition, women get opportunity to network and facilitate conditions for creating the 'social capital'. These conditions get reinforced with another set of forces which also involve a large number of women through micro-credit programme. In the private sphere, their working relations change. The area of cooperation increases at the family level also.

Beneficial Scheme

At this point, a reference can be made to the implementation of an important scheme, namely, SGSY through the panchayats and its impact on the poor in general, and poor women, in particular. The main features of the scheme are that it lays stress on a few select activities in each developmental block and attends to all aspects of these activities ranging from availability of raw materials, upgrading skills to marketing. The main objective of the scheme is to augment a sustainable income of the *Swarozgaries* (Self-earners) through the above investment. A major component of the scheme was in operation since the eighties in the form of

Development of Women and Child in Rural Areas (DWCRA) and had created some successful groups in one of the states of India—Andhra Pradesh.

The scheme was initiated by the government being encouraged by the women's conference in Nairobi. Of course, the government is not sole agency in initiating the micro finance programme. It is not always routed through the panchayats. World Bank, NABARD and other funding agencies have taken up the micro-credit programme in a big way. The revised scheme has borrowed a few innovative concepts from the Grameen bank, Bangladesh such as flexibility in payment. In addition, the above scheme emphasises social mobilisation of poor in the rural areas. Several women entrepreneurs have emerged as a result (Government of India, (nd) SGSY: Guidelines). In order gauze the magnitude of women's involvement in micro-credit programme, it would be sufficient to mention here that in Dhaka Declaration of the South Asian Coalition for the Micro- credit Summit1996 articulated the collective consensus among 21 networks which deliver financial services to 4.5 million poor people in Nepal, India , Bangladesh and Pakistan.

Studies conducted on the impact of Self-Help groups (SHGs) show that women's group formation, new knowledge and moreover, group mobilisation is capable of creating an alternative to women's traditional status in the family. Group mobilisation also enables women to speak out in the village meetings (Vijayanthi 2002). The micro-credit scheme has also caught the imagination of various funding agencies as has been referred to earlier.

Several studies have been conducted to assess the impact of micro-credit on the status of women. (Kabeer 2005).It is agreed that even though it doesn't lead to 'virtuous spiral of economic, social, and political empowerment of women', it does lead to empowering some women. In economic terms, it also reduce the vulnerability at the time of natural calamity so to that extent the power relation at the family level changes. It is also noticed that if men are involved in the programme women's 'practical needs' are met. In addition, the programme helps in creating the 'social capital' in a community since it encourages collective action. The social mobilisation created by the SGSY/SHGs gets reinforced by another factor namely, women's participation in the political process through campaigning, addressing the meetings and going to cast their votes.

Reserved Seats

Sen has mentioned that the family is an arena of cooperation and conflict. It is observed that the reservation of seats in the local governments has increased the areas of cooperation at the family level (Monitoring and Evaluating Study referred to above).The in-laws help the EWRs in finishing the household chores and look after the small children to allow them for attending the panchayat meetings. Some times, the husbands take them on bicycles if the panchayat office is far away from their own villages. The results of the Census of India, 2001 shows that the female life expectancy at birth has exceeded that of males marginally. It indicates that women's self-perception has changed and they look after their health and nutritional status.

Similarly, the female literacy rate has jumped from being 39 per cent to 53 per cent within a decade. A part of this quantum jump could be explained in terms of the women's excitement to become literate after getting elected. Because, it was noticed that women came to National Literacy Mission camp in large number at night to get them selves educated (Saldanaha 1995). Same kind of enthusiasm was noticed when they were asked about getting educated and sending their daughters to schools.

Constraints

The constraints are many. The most important constraint of women's empowerment through panchayat is that they are not a homogenous category. They represent different interest group depending on their class and caste, which get perpetuated through patriarchy.

However, one redeeming factor in uniting the women is the access to the basic services such as drinking water, health care facility and education, the practical needs. Secondly, predominant trend of Indian culture is still very patriarchal and the women are looked down upon. The EWRs are not taken seriously by their male colleagues and the bureaucrats and they get very scant information about the functioning of the panchayats. In some places EWRs get over burdened because of household chores as well as that of panchayats. Even though theoretically one may dismiss the notion of 'proxy women' in the real world husbands do take advantage of the ignorant women and work on behalf of them without giving any space.

Dirty Politics

Again, in many places, the women are not immune to systemic corruption though as beginners they are relatively more cautious. Joining politics is still considered 'dirty' and is frowned upon. The community leaders of the village try to choose candidates who are non-performers or would toe their line. The women themselves do not come forward. It is always the family members, or party leaders who push them to contest. The selection of seats for reservations—which are done on a lottery basis and only for one term-does not provide much scope for nurturing a constituency.

Even if the women perform well during the first term, the men do not allow them to contest from the same seat again. The panchayat institutions are used as an implementing agency. So the bureaucrats feel that they are the bosses and the first timer leaders are there to obey them.

Violence Against Fairer Sex

Violence against women has also increased. A woman chief of the panchayat was killed in one of the states because she defied her husband and called the meeting of the village assembly to discuss the agenda of the budget. In some cases, women representatives do not know that they have been elected from certain constituencies. The inter-caste violence has become more acute and so much so that a woman member of a *nagar palika* (township government) in an urban part of Tamil Nadu was murdered because she wanted to bring piped water to her ward. She belonged to a low caste community. In yet another case, another woman was forced by the villagers to quit her menial job because it did not suit her status as elected representative.

In a nutshell, men support women in panchayats so long as women do not challenge them to fulfill the 'practical needs'. But men feel threatened as and when the women try to fulfil the 'strategic needs'. Apart from the specific constraints, the PRIs system as a whole face several structural constraints, such as limited power and resources, the absence of appointed cadre and hence, dependence on the state level functionaries and so on. Again the panchayats are given 29 subjects which are included in different departments. But the policy matters are not conveyed to the elected representatives at all. So the elected representatives can not take decisions on their own regarding any subject, such as, agriculture, irrigation, family welfare etc. except only in implementing schemes or acting as the spokespersons of the state governments.

Besides, there are a number of parallel structures such as Janmabhumi programme in Andhra Pradesh, *Vana* panchayat (Joint Forest Management), Uttar Pradesh and Water Harvesting Management, etc. which try to ignore the involvement of the PRIs. All these systemic constraints also affect the functioning of the women in panchayats.

On the whole, however, it can be argued that reservation of seats in the local council has provided a critical mass of women with an opportunity to empower themselves by being partners in decision-making process.

Conclusions

The MDG has set various goals such as eradication of poverty which includes access to primary education, sanitation, drinking water, reduction of maternal mortality, empowerment of women etc. to be achieved within a span of a decade. In India, a bold experiment has been taken up in the form of giving more power to the village councils or panchayats which in turn will be responsible to local level of development by involving the entire village.

Not less than one-third seats have been reserved for the women in all three tiers of panchayats. In the process, three million elected representatives have been elected per term of five years out of which one million are women. In other words, women and men at the grassroots level are the planners for realising the MDG on their own terms. Debates on decentralisation and poverty are not conclusive but it is agreed that the delivery of basic services become more targeted if they are routed through the panchayats.

The impact of panchayats in the lives of women has been quite significant because it affected women's lives socially, politically and economically since they got enough space to negotiate at the private and public space. They could cross the four boundaries of the hearth which has been assigned to them traditionally. The presence of a large number of women in panchayats as well in the micro-credit programme has led to social mobilisation and created conditions for social capital. The patriarchal values which permeate all the institutions of India also affect the panchayati raj institutions.

Women who get elected to the panchayats become subjected to the caste, class and patriarchal values. Domestic violence has increased against women since some of them try challenge the male bastion by entering into politics. The panchayats also suffer from systemic constraints such as lack of financial and administrative power. Corruptions is also rampant among the elected representatives. Nonetheless, a space has been created for Asian women to emerge as a formidable force to fight for social justice and human rights.

NOTES AND REFERENCES

Bardhan, P. and Dilip Mukherjee. 2004. 'Poverty Alleviation efforts of Panchayats in West Bengal', *Economic and Political Weekly*, 39 (9).

Bose, Ashish, 2001. 'Promoting Health and Family Planning through Panchayats', in Bidyut Mohanty (ed.), Women and Political Empowerment 1999, *Women's Political Empowerment* Day Celebrations on Panchayats, Women and Family Welfare, ISS, New Delhi.

Buch, Nirmala. 2000. 'Panchayats and Women', in George Mathew (ed.), *Status of Panchati Raj in the States of India.Concept,* New Delhi.

Chattopadhyay, R. and Esther Duflo. 2004. 'Impact of Reservation in Panchayati Raj: Evidence from a Nationwide Randomised Experiment', *Economic and Political Weekly*

Datta, Bishakha. 1998. And Who will make Chapatis? *A Case Study of All Women Panchayats in Maharashtra*, Calcutta: Stree Publications.

Dreze, J. and Mamta Murthy. 2001. 'Fertility, Education and Development : Evidencefrom India', *Population and Development Review*, 27 (1).

Government of India. 2001-02. *Economic Survey*, Ministry of Finance, New Delhi.

Government of India. 2002-03. *Annual Report,* Ministry of Rural Development, New Delhi.

Haq,M Human Development Report. 1997. *Human Development Report*, United Nations Development Programme, New York: Oxford University Press.

Issac, T.M. Thomas. 2003. 'Women Elected Representatives in Kerela (1995-2000): From Symbolism to Empowerment', Paper presented at the workshop on 'Women's Empowerment through Seventy-third Constitution Amendment Act', Institute of Social Sciences, 20-21, October, New Delhi.

Johnson, Craig. 2002. 'Decentralisation and Poverty: Exploring the Contradictions', *The Indian Journal of Political Science*, 63 (1).

Kaushal, Avdhash and Bindu Kalia. 2003. 'Uttaranchal: Betrayal of grassroots democracy', *Panchayati Raj Update* (March).

Mathew, George. 2000 (ed.) *The Status of Panchayati Raj in India*, New Delhi: Concept Publishing House.

Mathew, George. 2002. *Panchayati Raj : From Legislation to Movement*, New Delhi:Concept.

Mohanty, Bidyut. 1998?. 'Women and Family', in Tan Chung (ed.) *Across the Himalayan Gap, India's Quest for Understanding China*, New Delhi: Gyan PublishingHouse.

Mohanty, Bidyut and Vandana Mahajan. 2004. 'Women's Empowerment in the Context of the Constitution (73rd and 74th Amendments) Acts 1992: An Assessment', Background paper in ISS and SAP Canada (2003) (ed.) *A Decades of Women's Empowerment through Local Government in India Workshop Report*, New Delhi: ISS.

Mohanty, Manoranjan and Mark Seldon. 2003. 'Reconceptualising Local Democracy: 1 & II Preliminary reflections on democracy, power and resistance', *Panchayati Raj Update* (April and May).

Mohbub Haq, Human Development Centre. 2000. Human Development in South Asia 2000: *The Gender Question*, Karachi: Oxford University Press.

Pal Mahi. 2002. Swarnajayanti Gram Swarozgar Yojana, Evolution, Assessment and Future Prospects, *Kurukshetra* (June). Government of India.

Rai, Manoj *et al.* (eds). 2001. The State of Panchayats: A Participatory Perspective, New Delhi: Sanskriti. Rai, Sirin. 1994. 'Gender Issues in *China: A Survey*', China Report, 30 (4)Saldanha, Denzil. 1995. 'Literacy Campaigns in Maharashtra and Goa, Issues, Trends and Direction', *Economic and Political Weekly* (20 May).

Sen, A.K. 1983. 'Conflict in Access to Food', Mainstream, 21 (8).

Sethi, Geeta. 2004. (ed.) *Fiscal Decentralisation to Rural Governments in India*, The World Bank, New Delhi: Oxford University Press.

Sharma, Kumud (ND). 'From Representation to Presence, The Paradox of Power and Powerlessness of Women in PRIS', Occasional Paper, CWDS, New Delhi.

The Economic Times, 30 June 2004, Delhi Edition Vijayanthi, K.N. 2002. 'Women's Empowerment through Self-Help Groups: A Participatory Approach', Indian Journal of *Gender Studies*, 9(2).

4

WOMEN AND EDUCATIONAL DEVELOPMENT

Introduction

Developmental policies and programmes that do not address gender disparities miss critical developmental opportunities. Education of girls is vital not only on grounds of social justice but also because it accelerates social transformation. Promotion of gender equality in education is essential for human resource development. By educating a woman we educate the whole family. Given that a woman has the responsibility of the whole family on herself, an educated woman is better capable of taking care of the health, nutrition and education of her children and more so be an active agent in the social and economic development of the country.

It is evident that economic success everywhere is based on educational success. Literacy is the basic building block of education. It is a basic component of social cohesion and national identity. It leads to an improvement in the depth and quality of public opinion, as well as to more active participation of the marginalised in the democratic process. No society has ever liberated itself economically, politically, or socially without a sound base of educated women. Education has a direct impact on women empowerment as it creates in them awareness about their rights, their capabilities and the choices and opportunities available to them. Studies have indicated that there is a strong correlation between female education and several developmental indicators such as increased economic productivity, improvement in health, delayed age at marriage, lower fertility, increased political participation, and effective investments in the next generation.

Indian Context; Policies and Programmes

In India, providing education to all the citizens is a constitutional commitment. The principal of gender equality is enshrined in the Indian Constitution, in its Preamble, Fundamental Rights, Fundamental Duties and Directive Principals. The Constitution not only guarantees equality to women, but also empowers the State to adopt measures of positive discrimination in favour of women. Just after Independence, in 1951, literacy levels were very low (25% for men and 9% for women). In the next ten years, there was not much progress in the literacy levels.

It is only after the recommendations of the Indian education commission (1964) and the National Policy of Education (1968) that the education of girls was seen as a means of accelerating social transformation. The policy placed special emphasis on initiating programmes to give equal educational opportunities to all the groups and both sexes. The Constitution also gave primary responsibility for elementary education to the state governments, while the central government was given responsibility for technical and higher education. This situation changed in 1976 after the 42^{n} Amendment to the Constitution was passed, making all education the joint responsibility of the central and state governments. One of the consequences of this was that the foreign assistance, so far restricted to technical and higher education, now began to flow into primary education as well. Between the mid-1960 and the early 1980s, the proportion of resources going into elementary education showed a steady increase.

Empowerment through Education

National Policy on Education (NPE), 1986 and its Programme of Action (POA) gave high priority to gender equality and committed the entire educational system to work for women's empowerment. The National Perspective Plan 1988-2000 reiterates this point of view and states that women themselves must overcome their handicaps. Thus, there has been a careful articulation of education for equality for women, which is reflected in the educational policy discourse. Central and State governments attached lot of significance to actually operationalising the NPE's Programme of Action and in a series of regional meetings with the State Governments, a special review of gender issues in education was undertaken.

At the same time, it was emphasised to the States, that gender concerns must be built into all educational processes. Monitoring committees for women's/girls' education at the Ministry of Human Resource Development level and also state level were formed to monitor the indicators of gender concerns in all policies and projects. Emphasis was laid on enrolment and retention of the girl child in formal and non formal schooling; recruitment of rural women teachers and removal of gender bias in the curriculum.

Mass literacy campaigns in different parts of India were launched which brought out volunteers from all sections of society as instructors, master trainers and organisers. Adult Education Programmes, Total Literacy Campaigns, Post Literacy Programmes, and continuing Education Programmes were also started. Nationwide gender sensitisation programmes were undertaken to cover a large number of educational personnel to include educational administrators, teachers and teacher educators. Complementary to this strategy, media campaigns and parental awareness programmes for generating a positive climate for girls' education were also started. Mobilisation of women's groups and projects like *Mahila Samakhya* (Education for Women's Equality) with focus on the constraints that had so far prevented women and girls from accessing educational inputs were launched.

The purpose of these groups was to address issues of self-image and self-confidence of women and alter societal perception about them. Its overall goal was to create circumstances to enable women to better understand their predicament, to move from a state of abject disempowerment towards a situation in which they could determine their own lives and influence their environment, and simultaneously create for themselves and their family an educational opportunity which enhanced the process of development.

Profiling Gender Gap in Education

Gender gap has been well documented and analysed by governmental agencies, international organisation, university departments, NGO'S and individual researchers. Some recent publications that provide a panoramic view of this subject include, World Bank (1997), which charts the terrain occupied by primary organisations; Ramchandaran (1998), which provides the comparative perspective on girls' and Women's education in South Asia; Shukla and Kaul (1998), Bhattacharya (1998), which looks more generally at the status of education in India; and finally Haq and Haq (1998), which analyses education within the context of human development in South Asia.

The past five decades have produced mass of information on innovative practices and experimental programmes. There are also innumerable guidelines and policy statements on why gender gaps persist in education and how these can be reduced.

Negative cultural and societal attitudes , different standards, roles for boys and girls, competing demands on the girls' time, economic reasons like—lack of resources, distance from school, lack of facilities in schools for girls, lack of female teachers, lack of security both in and outside the school curriculum not relevant and flexible, gender stereotyping in curriculum ,gender unfriendly classroom environment, early marriage and child bearing, absence of women role models, fear of deterioration of social structure, are the most frequently quoted stumbling blocks to female education.

In response to this, developing flexible school calendars, encouraging community participation, promoting parental awareness, creating gender neutral textbooks, training teachers for promoting gender equality, promoting girls access to science and math's education, reliance on multiple delivery systems and increasing resources of primary education are the strategies most often recommended for overcoming these hurdles. (Haq and Haq, 1998). In fact, there is a certain degree of agreement about the constraints to education and about strategies that "work". But despite this convergence, these problems persist. The discourse on strategies needs to be located in a dynamic perspective. Revision and reflection are required to analyse this changing scenario, to identify its impact and to develop strategies to adjust to it.

The 93rd Constitution Amendment with the insertion of new article (21A). "The state shall provide free and compulsory education to all children of the age of 6 and 14 years in such manner as the state may, by law, determine." enables any citizen to seek the enforcement of the right by way of resort to writ Jurisdiction under Article 32 and 226 of the Constitution. Thus the 93r Constitution Amendment fulfils the mandate of the CRC (The convention on the rights of the child which was adopted by UN General Assembly on November 20, 1989).This initiative of the government has had far reaching consequences and has been a major catalyst in increasing the number of enrollments in primary classes.

Data from Demographic and Health Survey (DHS) shows that the primary school attendance rate has increased by more than one percentage point annually since the beginning of the decade. In 2000, 76 per cent of all children of primary school age (6-10 years) were in school. By 2006, this value had increased to 83 per cent. The attendance rate of girls increased by 9 per cent over the 2000-2006 period and the attendance rate of boys by 6 per cent.

School attendance rates also grew in urban and rural areas, and across all household wealth quintiles. However, close to 17 per cent of all children of primary school age still continue to be out of school.

Rural-Urban Divide

Experience of the last sixty years has shown that placing a high priority on education in policy statements has, to a certain degree ensured availability of adequate resources, but it does not ensure that marginalised groups benefit by national programmes The expansion of the educational system has been uneven and inadequate There is a gender gap in the educational status of boys and girls and more so amongst the disadvantaged castes and tribes. Wage labourers have lower literacy levels than other occupational groups. There is also a marked rural-urban differential. The lowest educational achievement can be expected among rural women belonging to scheduled caste or tribe.

India represents a picture of contrasts when it comes to education and employment opportunities for girls in the rural and the urban areas. Cultural, social and economic factors still prevent girls from getting education opportunities and so the question of equality is still a mirage. The status of the girl child has been a subject of much discussion, controversy and debate. While more and more families are beginning to value girls as equals to boys, there are still overwhelming cultural and economic reasons why female children are not receiving the same medical, emotional and educational attention as their male counterparts.

From the start, girl child is seen as burden rather than a blessing, bearer of exorbitant dowry, who will eventually move into the home of her husband. As a child; a girl receives less food, attention and emotional support than her male counterpart; as an adult, less attention is paid on developing her potential and more on matrimony and motherhood as these are regarded the essential and overarching goals of her life and all education is a preparation for that.

Multitask Role

In the rural areas, the girl child is made to perform household and agricultural chores. This is one of the many factors limiting girls' education. Cleaning the house, preparing food, looking after their siblings, the elderly and the sick, grasing the cattle and collecting firewood are some of the key tasks they have to perform. Households are therefore reluctant to spare them for schooling. Physical safety of the girls, especially when they have to travel a long distance to school and fear of sexual harassment are other reasons that impede girls' education. In the urban areas, however, there is a discernible difference in the opportunities that girls get for education and employment. There is an element of awareness of gender issues in the more educated sections of society in certain regions. Moreover, urban spaces permit greater opportunity for personal autonomy to girls. Though the figures for girls would still be low as compared to boys, what is heartening to see is that whenever given the opportunity, girls have excelled more than boys. For instance, in the Central Board of Secondary Examinations (CBSE) for grades 10 and 12, which are at an All India level, girls have for over a decade now, bagged all the top positions and secured a higher over all per centage compared to boys.

In employment opportunities too, women in our country today have stormed all male bastions. Be it piloting aircraft, heading multi-national corporations, holding up top bureaucratic positions, leading industrial houses, making a mark as doctors, filmmakers, chefs, engineers and even as train and lorry drivers, women have made their presence felt in every sphere of life.

However, this is not reason enough for us to cheer. For the number of girls and women who have been left out of education and employment opportunities still far outweighs those who have got them. It is important to realise that fewer girls survive in the system long enough to reach the end of secondary education. And what is needed to change this scenario is not just governmental efforts but a change in societal norms, in cultural and traditional biases and in general mindsets of people. And in this the media, the civil society, and the youth, the women and girls have a lot to contribute.

Higher Education for Girls

Indian higher education system is one of the largest in the world. It consists of colleges, universities, institutions of national importance (such as Indian Institutes of Technology (IIT), Indian Institutes of Management and Indian Institutes of Science, etc.), and autonomous institutions with the status of deemed universities. In 2002-03, there were 300 universities; of which 183 were provincial, 18 federal, 71 deemed universities, and 5 were established through central and state legislation and 13 institutes of national importance. The enrolment was 9,227,833 (about 7.8% of the relevant age group). There were 436,000 teachers in 2002-03 as against 457,000 in 2000-01. Of these nearly 83% are in the affiliated colleges and 17% in the universities. Gender wise data is not provided by the UGC. However, the 2001-02, MHRD (2001-02) provides information on the women teachers in the 12 open universities which is 18.4% and 21.5% in the institutions offering correspondence courses.

There has been phenomenal expansion of educational opportunities for women in the field of higher education both general and technical. Women education at the university-levels has been diversified and reoriented in tune with the changing requirements of the society, industry and trade. The number of women enrolled in institutions of higher education increased from 40,000 in 1950-51 to about 14,37,000 in 1990-91 recording an increase of more than 36 times over the forty-year period. And in the year 2004-05 the number increased to 3,971,407. Proportion of women entering higher education l950-51 was l0.9 per cent and in 2002-03 it was 40.04 per cent. The number of women per 100 men in 1950-51 wasl4 which increased to 67 in 2002-03.

There are also wide disparities in enrollment by region, caste, and tribe and by gender. These differences impact on women from the disadvantaged groups. In 2001-02, the proportions of SC/ST students were as follows: Scheduled Castes 11.5 per cent (1,016,182) SC men 8 per cent (7, 06,769) and SC women 3.5 per cent (309,813). The ST students constituted 4 per cent (351,880) of total enrolment; men 2.7 per cent (240,495); women 1.3 per cent (114,168). In M.Phil/Ph.D. programmes, there were 53,119 students all over the country. Of these, 36.3 per cent (19,299) were women; 5.9 per cent (3,133) SC students; and 1.80 (951) ST students. There were 824 SC women and 344 ST women, i.e. 4.3 per cent and 1.8 per cent respectively of all women research students. It is quite well known that in spite of a very well formulated policy of positive discrimination, the representation of SC/ST students is not adequate and the proportion of women is negligible. They generally join general education courses and are denied access to elite/courses and institutions.

Further, disciplinary choices are affected by socio-economic factors especially in the case of Scheduled Caste/Scheduled Tribe students whose representation remains marginal in higher education. But they too, are better represented in states in which women have better representation and in which higher education facilities have expanded in recent years.

Disciplinary Choices for Women

The relationship between availability of disciplinary choices and women's ability to accessthem are not directly related, nor are they dependent on women's academic achievement. The reasons cited for this are mainly due to social ethics. Large majority of women may be deprived of exercising free options in selecting subjects of their choice in school, as in case of girls, parents generally take the decision regarding the academic stream to be pursued. This decision is guided by the consideration that girls are not expected to work or earn before marriage and education is only an investment to fall back upon in case of the daughter becoming a widow or being deserted (Chanana 1998). The poor parents have another problem; even though they perceive the significance of education, many a times they are not able to finance it.

Besides, there is lack of role models and socialisation support at home. Women from these social categories are the most affected by the stratification of disciplines, programmes and institutions. Further, the social and economic disparities are reflected not only *vis-a-vis* caste and tribe but also at the regional level, i.e. in different provinces. Discipline boundaries not only limit choices but choices are further limited by future options of "life chances" of women. Higher Education is further denied to the disadvantaged groups and especially women from rural poor homes. Because of social and economic reasons, parents may be unwilling to spend on education as well as the dowries of their daughters

A perusal of the disciplinary choices depicts that the proportion of women in some of the masculine disciplines was miniscule soon after Independence and remained so till

1980s.This is evident as the proportion of women in science decreased from 33.3 per cent in 1950-51 to 28.8 per cent 1980-81. This was the period when natural science was at a premium, especially physics and chemistry. Till the eighties, they were the first choice for male students and while competing with men, women were pushed out.

It is also possible that science was not, in any case, the first preference for young women whose parents perceived marriage as a priority over higher education. An undergraduate degree of any kind only helped in the marriage market by raising the social status. A science degree required a longer investment of time and other resources, therefore was not desirable. The young women were also socialised to perceive higher education from that view point.

The proportion of women in 2002-03 in arts was 44.2 and has been increasingly steadily since 1970-71. The proportion of men, on the other hand, has decreased gradually during the same period from 83.9 per cent to 54.6 per cent. In teacher's education, another feminine discipline the proportion of women has gone up from 32.4 to 50.6 per cent. Science, a masculine discipline, provides an interesting insight on disciplinary choices of young women and men. For example, in science the proportion of men which was around 80-90 per cent till 1980-81, has come down to 59.8 per cent in 2002-03. (Chanana 2004).

Higher education for young women is taken for granted nowadays among the upper and middle strata in the cities but it is still not viewed as an immediate investment in their careers. Social role expectations affect the aspirations of women. For example, in the patriarchal social structure, parents are not expected to use the income of their daughters. Therefore, even educated daughters are not encouraged to work and if they do so, it is for a short period before marriage. After marriage it is the right of the groom's family to decide whether she will work or not. Therefore, for a majority of young women in the academia, higher education is not linked to careers. This is the reason why women join arts and humanities as they are cheaper, softer, easy to understand and shorter than the professional courses. But lately the number of those who are entering the professional subjects is growing.

Public *versus* Private Education

Until the liberalisation of the economy in the early nineties, higher education was publicly funded by the federal/central and provincial/state governments. However, since 1991, the policies of the government have dramatically changed with regard to seemingly privileged position of higher education. The government began to remove public support to higher education and make it self financing while privatising it. Higher education has also become a non merit good. However, Since the early nineties, private autonomous institutions were permitted to be set up on a liberal scale without a clearly defined policy to regulate the private institutions (Anandkrishnan 2004).

Most of the private institutes offer professional courses as these are more popular and lucrative. Privatisation of education has increased the intake capacity of specific kind of professional education; especially skill oriented undergraduate degrees, which lead to a career and a job. Earlier an undergraduate degree, except in engineering and medicine, was a step to further higher education and was not a finishing degree. Young men and women were not expected to work and earn soon after finishing undergraduate education. Those who did so, belonged to the lower middle strata and needed to work and to earn to support the family and themselves. The middle and upper strata, on the other hand, could postpone income generation until further education. This was more applicable to most women across strata, that is, they were not studying in order to earn and to take up jobs. It was an investment in their social status as well as additional criteria for marriage.

Privatisation has deepened the gender gap further. Professional Education is denied to the disadvantaged groups and especially poor and rural women because of social and economic reasons. Resultantly, more women are taking up courses in general education as these are easily available and are cheaper as compared to professional courses. Professional education requires several years of studentship and higher financial investment than the general education. Many women join general courses as these provide them an opportunity to enhance their qualifications as well as wait for the right match for matrimony.

Secondly, parents may be unwilling to spend on education of their daughters as they are expected to spend money on their marriages. According to Indian tradition, it is obligatory for a girl's parents to offer gifts and money to the grooms family at the time of marriage.

Recent Trends

In recent times there has been a change in the aspirations of young persons. Both men and women are in a hurry to finish studies and start earning. Money making has become the most important value for them. For this reason, they prefer to take up courses which are linked to jobs and pursuing studies for academic purposes is no longer the aim.

The revolution in values cuts across strata, i.e. young persons even from the upper and middle strata want to earn as early as possible. The daughters of city-based professional parents have really undergone a sea change in their socialisation. Parents are giving the best education to their daughters and expect them to be independent and follow careers.

This revolution in values contrasts with those values which dominated prior to the nineties, i.e. education and its linkage to the job market early on in life was only for those men who needed jobs and was certainly not for women. In this changed scenario, the priorities of women have also changed. They too want professional education and are, therefore, entering the so called masculine disciplines.

There are two simultaneous trends of clustering and dispersal that can be seen in the participation of men and women in higher education. During the first three decades while women tended to be clustered in the general disciplines of arts and sciences (nearly 90 per cent); men's participation was characterised by both clustering in arts and sciences disciplines but also significantly dispersed in others such as commerce, engg/tech and law. Lately, however, women's participation too is marked by clustering as well as dispersal.

Once women enter higher education at the undergraduate level, they move on the next two levels, namely, the graduate and research level. In other words, their transition from one level to another has increased which highlights their staying power. In 1991-92,14,79,231 women were enrolled for undergraduate programmes which increased to 3,285,544 in 2002-03; 169,267 women were enrolled for graduate programmes. In 1991-92 as compared to 355,893 women in 2002-03; from and 19,894 in 1991-92 to 23,609 in 2002-03 for research programmes.

During these years their proportion has also increased from 32.8 per cent to 39.9 per cent in undergraduate programmes; from 34.7 per cent to 42.0 per cent in graduate level progammes; and from 37.1 per cent to 38.0 per cent in the M.Phil and Ph.D. programme.Their proportion is highest at the graduate level while their proportion in research programmes has marginally declined from 39.2 per cent in 1995-96 to 38.0 per cent in 2002-03.

Until 1950-51, only 20.2 women had enrolled for research degrees which increased in the next three decades to 8,780 in 1980-81 (Chanana 1993). Their number nearly doubled to 15,018 in 1988-89. Now, it stands at 23,609 in 2002-03. The

University Grants Commission (UGC) has been providing financial assistance to universities for undertaking well-defined projects for research in women's studies and also for the development of curriculum at the undergraduate and postgraduate levels and relevant extension activities.

The Commission has also created positions of part-time research associate ships for women candidates in Science and Humanities including Social Sciences and Engineering and Technology. Research projects related to the theme of women's studies were approved. Also, assistance was provided to 21 universities and 11 colleges/university departments for setting up women's studies centres and cells The slightly higher percentage at the graduate level indicates that more women are transiting from undergraduate to the next higher level courses. It may also have something to do with the popularity of master's programmes in management, computers and IT, media, advertising, fashion technology etc. which are proffered in the metropolitan cities. But in the absence of statistics, it is difficult to arrive at a conclusion.

In fact, there is a general trend of moving away from the general courses to the professional courses which lead to jobs and careers. There is also a big demand for vocational courses at the undergraduate level. As observed in the departments of Management, women seem to prefer human resource management (HRM) and development (HRD) as fields of specialisations. It is likely that jobs involving public relations, personnel management, marketing, and advertising in the corporate sector, such as the banks, IT firms, BPO companies are becoming feminine jobs and specialisations. It seems that women are moving from discipline choices to specialisations within disciplines. One could treat post 1991 phase as a period which set forth a change which increased the social demand for specific kind of professional education, especially skill oriented undergraduate degrees which lead to a career and a job. Earlier boys and girls were not expected to work and earn soon after finishing undergraduate education. Those who did so belonged to the lower middle strata and needed to work and to earn to support the family and themselves.

The middle and upper strata, on the other hand, could postpone income generation until further education. This was more applicable to most women across strata, that is, they were not studying in order to earn and to take up jobs. It was an investment in their social status as well as additional criteria for marriage. Although, this may still be true of a large majority of women and their parents, that is, they do not expect their daughters to earn after receiving a degree, there are changes in the expectations of parents and of young women in big cities.

Therefore, parental expectations and young women's aspirations have been push factors in the shift of disciplinary choices in the mid 90s. It is related to the change in values as mentioned earlier and as a response to market demands in the post liberalisation phase. More women are enrolling in engineering and law but the preference for management degrees and computer related degrees and skills is higher. These subjects are available in the fast expanding private sector which responds quickly to the unmet demand for specific skills. Informal discussions with key persons reveal that computer applications and software computer engineering as compared to other specialisations are popular among women. It will, therefore, have to be seen if women are getting professional training which leads to jobs and careers?

There are hardly any micro studies for macro data to fall back upon to answer this question. But as mentioned earlier, there are now differences in the specialisations within disciplines which have career implications. For example, HRM requires interaction with the public and there are several others of this kind. In the last few years women have become visible in the call centres; telemarketing; front desk jobs in the multinational/private banks, hospitals, hotels, etc. Quite a few of these jobs are short term and contractual and, therefore, suit the social role expectations of women.

Current framework of National Development recognises women as a unique power unit and a potential resource and has played crucial role in social reforms, economic development and also in the political process. Women's development is a pre-requisite for all the round development of the society. In a package of developmental inputs available to community, education should form an effective means to improve the physical quality of life of the masses. Many studies have shown that there is a strong correlation between several developmental indicators and level of literacy of the population. Correlation is particularly strong with the level of female education.

It is found that the relation between the age of marriage of a girl and her achievement in education is positive. On the other handy infant mortality rate, birth rate and total fertility rate are negatively correlated. Though school enrollment ratios have been rising, high rate of dropouts, particularly of girls, still continues to be a major problem. The Mass Scale Adult Education Programme for women in the age group 15-35 years, Non-formal education for the age group 6-14 years and the formal school system—these three systems of education have to be integrated and coordinated to eradicate illiteracy among females. Continuing education centres should be strengths to provide training and for retention of literacy skills.

Create Public Awareness

Corrective measures must be taken to increase public awareness for the value of the girl child, to ensure their participation in programmes of Child development, health, nutrition and education and to create a positive environment to allow girls to develop into productive young women.

The biggest challenge before the Government and NGOs is to create awareness and sensitisation among people of all levels, especially in rural areas, about the special needs of women and girls. They need to be made aware that imparting education to women is a great service to society. This vital section of society has remained bound in the shackles and been deprived for far too long. There is a need for affirmative and real action in their favour which will ensure the women to right to food, shelter, health, education and employment. However, the recent changes and developments are kindling hopes for better and promising future.

NOTES AND REFERENCES

Anandkrishnan, M. 2004. *Private Investments in Technical Education.* In K.B. Powar and K.L. Johar (eds.). Private Initiatives in Higher Education, Sneh Prakashan & Amity Foundation for Learning, pp. 202-25.

Bhattacharya, Sabyasachi (ed) 1998. *The Contested Terrain: Perspectives on Education in India.* New Delhi: Orient Longman.

Chanana, K. 2004. Gender and Disciplinary Choices: Women in Higher Education in India.Paper presented in Colloquium on RESEARCH AND Higher Education Policy 'Knowledge, Access and Governance: Strategies for Change', 1-3 December, 2004, UNESCO.

Chanana, K .2001. Female Sexuality and Education of Hindu Girls in India. In *Sociological Bulletin 50 (1), Marc.Also in* S. Rege (ed.), *Sociology of Gender: The Challenge of Feminist Sociological Knowledge.* New Delhi: Sage Publications, 2003, pp. 287-317.

Chanana, K. 1988. 'Social Change or Social Reform: The Education of Women in pre Independence India', in K Chanana (ed) *Socialisation, Education and Women: Explorations in Gender Identity, Orient* Longman, New Delhi.

Census of India. 1881. Primary census abstract, General Population. Part II(B) series 1 India. Chanana, K. 1990. 'The dialectics between tradition and modernity and women's education in India.' *Sociological Bulletin,* 39 (182), March-September, pp.75-91.

Chanana, K. 2000. Treading the hallowed halls: Women in higher education in India, *Economic and Political Weekly,* vol. 35(12), March 18, pp. 1012-22.

Chanana, K. 2003. Visibility, Gender and the Careers of Women Faculty in an Indian University. *in McGill Journal of Education,* vol. 38(3), Fall 2003, pp. 381-90.

Christopher Colclough with Keith M. Lewin, *Educating All the Children,* Oxford University Press, 1993.

Christopher Colclough with Keith M. Lewin, Educating All the Children, Oxford University Press, 199 Elizabeth M. King and M. Anne Hill, eds. Women's Education in Developing Countries: Barriers, Benefits, and Policies, World Bank, 1992.

Government of India 1993, Educational for All, The Indianscene, Widening Horizons, Dept. of Education DMD, Dec. 1993.

Government of India, 1998 National perspective plan for women. 1988-2000, Dept of women and child development MHRD, Delhi.

Haq, Mahbubul & Khadija Haq, 1998 Human Development in South Asia 1998 Dhaka: Oxford University Press.

India, Government of. 1974. *Towards Equality: Report of the Committee on the Status of Women,* New Delhi: Ministry of Education and Social Welfare.

India, Government of 2002. *Selected Educational Statistics 2001-02.* New Delhi: Department of education, planning, statistics and monitoring division, New Delhi: Ministry of Human Resource Development. Kaur, Ravinder, 2002.

Social Framework for Technical Education: Appraisel of Social Issues in Engineering Education. Report, mimeographed. NCERT 1993, Universal Primary Education of Rural Girls in India, New Delhi, Population Action International, "Closing the Gender Gap: Eucating Girls", 1993 Report on Progress Towards World Population SDtabilisation.

5

RURAL WOMEN AND TECHNOLOGY

TECHNOLOGY AND RURAL SECTOR

There is a global movement of economic integration through technology. The impact of this globalisation process has become all pervasive and inexorable. All sectors of developing countries seem to be vibrating with económic buoyancy. It has generated an impervious atmosphere of over optimism of instant economic growth. There is expansion of trade, investment, market, and increase in GNP, productivity, per capita income, profit, efficiency, salary etc. Lifestyles of metro people in India have become more attractive, comfortable and fashionable than ever before.

There is worldwide process of overproduction but unemployment and dramatic contraction of purchasing power of people. The global economic system is thus characterised by two contradictory forces: the consolidation of cheap labour economy on the one hand and the search for new consumer markets on the other. Unfortunately the former undermines the latter in the long run.

It generates social apartheid and undermines the rights of women. It is an insidious and inscrutable process, which is conducive to globalisation of markets, which ultimately undermines human livelihood and destroys civil society in the south.

After India's Independence and a long period of planning and development exercise, spanning over more than sixty years of in India, it is saddening to observe that the incidence of poverty and livelihood insecurity have remained as grave as ever. There is pronounced urban bias and rural neglect in the development process. The economic development has created an urbanisation process, which is dysfunctional, and an industrialisation pattern, which is regionally concentrated. The development planners have remained broadly myopic and complacent with trickledown effect for the rural sector. The result of the development exercises have been the persistence of a huge low productive primary sector, slender industrial sector and a bloated tertiary sector. All the benefits of the welfare measures have gravitated willy nilly towards the elite class and such other groups with political visibility. The rural sector of India has remained closed to the subsistence level and sensitive to the vagaries of nature—flood, cyclone and drought etc.

With the euphoria of 'high-tech civilisation', the concern for rural development, rural poverty, hunger and inequality virtually are dismissed as an obsession of egalitarian romantics. This insolent attitude and insouciance have generated dangerous consequences. It has spreaded an excitement of over optimism of instant change and pragmatism of high-tech-efficiency. It appears to be very logical and attractive. But, its socio-economic impact and implications are not uniform across social groups, genders, regions, sectors, and generations. Its statistical mirage underestimates the ground reality and depicts a misleading picture.

When one aims at gender equity, neither the earlier panacea of central planning nor the virtues of free marketism appears to carry much conviction for the common man of backward regions of India. The problem of economic vulnerability, livelihood insecurity and malnutrition among village people is becoming more pronounced.

WOMEN AND ECONOMIC DEVELOPMENT

The millennium development Goals (MDGs) aims at eradicating poverty and promote gender equality and empower women by 2015. There is need to improve the policies and implement them with greater impetus. But, poor women in India remain in traditional fields of employment. When traditional jobs become unavailable due to number of factors, women are forced to seek employment in other areas, which may have no relationship with their original experience and expertise. Women have a marginal role in family decision-making, they are primarily responsible for keeping the hearth going. They are occasionally consulted on marriage negotiations but not on any financial matters in the villages. Women's economic contribution has been invisibilised in the industrial process of economic development. This trend is not linear or unidirectional. Women are also displaced and lost their share in the industrial workforce due to upgradation of technology, and reduction of labour intensity of production through automation and adoption of high-tech .

Employers in the private sector, in the process of modernisation, eschew the responsibility for workers well being in the name of eliminating market distortions. Moreover, in the current globalised economy, women's social subordination coincides with the absence of economic alternatives. Employment of women in industries has been accompanied with deregulation of labour protection. Women fail to defend or promote their interest both as women and as workers. Even male-led labour unions either ignore or consider women's demand as divisive and irrelevant to the interest of the 'real working class'. The women-heads in the families face serious challenges in village economy due to low literacy levels, low asset holdings, lower productivity of land, lesser access to avenues of income-earning and governmental help and the declining kinship supports. The differential social evaluation of the sex roles, the male-orientation in running households coupled with rural poverty and household poverty enmesh in narrowing choices open to women heads of households. The capital intensive technology has rather trivialised the gender issue. The whole host of economic and social structures and processes that reinforce patriarchy, devalue and commodify the women. The confluence of modernisation does not improve the fate of women.

TECHNOLOGY AND WOMEN OF INDIA

Modern technology is supported and directed by powerful institutions and interests. Men gravitate to science and technology. We must question, whether technology is male-dominated because it demands some essentially masculine traits, or 'simply' because technology is where the power is? Technology is socially constructed, or co-produced, alongside gender. Technology itself gets gendered in the eyes of would be technologists. The continued male dominance in science and engineering is due in large measure to the enduring symbolic association of masculinity and technology by which cultural images and representations of technology converge with prevailing images of masculinity and power.

The use of technology is always discriminatory. Technical prowess is what defines them as engineers *and* what gives them a sense of power. The symbolic gendering of technology extends beyond the artifactual, but it has material consequences. Within the masculinity-technology association, one can discern a series of highly gendered dichotomies. Most obvious of these is the distinction between being people-focussed and machine-focussed. It corresponds to the division between feminine expressiveness and masculine instrumentalism. Most women routinely interact with people *and* technologies. For example computer is implicitly rather than explicitly gendered. 'Hard' technology is inert and powerful, while 'Soft' technology is smaller scale. So the world of technology is made to feel remote and overwhelmingly powerful because of the hard-soft dualism. The hard-soft dichotomy also extend to styles of thought in technology. On the masculine side of those dualisms we have an objectivist rationality associated with emotional detachment. On the feminine side, we have a more subjective rationality associated with emotional connectedness. Males have dominated the 'internet culture' since its inception. The Internet culture can be discomforting and alien to females.

Technological Advancement

India has achieved higher technological advancement during last decade. The Green Revolution, which focuses on increasing yields of rice and wheat, entails a shift in inputs from human to technical. Women's participation, knowledge and inputs are marginalised, and their role has shifted from being "primary producers to subsidiary workers." Women work longer hours and their work is more arduous than men's, yet their work is unrecognised.

Men complain that "women, like children, eat and do nothing." Technological progress in agriculture has had a negative impact on women. There is tremendous effects of information technology on women's employment and the nature of women's work in all third world countries including India . But, in areas of technology, till today women represent about 10% of researchers and about 5% of manager. The impact of information technology on society has not been uniformly beneficial, and the technological divide is being increasingly felt, especially in the developing countries. Serious obstacles still continue in achieving gender equality. The gender implications of digital divide is very serious in India. Access to and use of the Internet has important economic, educational, and social benefits, and those who are excluded from Internet participation will also be excluded from several benefits.[9] Lack of training does not allow them to escape from their sex-typed slots.

The women from poorer families face challenges as they adjust to new technologies. Their jobs do not reintegrate them, levelling the hierarchies and adding responsibilities. It is still believed by the elite class of Orissa that science improves their role and make them better mother, better wives, enriching their domestic lives. They do not think beyond that. Women still face subtle resistance to their participation in science and technology, no matter how talented she is, from all corners, particularly from the husband, how so ever educated he may be. Women are expressly excluded from many activities. Because marriage has remained indispensable goal for the women, particularly in Orissa. All her achievements culminate in a good marriage and proving her motherhood. Not being married is a great social stigma both for the family and the girls.

Not becoming mother is considered greater ominous. Therefore, getting higher education for girls is an accident. Ninety per cent of marriages are caste-based, arranged by the parents. Therefore, parents feel it as a burden or duty. Girls continue their studies till the parent get a good boy for them. Education reduces the set of choice for the parents. So, it is perceived as a problem for many girls. It is increasingly difficult to marry and get a partner. A good girl student experiences very encouraging motivation from the teachers, but cold attitude from the parents and relatives. Besides this, the amount of dowry-offer proportionally increases with the girls schooling for the parents. Even today many educated people (including the potential husbands) think that educated women would engage in deviant social and political behaviour. It is perceived that she would refuse to do household work and disobey their husband, if their education is too higher than the husband. They would become musculinised and expect to be included in men's activities. Advocates of women's education argue that education will help women to fulfil their God-given duties toward their husband and family. Therefore women suffer greater subordination and deprivation both at home and in society. Oppression of women in Orissa can be described as hypocritical at its worst and schizophrenic at its best.

Women should be given various (both farm and non-farm) training to escape from their sex-typed slots. The aim with jobs should be to reintegrate them wherever possible, levelling the hierarchies, adding responsibilities to lower grade jobs and building in more interaction with the technologies in the case of routine operations and jobs. It should provide pathways for lower skilled women workers to learn and progress. The aim of training should be to encourage women of any age or occupation to consider on-the-job or off-the-job training for more technical work. Otherwise they are more susceptible to displacement and deskilling by emerging push-botton technology.

Technology should liberate women potential instead of hooking them up, or tying them in side the virtual prisons. Community-based women's organisations should be instrumental in the process of enabling women to cross the so-called digital divide .Technology should be powerful tools for women to overcome discrimination, achieve full equality and higher well-being.

RURAL POVERTY AND WOMEN IN ORISSA

India consists of 28 states and six union territories of which 17 are major states with a population of one billion. Orissa is the poorest state of the country. It is the state which depict the paradoxical situation of economic growth and coexistence of poverty and livelihood insecurity of people. Livelihood Security refers to the poverty line defining inadequate income, consumption, nutritional level, health status, life expectancy, and asset holding of the people. Livelihood consists of both generation of income as well as the ownership of productive assets that reduces the vulnerability of marginalised communities. It involves the capabilities, assets of both material and non-material resource required for a means of living.

A majority of the population is still dependent upon the agricultural sector for their income. The income derived from farming is too little to improve their economic status. The rural poor are unable to save and do not have access to credit in order to invest in creating assets. The livelihood strategies of poor people in the villages are in reality different from those of rich people. The reduction in poverty in India is a myth. One fine morning the poverty level of India reduced from 36 % to 26% without any commensurate results. The definition adopted by the government at present has conceptual problem and therefore poverty is consequently underestimated.

The government uses that statistics to camouflage the real state of affairs. Orissa is the poorest state of the India having 48% of its population below the line of poverty. The deprivation Index estimated for all states depicts the Indian scenario and place of Orissa in the national map. Orissa has the highest IMR, MMR and high rate of illiteracy. It has the maximum concentration of tribal population. Incidence of poverty is the severest on Women and children of Orissa. The standard prescription for growth have not ended poverty or hunger anywhere in the state. Poverty reduction is the bench mark against which success of development institutions must be measured. Poverty, hunger and starvation deaths persist in KBK districts of Orissa despite large sums are spent in various government programmes. The ongoing poverty alleviation programmees of the govt do not attack the poverty at its roots. Rather they tend to polarize the society by concentrating income in the hands of few and narrowing the social and economic opportunities for the poor. Land degradation, water scarcity and growing vulnerability to economic stress are real threats to food security. Hunger is considered as the result of underdevelopment.

Therefore there is need for appropriate mix of resources, food, water, land, credit, training, market and technology in order to create enabling condition for the poor people. Policy makers of India attempt to fight against 'Feminisation of poverty'. It does not mean that poverty is a gendered experience but that the poor are mostly women. The poorer the family, the more likely it is to be headed by a woman. But, poverty can not serve as the proxy for subordination of women. Therefore, anti poverty policies can not be expected to necessarily improve the position of women.

Feminisation of Jobs and Village Economy

Independence in all countries has brought radical changes in the traditional hierarchy for men but much less for women in Orissa. For example, modernisation of agriculture resulted in mechanisation, which had reduced the work burden of male. But, women of Orissa continue to perform their drudgery-ridden traditional hand operated tasks unless their family income is sufficient to shift some work to another women from less well-off families. Advocates of globalisation argue that there is feminisation of jobs by looking at the rising work participation rate among females. But, it does not solve the problem of gender inequality in Orissa.

The ergonomics and working condition of employment in the urban informal sector is becoming worse. There is lack of training, job insecurity, health hazards, low wages, longer working hours, intensive supervision and contractual tasks etc, irregular salary and absence of social security benefits. This entails heavy exploitation of women workers of Orissa. Sometimes young girls are pressurised by the family to work in factories or offices. Sometimes they choose 'bad jobs' on their own in the face of strong parental oppositions. They see their job as a route to escape and find personal liberation. Employers take the advantage of their psychological/economic insecurity. Social dynamics so operate in side the house that even working women are not happy either. Given the opportunity they prefer to leave the job and remain as idle mothers. Some of them even cherish the 'comfort and care' of the husband for their non working wives.

The gender inequality in Orissa has remained very sharp within both rural and urban households. It manifests also in the labour market. Since the employment options available to women are severely limited and since the opportunities for skill acquisition and job mobility are more limited for the female than the male, the work force participation for the female means the relentless weariness of multiple burdens.

The economic citizenship has failed to improve the situation either. Both technology and labour market imperfections have been continuously displacing the female workers from high productive activities to low productive activities, through casualisation and contractualisation of jobs. Growing industrialisation and cut-throat market economy suits and reinforces the image of the female home makers par excellence. The work participation rate of female is rising in the informal sector only. They are ill-paid but don't leave the job due to increasing unemployment. This need for survival drives the woman to a virtual rape situation.

Harassment at work place is real and pervasive. The women have no courage to report due to the fear of further harassment, trauma and re-victimisation. Even earning women do not have the freedom to spend or regulate their lives. They are expected to hand over their salary to their husband or in-laws. The problems of managing both the employment situation and the home, and the suspicions about the woman's character continue to make matters worse. The male dominance is all-pervading and there are implicit assumptions that the wife should have a lesser designation at the workplace. The gender bias at work expects a woman executive to "look like a woman, behave like a lady, think like a man and work like a donkey".

The gender division of labour within the household of Orissa has remained culturally stubborn, till today. Women as a class are oppressed and subdued by the hegemony of social patriarchy. In Orissa, new labour saving devices have not changed the patterns of life and labour of farming community. State policy treats farm women as consumers, not producers. Farm women perform their field labour under a patriarchal system in which their work "belonged" to male family members. Their household labour remained unaffected by the technological revolution which changed lifestyle of urban women. Ironically, all home appliances and cooking gadgets encourage women to adopt the full-time homemaker role taken by urban housewives. But, village women of Orissa prefer their productive roles on and off the farm. The village society of Orissa recognises farming as a male occupation, so many of women's contributions to modernising farm life have been ignored or underestimated.

LIVELIHOOD SECURITY FOR WOMEN IN ORISSA

The concept of livelihood is defined as a means of living or supporting life and meeting individual and community needs. It involves the capabilities, assets of both material and non-material resources required for a living. It refers to poverty line defining adequate income, consumption, nutritional level, health status, life expectancy, and asset holding of the people. Livelihood consists of both generation of income as well as the ownership of productive assets that reduces the vulnerability of marginalised communities. A majority of the village population is still dependent upon the agricultural sector for their income.

The income derived from farming is too little to improve their economic status. The rural poor often are unable to save and do not have access to credit in order to invest in creating assets. As a result, there is over exploitation of natural resources such as water and forests in people's attempts to invest inputs into their agricultural production. The livelihood strategies of poor people in the villages are in reality different from those of rich people. Rich people always have the capacity to diversify their livelihood strategies because of the risks involved. The success of a livelihood strategy depends on both physical and human factors.

In state like Orissa, which is economically not developed, the sustenance and management of a good standard of living and maintenance of secured livelihood is really difficult. The poor villagers are subjected to the prey of vagaries of nature and variance in monsoon, which lead towards very low level of production of crops and family income.

The livelihood becomes sustainable when it can cope with and recover from stresses and shocks and maintain or enhance its assets both now and in the future, while not undermining the resource base. Sustainable Livelihood System promotes equity between and among generations, races, gender, and ethnic groups; in the access to and distribution of wealth and resources; in the sharing of productive and reproductive roles; and the transfer of knowledge and skills. Sustainable livelihoods are based on the functional interrelationships in which every member of the system is needed and participates. Sustainable livelihood supports meaningful work that meets the social, economic, cultural and environmental needs of all the members of a community—human, non-human, present and future and safeguard cultural and biological diversity. It stimulates local investment in the community and help to retain capital within the economy.

A futuristic nightmare is visualised for women in the villages, where widespread unemployment leads to economic insecurity and cuts in government spending and employment mean, worsening health services, lesser access to education and deterioration in civic services. Since gender relations at the household level governing the sexual division of labour tend to remain rigidly in place, young women are forced to give up their education or prospects for gainful employment in order to help their mothers in household maintenance. Thus, economic reforms, by ignoring the crucial cultural and structural aspects of gender, interact with the existing gender asymmetries affecting women of Orissa in negative ways. Some of these factors especially those that concern gender ideology are indeed very difficult to measure quantitatively.

TECHNOLOGY AND WOMEN'S OCCUPATION IN VILLAGES

Livelihood options and occupational pattern of the people are directly and indirectly related with market mechanism. Sometimes, market works friendly to the poor people and also sometimes expanded market access creates problems of livelihoods for them. Many social and cultural factors which influence women employment opportunities are persisting in the villages. Poverty and gender are not entirely separate social phenomena. The term "feminisation of poverty" does not mean that poverty is a gendered experience. Previous studies used to focus on vulnerability context, livelihood assets, policies, livelihood strategies and outcomes. They never perceive the gender dimension of the issue.

Women belonging to land-owning rich class, being mostly dependent housewives, run the risk of higher livelihood insecurity with worst fallback position. Our survey focuses on both endogenous and exogenous processes that influence the livelihoods of rural women. It identifies the crucial variables that influence the livelihood pattern among both land-owning and labour-selling class of women in the villages of Orissa. It analyses various farm and off-farm activities, which contribute to the family earnings, pursued by village women. It explains various livelihood needs, potentials and opportunities for village women.

During our field survey, we examine the links between technology and gender within the villages of Orissa. It analyses the occupational pattern of women, the level of female education, and identifies the factors that influence women employment. It assesses employment potentials and opportunities for women in both farm and non-farm activities in the villages. Orissa belongs to the coastal belt of eastern India. It has 30 districts. This study is based on the census study of two villages of two districts of Orissa .Two villages of Orissa have been selected purposively. The economy of both the villages centers around agriculture where as the first village has higher share of non farm activities. The first village is nearer to the town, second village is a remote one. It analyses the occupational pattern of women, their decision making power and contribution towards to the family income. It analyses how women are contributing to their family income through various farm and non farm works. Mostly, women are engaged in handicrafts, appliqué works and other small scale cottage industries.

CHARACTERISTICS OF THE STUDY VILLAGES

The study focuses on the scope, potentials and opportunities of income generation among women in both the villages. It analyses, how women are utilising these opportunities for getting employment and improving their earnings in the village economy. We observe the following difference between the two villages.

- The average family size is lower in the occupationally diversified village, Nuasasana.
- The dependency ratio is higher in the agricultural village, Madhusudanpur.
- The percentage of housewives is higher in the pure agricultural village.
- The work participation rate among women is higher in the occupationally diversified village.

- Higher literacy among the people motivates the people to diversify their livelihood in the first village .
- Lack of or lesser irrigation facility fail to motivate the people to purse non-farm activities.
- The higher percentage of marginal farmers encourages non-farm activities.
- The higher the percentage of wasteland, higher is the motivation for off-farm activities.
- The land-man ratio is lower in first village where people have high propensity to carry out non farm activities. The lesser the LAP higher is the propensity to carry out non-farm activities.
- The occupational concentration is higher in second village and occupational diversification is high in the first village.
- The dependency ratio is higher among higher caste and rich households due to many social constraints.

Employment of Women Outside the Village

There is high degree of seasonal unemployment and disguised unemployment in both the villages. The agricultural productivity is lower in Madhusudanpur than Nuasasan. Among the hired agricultural labour of Madhusudanpur 56% are men and 33% are women. On the contrary, among the hired agricultural labour of Nuasasan 55% are men and 53% are women. Therefore, the work participation rate among women in Nuasasan is higher than that of Madhusudanpur. But, , there is male-female wage differential in the farm sector of both the villages. It is observed that 21% of the house holds of Nuasasan are getting employment in service sector out side the village.

While 11% of the households of Madhusudanpur are doing services outside the village. But, 9% of households of Madhusaudanpur and 16% of households of Nuasasan are engaged in wage labour works outside the village. Mostly, women are found in the category of wage labour, working inside or nearby village. Women belonging to higher caste or rich class do not work outside the village at all.

The off farm activities of Nuasasan are mostly done by the women, while the off farm activities of Madhusudanpur are done by both, since they are family or caste-based occupations like carpentry, pottery, basket making etc. The orchard plantations and beetle vines supplement the livelihood system of the village economy. About 30% of farming households of both the villages have marketable surplus. The marketable surplus is generated from both non-cash crops like paddy and cash crops like vegetables, potato, pulses, fruit crops, groundnut and sugarcane. But, lower agricultural productivity in Madhusudanpur reduces the marketable surplus of the farmers of this village.

Village Credit System

1. The credit system differs between two villages. In Nuasasan, 83% of households, who borrow from commercial banks, use the credit for buying products and raw materials, which they need in their non-farm enterprises. But, it is different in the second village, where people get the cash credit from the cooperative banks. They do not borrow for buying raw materials from the outside market.
2. The Cooperatives encourage many non-farm activities and provide training opportunities for women workers engaged in appliqué, chalk manufacturing, agarbati, candle making etc. About 31% of households of Nuasasan and 12% of households of Madhusudanpur get training from the cooperatives
3. In the entire sample, about 29%, 13% and 8% of the households have borrowed for health problems, appliqué works and purchasing livestock respectively. Other purpose of making loan includes investing in various

types of non farm activities like candle, agarbati and chalk making. Loans for unproductive purposes amount to 24% of the total credit.

4. The investment in off farm activities is mostly self-financed in Madhusudanpur, while it is mostly loan-financed in Nuasasan. This difference has strong association with the nature of non farm activities. Family based on non-farm activities depends more on self-finance, while skill-based non-farm activities depends more on loan-finance.

Income and Expenditure Pattern

5. The occupational diversified village has higher average income than the agricultural village. It is due to two reasons; (a) The agricultural productivity is lower and (b) the average earnings from farm activities are lower than that of the farm activities.

6. But, when we observe the expenditure pattern of villages separately, we notice the difference that C is the modal expenditure class of Nuasasan while D is the modal expenditure class of Madhusudanpur. There is substantial difference in the average annual expenditure of two villages. It is due to the difference in the level of average earnings of the people.

7. When we examine the saving potential, we find that D is the modal group of both Madhusudanpur and Nuasasan. The average savings amount of household of Madhusudanpur is less than the average saving of the entire sample.

Women in Farm and non Farm Activities

8. The non farm activities of Madhusudanpur are mostly family-based and self-employed occupations. While in Nuasasan, the off-farm activities are mostly contractual and based on skill, knowledge and external supports.

9. The non farm women workers of Madhusudanpur obtain raw materials from the same locality, while the off farm women workers of Nuasasan procure raw material from outside the village. The network of intermediaries exist for supplying the raw materials to the non farm women workers of the first village.
10. The off farm activity in Madhusudanpur are mostly seasonal while in Nuasasan the non farm activities have no seasonality. It has connection with the nature of activity. When the occupation is family-based, then there are seasonal variations in production and demand. When the occupation is skill-based then there is no seasonal effect on production or demand.
11. The market for the products of family based non farm occupations is local, while the markets for the products of skilled based occupations are outside the village. The network of intermediaries exist for supplying the product to the marketing destinations.
12. Rise in household income and higher production are the main motivational factors for women to pursue off farm activities. There is inter-village difference in the impact of motivational factors.
13. Lack of or lesser irrigation facility has indirectly motivated the male to purse non-farm activities. Lack of irrigation is the cause of low land productivity. Therefore, it constitutes a push-factor for the villagers to undertake off-farm jobs.
14. The higher percentage of marginal farmers and landless peasants encourages more non-farmers activities. Nuasasan having higher percentage of marginal and landless farmers has more off farm activities.
15. Average earnings from non-farm activities of households are higher than that of second village. But, average

earnings from farm activities are higher in Maddhusudanpur than Nuasasan.

Socioeconomic Status of Women

16. The percentage of housewives is higher in the pure agricultural village i.e Madusudanpur. And the proportion of women engaged in non farm activities is more in Nuasasan. The socio-cultural factors are more restrictive in Madhusudanpur where women are demotivated to earn from any economic activity.
17. The work participation rate among women is significantly higher in Nuasasan than in Madhusudanpur. It has brought occupational diversification in the first village. But, the women of second village are mostly housekeepers. It is both the cause and effect of occupational concentration in second village. But, there is no inter village difference in male work participation rate. It is almost the same in both the villages.
18. Higher literacy among the people motivates the people to face the challenge and diversify their livelihood base in the village economy. Higher female literacy encourages the women to seek alternative sources of income. Therefore, Nuasasan having higher literacy has more non-farm activities.
19. The gender divisions of labour are socially rigid in both the villages. Women in all families of both villages are found to do the full responsibility of many jobs like cooking, cleaning, washing, child care, waste disposal and gathering fuel, carrying fodder and water.

Participation of Women

20. None of the non farm women workers is very satisfied. In terms of fair price the non farm workers in both villages are marginally satisfied. It indicates the

exploitation involved in the contractual arrangements with these women workers. The non producers expropriate the profit margin of the women workers.

21. The participation of women in decisions making pertaining to farming, village meetings, selling of crops, and purchase of animals, orchard plantation and purchase of durables in of sample households is very low.
22. Lower educational status and village tradition and caste system are the main constraining factors for availing employment opportunities of women in both the villages. Reduction in the rigidity of social and caste system leads to increase in women's' freedom to undertake some economic activity in order to supplement the household income.

Agricultural operations are mostly done by men. Off farm activities are mostly done by women. The seasonal and disguised unemployment is very high in both the villages. The male-female wage differential is higher in the farm sector of both the villages. There is no inter village difference in male work participation rate. But, the work participation rate among female is directly connected with agricultural productivity.

The higher caste households used to lease out their land to landless farmers or marginal farmers. People have high propensity to carry out non-farm activities due to: (a) low agricultural productivity (b) lower land-man ratio or land availability per household (LPH) (c) higher percentage of upland (d) higher percentage of wasteland. The dependency ratio is higher among higher caste and rich households. Due to many social constraints and traditional values, the women belonging to higher caste and richer class are compelled to remain as housewives. Awareness and poverty among people encourage them to supplement their farm income and diversify their livelihood base.

The orchard plantation, fishery, appliqué, candle making and basket-making constitute a sustainable source of supplementary livelihood of the village people. The structures of landed property vary but the structure of non productive household assets does not vary according to the village category. The occupational diversified village has higher average income than the agricultural village due to: (a) irrigation facility (b) higher size of land holding, (c) high income from non farm activities. Correspondingly, level of expenditure and saving are higher in the occupational diversified village. But, the contractual arrangements in the non farm activities involve exploitation of the women workers. The borrowing for non productive purposes among village people is high.

Higher occupational concentration in a village does not encourage the women to be economically productive. The gender divisions of labour are socially rigid in the villages. Higher literacy among the people motivates the people to face the challenge and diversify their livelihood base in the village economy. Lower educational status and village tradition and caste system are the main constraining factors for village women in availing employment opportunities outside the village and carrying out non farm activities. Thus, it is inferred that livelihood security of women in the village economy is determined by the following five factors: (a) Economic factors, (b) Social Factors, (c) Demographic factors, (d) Institutional Factors.

STATUS OF WOMEN IN VILLAGES

Although gender empowerment has been a buzzword in development circles, the concept has been used in so many different ways by different agents that it remains ambiguous. Conceptualising power and gender adequately entails understanding its multi- dimensional nature, the complex ways in which women experience subordination and the ways in which they negotiate or manage this state of affairs. The gender-gap in indices such as life expectancy, literacy and earning has in fact increased from sixties to eighties in entire south Asia. The UNDP developed Gender Development Index (GDI) as a tool to capture gender inequality.

It notes the inequalities between men and women on the same variables that make up the Human Development Index related to the over all achievements in that society. It considers only three variables: health, education and income. It fails to take into account important dimensions such as the quality of community life access to basic amenities and human rights. Important dimensions relevant for women such as safety and security, household allocation of resources, unpaid labour, mobility constraints and on sexual and reproductive freedom by patriarchal ideology do not find any place. Raising income of women may not indicate improved status for women.

The GEM (Gender Empowerment Measure) is again based on three variables. It is built on a very narrow conception of empowerment. It does not include legal and human rights nor does it reflect the ways in which cultural constructions of gender identity are made. Thus, it is clear from the above discussion that if one attempts to assess the impact of economic reforms differential on men and women, the conventional parameters used to measure gender disparity is not enough. It is therefore, necessary to consider research methodologies that go beyond the quantitative in order to do justice to the complexity of these phenomena.

The situation in Orissa is counter logical. Paradoxically it is observed that in Orissa, there is a trade off between women's material well being and their autonomy. When the family becomes richer, the women lose her earning power and social autonomy. Therefore, poverty and gender development can not be approached synergistically with the same policy instruments. When rising household income has a perverse effect on women's well being then policies which promote women's work participation rate even if successful, may not increase women's well-being. Thus, money is neither necessary nor sufficient for transforming the existing gender relations in Orissa.

In villages of Orissa, the child marriage practice still prevails in some communities. Dropout rates in village schools for girls has been increasing. Practice of girl child labour has been endured as the "harsh reality". Case of selling of girl child Karlekar, Malavika (1995), Search for Women Voices, *Economic and Political Weekly* 29 April has increased. Rape cases have been increasing. It is sheer hypocrisy that the so-called modern civilisation with its pretensions to high thinking considers that to be born as a girl is a crime and burden.

Unfortunately, education among women has not produced a reformative effect on the social outlook, nor encouraged any change conducive to social upliftment. Discrimination against women does not end by merely bestowing of judicial rights or by making women literate. The social problem can not be solved by legal cell or economic independence. Most urban women are literate today but they are also victims of domestic violence and social discrimination.

SOCIAL DYNAMICS AND FEMALE EDUCATION

While science and technology are advancing economic and social problems of backward states are worsening. In Orissa, discrimination and violence against women takes a dismaying variety of occurrences. All are violations of the most fundamental human rights. The pitiable condition of womanhood in Orissa trapped in the web of socio-cultural factors such as superstitious and blind faith perpetuated by male dominance. Her struggle for survival continues from the womb to the grave without respite. The struggle for survival continues throughout the woman's life beginning with the female foetus. Although, there is anti-abortion Act, private practitioners continue to conduct abortions with a sex bias. Though the technology has supported to help women to have safer births, it has resulted in female foetus being aborted and the practice is spreading in an alarming manner.

In fact, prenatal Diagnostic Centres have become sex determination clinics. The legislation to curb the misuse of amniocentesis for sex selection and abortion of female fetuses calls for further punishing the women because they are under pressure to bear a male child. Son preference dangerously affects the women. Its consequences can be anything from foetal or female infanticide to neglect of the girl child over her brother in terms of such essential needs as nutrition, basic health care and education.

Victim of Cruelty

Orissa is a mosaic of many social riddles and contradictions. One such paradox is the gender inequality. There is a snark syndrome, where there is no credible empirical base for the prejudices against women. Educators and policymakers have internalised repeated social assertions. Even they do justify and implement such policies such as reservation of seats, women day celebration, welfare measure for widows, etc. The land which worships the woman most, has the highest violence against women. She is not only robbed of her dignity by the men outside, but also become a victim of cruelty by her saviours, within the four walls of her own house. However, her trauma does not end here, it may even go to the extent of forcing her to commit suicide or she may be burnt to death for various reasons. In the age of cyber culture and nanotechnology, the horrendous phenomena as dowry in Orissa has also been increasing. Girls are treated as commodity in the market. It transcends the rural urban dichotomy. Its incidence cuts across all caste and class boundaries. The cases of bride burning has been increasing. Many such case twisted as suicides. Some ideal parents who prefer not to take dowry for their well-qualified sons, are, in fact, considered 'strange' by the society and doubts about 'the respectability of the groom's family' are usually raised. Even on the final day, the marriage is cancelled on the suspicion that the boy may be impotent or having some ulterior motives. He may not find a girl to marry.

Domestic Violence

The most common type of violence against women in Orissa is "domestic violence". Although the family is a source of love, sympathy and support, it is also the great source of inequality, exploitation and violence. Domestic violence in Orissa is a horror they have to cope with in silence. The woman in Orissa is a slave to the so-called institutionalised cultural shackles. Her mobility is restricted, her self-expression is monitored and her thoughts influenced by others in her milieu. She becomes the victim of suspicion by her brothers, parents, husband and in-laws. Domestic violence is one of the greatest obstacles to gender equality and right to life and liberty. Wife beating is generally accepted as a cultural phenomenon. Most men take it upon themselves to beat their wives to 'improve them.'

Women too accept it as a part of life. The police, the doctor and the teacher all view it as a societal norm. The legal system is also hopeless in Orissa. There are pertinent rules and laws. But, there are so many factors that prevent women of Orissa to seek justice through legal exercise such as: (a) Her apprehensions relating to ultimate consequences, (b) Unreliable and expensive legal system, (c) Lack of support from her parental family and (d) Cultural and religious forces. Thus, it is imperative that women themselves must be morally strong and empowered. Educational system should make them mentally strong.

Institutionalisation of Neo-patriarchy

The patriarchy is very strong among high caste households of Orissa. The women cannot take the full advantage of their increasing access to education in order to enhance their autonomy.

The most important factor affecting women autonomy is social prestige associated with higher caste Hindu families. In spite of being an essential economic contributor, there are social constraints, which work against the women to improve her status and position within the household. Female labour who work and earn do not automatically enjoy same rights and liberties. It is again dependent on caste hierarchy. A variety of cultural and socio psychological factors determine her autonomy. Even today, man continues to exercises his subtler control on the family production and reproduction system. It is gradually institutionalised at several spheres: work, culture, customs, religion and education.

Therefore, liberation of women will not be easy or complete without the destruction of 'neo-patriarchy'. The social and economic structures that locks production and reproduction together, perpetrate male dominance and female submission. Thus, liberation of women in the villages does not automatically follow from their economic citizenship. It can only be achieved if all structures in which women are integrated are transformed simultaneously. A modification of any one of them can be offset by a reinforcement of another, so that a mere permutation of the form of inequality is ultimately achieved.

Housewife in the Age of Globalisation

The gender division of labour within the household of in India has remained culturally stubborn, till today. Women as a class are oppressed and subdued by the hegemony of social patriarchy. The gender inequality is very sharp within both rural and urban households. It manifests also in labour market. Both technology and labour market imperfections have been continuously displacing the female workers from high productive activities to low productive activities, through casualisation and contractualisation of jobs. The fate and fortune of working women is not better off either. The working women is saddled with multiple burdens like: cooking, gardening, cleaning, tutoring, shopping, hospitality, rearing children, caring old and diseased, driving etc.

The modern women in the towns does every thing with out leaving the primary job of being the house wife. Yet, she has no voice or empowerment. Rather, her activities are remotely controlled by the husband. But, it safely goes in the name of husband's care and concern. It creates a snark syndrome of neo-houswifisation. After liberalisation of the last decade, there is more concentration of women in domestic works and non-market roles and activities. Each household has two clear roles to play: producing and consuming. The consumption activity has two components:

$$C = C_o + C_h$$

Where C_o means goods and services suppplied and consumed from outside the household. And C_h represents goods and services supplied from the household itself. The production activity has two components:

$$P = P_o + Ph$$

Where: P_o stands for the goods and services produced for the outside market and P_h means good and services produced for the house. Each household has no control neither over the C_o nor P_o. In the process of marketisation, the purchasing power of the common man has been decreasing. The globalisation of prices inflicts economic strain on the family, which ultimately spells further strain on the women and girls only. The economic strain is partially absorbed and neutralised by women by curtailing Ch and raising Ph. It only amounts to spell a heavier pressure on women, girls children and housewives.

Therefore, modernisation is generating a TRAP which is not very easily perceptible. T stands for tailoring, tutoring, R stands for jobs like receptionists, A means female engaged in producing *Achar* and *Papad* and *agarbati* and P stands for getting a job in the beauty parlours. All these jobs are palpably make the females more active. But, all these jobs belong to the inside spheres (outside the house but inside the gate) and semi domestic sectors. Most of these belong to the informal sector, which is unregistered, unrecorded and unprotected, subject to all types of exploitation and intimidation. It is unfortunate that greater availability of these jobs makes us believe in the feminisation of jobs. Therefore, economic independence is a myth for women in Orissa.

In fact, outside earnings is expected to give her:

- a better breakdown position
- a clearer perception of her individuality and well being and
- a higher perceived contribution to the economic status of the family.

The greater economic role for women definitely improves their status within and outside the family. However money is not sufficient condition for transferring gender relations in existing social order in Orissa. She remains as dependent both in thinking and action as before. The socio-religious and cultural influences on the girl child are so strong, both physically and mentally, that even with education and influences from outside, she is not free to think of herself as an individual.

CONCLUDING REMARKS

Although gender empowerment has been a buzzword in development circles, the concept is being used in so many different ways that it remains ambiguous. All studies and reports on women status have only remained as a source of data, which rather endorses the passivity of the state. We should reject the touristic observations of women in metro society, dispel misconceptions and portray the real scenario of Orissa. Effective policy design requires an accurate understanding of the gender issues within a broad social framework.

We need poverty-independent gender analyses and policies in order to rescue gender from poverty trap. Women's income earning activity should not be temporary, exploitative and reversible. Education and technology should ensure liberation and freedom for all human beings. It should break gradually the shackles of tradition that binds women in the man-made gaol. Technological development can be both a threat and an ally to women in their various roles. Therefore, we should integrate gender into technology and development. More nuanced discussion of the complex interrelationships between gender and technology is needed. Training programme for successful technology transfer is necessary to derive the benefits of existing market-driven technological promotion. The new technology should be used as a vehicle for gender equality in the backward societies like Orissa.

The gender issue should be delinked both from myopic economics and insensitive politics. There is no substitute for a gender analysis, which transcend class divisions and material definitions of deprivation. Therefore, 'adding women' is not necessary, but an insight and rethinking development concepts and practices as a whole through a gender lens is necessary. We have to initiate debate on state non action on gender issues. Despite several rules and acts in place, all rights of women are being violated and they have been suffering in silence. A vigorous multi-pronged and multi-professional effort is needed to establish the woman as a human being in her own right. With the hosanna of modernisation, it is imperative to dispel myths, superstitions and misconceptions about woman and her duties and adopt a rational attitude towards the woman as a human being.

Social Transformation

Despite jamboree of techno culture we need a meaningful social transformation, which gives the equal independent human status to women. Economic citizenship is not sufficient for transforming existing asymmetric gender relations. In all backward states like Orissa, girls are educationally very successful but socially women are not. The wife may be happy but the women is not. The real progress should occur when the women become the producers of their own welfare and bounty, not the recipients of charity. The chance for a social transformation should begin and end with the womenkind in the ground, because, nothing grows from the top. Effective policy design requires accurate understanding of the gender issues within a broad social framework. Women development is a social process to be evolved from the society but not a technological product to be achieved by a triggered policy.

NOTES AND REFERENCES

Agarwal, Bina (1986). 'Women, Poverty and Agricultural Growth in India', *The Journal of Peasant Studies*, Vol. 13, No.4, July.

Agarwal, Bina (1994). *A Field of One's Own: Gender and Land Right in South Asia*, Cambridge University Press, Cambridge.

Agarwal, Bina (1997), "Bargaining" And Gender Relations: Within and Beyond the Households. Feminist Economics. 3(1), 1-51.

Bardhan, Kalpana (1979). 'Work as a Medium of Earning and Social Differentiation: Rural Women of West Bengal', Paper presented at ADC-ICRISAT Conference Hyderabad, India.

Bhalla, G et al (2003). Rural Employment and Poverty, *Economic and Political Weekly*, Aug 16th Chambers, Robert and Gordon R Conway (1992). Sustainable Rural Livelihoods: Practical Concepts for the 21st Century.IDS Discussion Paper No. 296.

Brighton Chattopadhaya, Molly and David Seddon (2002). Life histories and Long term Change: Rural Households and Gender Relations in a West Bengal village, *Economic and Political Weekly*, Vol 37(49) Dec 7.

Curie , Bob (2000)The Politics of Hunger in India, Macmillan India, Chennai.

Das, Kumar(1993) Rural Development in India, Discovery publishing.House, Delhi.

Desai, Sonalde. 1994. *Gender Inequalities and Demographic Behaviour: India.* New York: The Population Council, Inc.

Dorward, Andrew et al (2003) Markets, Institutions and Technology: Missing Links to Livelihood Analysis, Development Policy Review, Vol. 21(3), pp. 313-32

Dreze, Jean and Chen Marty (1995), Recent research on widows in India, EPW, Sept. 30, PP.2435-50.

Dreze, Jean and P.V. Srinivasan(1995). 'Widowhood and Poverty in Rural India, p. 234.

Dube, Leela and Rajni Palriwala (eds.) (1990). Structure and Strategies: Women, Work and Family, Sage Publications, New Delhi.

Dwyer, Daisy and Judith Bruce (eds.) (1988). A Home Divided: Women and Income in the Third World, Stanford University Press,Stanford.

Krishnaraj, Maithreyi and Karuna Chanana (eds.) (1989). *Gender and the Household Domain,* Sage Publications, New Delhi.

Kumar, V. (1997). *Economic Growth and Rural Poverty,* Concept Publishsing. House, New Delhi.

Kumari, Ranjana (1989). *Women-Headed Households in Rural India,* Radiant Publishers, New Delhi.

Lingam, L(1994) Women headed Households: coping with caste, Class and Gender Hierarchies, *Economic and Political Weekly,* March 19.

Lingam, Lakshmi (1994). 'Women-Headed Households: Coping with Caste, Class and Gender Hierarchies', *Economic and Political Weekly,* Vol. 29, No. 12, pp. 699-704.

Lipton and Jacques van der Gaag (eds.) *Including the Poor,* The World Bank, Washington DC.

Purushothaman, Sangeetha. 1998. *The Empowerment of Women in India: Grassroots Women's Networks and the State.* New Delhi: Sage Publications.

Saskia Everts(1998) *Gender and Technology: Empowering Women, Engendering Development,* Sed Books, London.

Sonpar, S and Ravi Kapur (2001). *Non conventional Indicators: Gender disparity under structural Reforms,* EPW, Jan 6

Swantz, Marja-Liisa (1995). Embracing Economies of Women: paths to sustainable livelihoods. *Development,* 3, 27-29.

Visaria, P. and L.Visaria (1985). 'Indian Households with Female Heads: Their Incidence, Characteristics and Levels of Living', in Devaki Jain and Nirmala Banerjee (eds.) *Tyranny of the Household,* Vikas Publishing House, Shakti Book Series, Delhi.

Faulkner, Wendy (2000), *The Technology Question In Feminism, Women's Studies International Forum,* University of Edinburgh.

Venkateswaran, Sandhya. 1995. *Environment, Development and the Gender Gap.* New Delhi: Sage Publications.

World Bank (1991). *Gender and Poverty in India, A World Bank Country Study,* The World Bank, Washington DC.

6

FEMALE POLITICAL LEADERSHIP IN INDIA

The main aim of this chapter is a recognition and exploration of alternative accounts of female leadership in India, other than dynastic succession. The chapter addresses dominant accounts of female political leadership in two ways. This chapter will examine why female political leaders become popular and hold positions of power, other than as "martyrs wives and dynastic daughters" (Thompson, 2002). Equating female leadership with the dynastic account of leadership of females in South and Southeast Asia does not adequately explain the varied paths to power that many female political leaders in India have followed, at least in the past two decades. It also does not reflect the changing political scene in India which has seen the growing importance of the state level parties, resulting in a regionalisation of politics, thus, allowing regional or subnational leaders to become more influential at the national level.

Therefore, this element of the chapter is an attempt to rebalance an empirical oversight in the literature. The second element of the chapter addresses gender stereotypes which emerge from essentialised accounts of behavioural styles of gendered leadership, such as the moral capital argument.

In order to address these two elements, the chapter attempts to synthesise relevant literature on Indian politics and the politics of gender. The chapter includes a brief contextualisation of the Indian political environment (women's political participation in the nationalist movement to present day) and the changing political institutional structure (the fragmentation and regionalisation of Indian electoral politics), a gendered analysis of sources of legitimacy in the Indian context, and a discussion of essentialised accounts of behavioural styles of gendered leadership. Prominent female politicians demonstrate the diverse manifestations of female political leadership in India. This chapter will focus on the leadership of J. Jayalalithaa, Rabri Devi, Uma Bharti, and Mayawati.

The chapter concludes that gender is an important factor of both the path to power as well as the exercise of leadership and the sources of legitimacy that leaders draw upon. Structural gender bias and gender-biased perceptions and expectations are understood to have a significant impact on assessments of behavioural style and performance. Yet, these sources of gender power can be utilised by leaders, reinforcing and legitimising stereotypes in exchange for political power. Identity politics and political discourse play important roles in the exercise of leadership. However, the implications for women's political participation suggest little short-term benefits for women in politics. The changing political system has only worked to catapult a few women into positions of power. Nevertheless, female political participation and leadership in the local panchayats does have potential implications for the future generation of political leaders and the political participation of women.

Dynastic succession is the most frequently used explanation for women's rise to political leadership in Asia. This consists largely of three elements relevant to this argument. Firstly, twentieth century dynastic succession in Asia has taken place in times of transformational change, resulting in emergency dynastic succession (as a result of a coup d'etat or process of democratisation for example). Secondly, martyrdom often means a transferral of charisma onto the successor. Thirdly, the relatively high presence of women successors, it is argued, is due to the (perceived or actual) higher moral capital of women as opposed to men; the former as less corrupted or corruptible than men.

Female Leaders

Comparative analyses of South and South-east Asian women leaders have frequently brought the dynastic succession account to the fore. Richter asserts "[i]n south and southeast Asia. the most important political posts open to women have been so because of *familial* ties to prominent male politicians—the opportunity for such women having been greatly enhanced by their husbands' deaths and often dramatic *martyrdom.* Although Thompson concentrates more on female leaders of democratic transitions in South and Southeast Asia, his study offers insights into how gender structures the dynastic account of female leadership.

He emphasises several features of dynastic succession including the symbolic representation of women as mothers healing the nation; women imbued with higher moral capital than men; and male chauvinism in the political sphere. However, Thompson's account of female political leadership is limited for three reasons.[1] Firstly, as a large-scale comparative analysis of South and Southeast Asian women leaders, some contextual detail is lost, particularly in how the political context varies spatially, temporally, and discursively. This is crucial to understanding how female political leaders in India gain access to and sustain power in contemporary times. Secondly, Thompson's account has limited applicability to the Indian context and this is reflected in his limited discussion of Indian female leaders[2]. As Mitraargues, "if we broaden the base of our enquiry and look at appointments to political office at all levels of the [Indian] system, succession by members from within the immediate kin will no doubt appear as the exception rather than the rule." Thirdly, in concentrating on female leadership during democratic transitions, Thompson does not touch on political leadership of career politicians, more representative of transactional leadership.[3]

A sustained professional career in politics is a more representative pattern and is thus becoming increasingly important for the study of female political leadership in India, not least so because of the recently enacted 73rd and 74th Amendments on panchayat reservations. Lastly, and this is not confined to Thompson's account of dynastic succession, arguments based around women's relatively higher moral capital compared to men rarely address their underlying essentialised assumptions.

The three criticisms of Thompson's work will be addressed in three ways. Firstly, to address the issue of contextual detail, an account of women's political role in India from the Independence struggle to the present day must be briefly outlined. This enables an understanding of the material and discursive *environment* in which female leadership in India is situated, the environment being a critical factor in the assessment of leadership.[4] Secondly, a discussion of the changing structure of Indian electoral politics will demonstrate alternative opportunities for the emergence of women leaders, other than the dynastic route. This provides the institutional and environmental backdrop to the changing situational context of political leadership in India. Thirdly, a discussion of the exercise of leadership will focus on a critique of accounts based on a gender-as-difference approach, such as the moral capital argument, and recognition of the structural gender bias that impedes women within institutional settings. A more contextualised understanding will be provided of how women leaders in India draw upon sources of legitimate authority and thus power. This situates leadership within a discursive context in which modern Indian women are perceived to act in a political dimension, which affects their perceived or actual style of leadership.

Alternative Paths to Power

Contemporary accounts differ somewhat in explaining a leader's path to power, but many accounts reproduce an insider/outsider dichotomy, which distinguishes between two sets of individuals. "Insiders" have risen through the ranks of the political institutional infrastructure whereas "outsiders", come to political leadership and/or formal political activity with little experience of the "rules of the game" yet may possess either popularity, expertise, ambition, or substantial interest in policy issues, or any combination of these. Gendered accounts of leadership highlight an additional category, the political 'surrogate', which, while similar to the concept of 'outsider', takes on its own unique significance in dynastic accounts of female leadership.

Hart outlines two features that are important in the accession to Indian leadership—those of *winning mandates* and a leader's *pathway to power*. The importance of an individual's pathway to power in determining their legitimacy is especially relevant to the critique of the dynastic account of female leadership because "the path taken to leadership in some part determines the power held by the leader, the legitimacy of his leadership, and, to some extent, support for his policies". Therefore, a leader's route to the top determines in part the legitimacy that he or she commands and has implications for the success and sustainability of that leadership.[5]

Hart also outlines the pathways to power offered by the Indian system as (1) the institutional ladder; (2) the move into politics of the "culture hero"; and (3) dynastic succession. The third path of dynastic succession has been outlined above. Hart's account generally concurs with other accounts in the literature. If we recall, the main characteristics can include martyrdom followed by a transferral of charisma onto the dynastic successor, symbolic representation of women as mothers healing the nation, women imbued with higher moral capital than men, and male chauvinism in the political sphere.

The author have attempted to synthesise some approaches to "paths to power" into a typology that is shown in Table 1 below. It is important to note the dynamic aspect of this typology in that different female leaders can represent different paths to power at different stages of their career. Also, these categories are not fixed and their boundaries not impermeable but represent ideal types.

The "institutional ladder" path can be equated to that of the "insider" who climbs through the ranks often from the grassroots and develops leadership capability over time with acquired experience and expertise. Promotion is obtained through merit or otherwise and the individual gradually becomes more aware of the "rules of the game". The "institutional ladder" route— which provides long-term exposure to male-oriented political organisations—demonstrates how structural gender bias can impede the career progression of women, offering them limited strategic choices. They can conform to the rules of the game and thus internalise male, or more accurately, hegemonic masculine norms[6]. This often means a woman has to "struggle to reconcile conflicting demands" to avoid violating gender norms and stereotypes. In short a woman has to "look like a lady, and act like a man". The second path is that of the transfer to politics of the culture hero. In India, this has been a marked phenomenon, particularly in the southern states of Andhra Pradesh and Tamil Nadu, where popular film stars have entered politics exploiting their mass popularity and cultural appeal, and have been successful as political leaders. While some have downplayed this as a phenomenon of Indian leadership, due to relatively few manifestations, others see this explicitly as the effect regional culture and populist politics can have on the appeal and legitimacy of political leaders.

To these three paths, the author has added the concept of the "proxy" leader which in India is a scenario more visible at the panchayat level but which has become symbolised by the leadership of Rabri Devi, former Chief Minister (CM) of Bihar, as a "proxy" for Rashtriya Janata Dal party leader Laloo Prasad Yadav. In this sense, women are elected but act as an agent on behalf of their male relations, and exercise power in their interests. This has become more common and widespread due to the reservation policy enacted in the 73rd and 74th constitutional amendment reserving for women a third of all seats in the panchayat institutions. The "proxy" phenomenon has emerged as a source of criticism of the legitimacy of both participating women and the system itself.[7]

As a concept, the "proxy" agent is similar to the idea of the 'surrogate' or dynastic successor as power is conferred not on the basis of the proxy's own ability but on whom they are acting on behalf of. It is dissimilar in that the proxy is an agent for someone who is active in politics through them rather than as the predecessor whose mantle the surrogate takes on.

The political mobilisation of women during the fight for Independence has been identified as one of the key factors in determining women's political participation in contemporary times. Several accounts of the women's movement in India which accompanied the nationalist struggle for independence from British rule, note the lack of an emancipatory outcome and the enduring subservient nature of women's role in society. Women were welcome to join the resistance to British colonial rule, but their political activity was encouraged only insofar as to support the traditional gender hierarchy within Indian society. As long as their political activity supplemented but didn't sacrifice their traditional duties as wives, daughters and sisters, their political activism was encouraged. However, several male supporters of reform for women's issues supported women's franchise.

Women in Politics

Crucially, the nature of the women's movement and the participation of women in politics in India must be understood in terms of the impact of colonialism. As Forbes notes women rejected the label of "feminist" for fear of being accused of as unpatriotic; the enemy in their understanding was not their male counterparts but the forces of colonial power and "foreign domination". While the nationalist leader M.K. Gandhi supported the notion of female suffrage, he emphasised the need for unity and solidarity against the British Raj. Gandhi consistently mobilised the Hindu goddess of *Sita* as the supportive and sacrificing wife; in the process, "Gandhi was constructing a new ideal for Indian women that rewrote passivity and self-suffering as strength."[8]

Despite successful mobilisation of women's organisations such as the All-India Womens' Conference, these organisations largely benefited middle-class women by providing experience of working within organisational structures. There were however, significant advances in women's legal rights and progress in addressing the need for women's education, and with Independence women did obtain the franchise. Furthermore, their demands for a place in the government of newly Independent India were legitimised by their involvement in the nationalist movement.

Women in Freedom Movement

The role of Indian women in post-Independence and modern Indian politics is directly related to the lack of a significant outcome for the women's movement after the achievement of Independence from British rule by the nationalists. While a liberal discourse of equality ensued upon Independence in 1947, by 1974 the Committee on the Status of Women in India produced a commissioned report titled *Towards Equality* which evaluated and acknowledged the enduring plight of Indian women.

Women's political participation was largely manifest through the women's movement, itself fragmented as a result of differing ideologies and issue-based protests, with only token numbers of women participating in "formal" politics, many of which were from higher class and caste backgrounds and had been supported by liberal progressive families. The women's movement has organised on diverse issues from dowry, arrack, violence, equal economic and employment opportunities, eco-feminism, and anti-development protests opposed to displacement in the Narmada valley and similar state-sponsored developmental projects[9].

In the last two decades, the Hindutva movement has also become a site of women's right-wing political mobilisation although with dubious potential for the empowerment of women, and has become particularly militant around communal issues.

Modern Indian politics has seen political parties appropriate women's issues, such as the concerns of the anti-arrack movement, and appear sympathetic towards them in order to capture the women's vote. By adopting the interests of what could be considered a sub-altern group in India, they are employing a populist strategy. Change may therefore prove elusive and sympathy may turn out to be pure rhetoric, as political U-turns on prohibition laws have demonstrated. As a consequence of this appropriation, much of the women's movement has fragmented along ideological and political lines as women's organisations operate as an offspring of the major political parties.[10]

Despite the movement-based nature of the women's political mobilisation, women are engaged in electoral politics with similar overall turnouts for men and women at assembly and Lok Sabha elections, with some regional variance. The Lok Sabha elections in May 2004 elected just over 8% of female candidates to the Lok Sabha, with proportions of contesting and elected women candidates varying considerably among political parties. As these figures show, the attitude and policy of the political party towards giving tickets to women to contest constituencies, and thus their symbolic manifestation for the participation of women in politics, is crucial in determining women's actual participation, especially with regards women's relatively lower economic independence and the financial resources required to run for political office.[11]

Many commentators have noted the rising importance of the state level parties in national politics in what many have called the "third phase of democratisation" in Indian politics. The last three Lok Sabha elections in India more than most have brought into sharp focus the importance of coalition-building and party alliances in order to win elections, so much so that it is recognised that they have 'become a central factor shaping politics in India". Some point to the changing political party system; others attribute this to India's vast diversity in terms of electoral demands, from the Dalit movement of Uttar Pradesh to the regional identity discourse of the southern states.

Many see both as factors causing change. The demise of the dominant Congress (I) party has seen the simultaneous dilution of the Congress-based dynastic succession through the Nehru-Gandhi dynasty yet the dynasty still remains central to the party's core supporters, with Sonia Gandhi as Congress party chairwoman, and the entry into politics of her children, Rahul and Priyanka.[12]

Secondly, populist politics in India is driven by discourse centred around a politics of identity, which fragments and destabilises the political agenda. Regional-based politics as a result of India's vast diversity and the federal structure of the Indian polity have also contributed to this fragmentation of the political agenda and has given rise to the emergence of a fickle and unstable coalition politics sometimes based more on expediency than ideology or policy agenda. Traditionally, this has presented a complex picture in terms of electoral alliances and campaigns.[13]

Recently, however, in states such as Andhra Pradesh, Tamil Nadu and the Northern Hindi states there are strong regional-based parties, founded on a cultural discourse of regional identity or a spatially concentrated representational base, these smaller parties have proved to be a crucial mechanism in the alliance and coalition-building process for the national catch-all parties to access supporters of these regional parties.[14] In exchange for increased power and representation at the national level, state-level parties enter coalitions with the national parties, and the latter in theory receive an amount of co-operation and support from the state level parties.[15]

As a result, changes in party politics in India present alternative opportunities for women in India. Several prominent female political leaders have occupied the office of chief minister in different states simultaneously, some for a longer period than others. As James Manor states, "chief ministers are much more intimately involved in the day-to-day dilemmas of governance than anyone in New Delhi... It is mainly their decisions that determine how, and indeed whether, the institutions of state are integrated with society. Most of the actual governing in India takes place at the state level and below, and at those levels, chief ministers are critically important.

State level politics thus provides a wealth of experience for female political leaders, and few year back five of India's states were governed by female chief ministers, totalling around half the population of India[16]. Despite their growing importance and political clout, due to changing Indian electoral politics, there is currently less published in academic circles on them with regards to their leadership, even less so in terms of the role gender has to play. Furthermore, arguments of women's higher moral capital support efforts to increase women's presence in electoral politics in light of India's apparent decaying morality in the political sphere.

Essentialised Accounts of Gendered Leadership

There is a burgeoning literature in many fields of the social sciences on the contested issue of whether women and men lead differently.[17] Some accounts rely on an *essentialised* conceptualisation of gender and leadership. Essentialised accounts can include biologically reductionist explanations which assert that not only do women and men lead differently, but that this is due to biological differences based on genetic and hormonal differences which produce different leadership styles.[18] They attempt to explain differences in leadership capabilities and style between men and women by arguing that women are *naturally* more caring and nurturing and men are *naturally* more aggressive because of differing hormone levels, the natural sexual division of childbearing, and female attributes bestowed upon them for use in motherhood[19]. Fundamentally, these accounts conflate sex with gender. Their biologically reductionist outlook rejects accounts that attribute any purported difference in male and female leadership styles to processes of socialisation, which work to internalise socially constructed discourse on male/female difference. These accounts are largely discounted among feminist theorists, some of whom have questioned whether "sex" itself is a social construction. Despite criticisms, their legacy still carries weight among some sections of society, particularly in India among eco-feminists.

Other accounts argue that it is *gender*, a socially constructed, relational process, that constitutes the reinforced stereotypical roles of, and expectations about, men and women in society, and thus determines their likely leadership characteristics and relative strengths and weaknesses. Yet, employing the concept of gender still does not guard against essentialised accounts of how men and women lead. As the *gender-as-difference* approach demonstrates, many feminist advocates of the approach celebrate difference and the strengths and opportunities that gender difference provides, such as the skills with which one is equipped as part of the inherently gendered socialisation process.[20]

Critics of *gender-as-difference* emphasise recognition of multiple intersecting inequalities such as caste and class which combine to manifest gender inequality in various ways. This intersectionality approach is characteristic of Third World, post-modern, post-structuralist and Black feminism that seeks to counter universalising and essentialised white, Western, middle class, feminist accounts that homogenise and essentialise women and do not represent the experiences of other marginalised groups. Many assert there are real material differences between men and women because of gender differences in socialisation, and results in differentiated cognitive and emotional development. Others would argue that these professed differences are more symbolic than real and that difference exists more substantially *among* women than it does *between* women and men. The internalisation of symbolic differences on an unconscious level has resulted in their materialisation through the everyday "performativity" of gender stereotypical behaviour.

Whether the style of leadership among men and women is actually different or is simply constructed as so, the significance lies in the effect this perceived difference has on the leader-follower relationship. Astin and Leland assert that "while studies show no clear pattern of difference in behaviour between male and female leaders, subordinates react differently to similar behaviour according to whether the leader is a man or a woman". Thus, the *perception* of a leader's behaviour is in part an outcome of gendered societal perceptions of men and women in leadership positions. This, in turn feeds into the individual's self-reflexive understanding of their own ability to lead. In cases of political leadership, this produces a unbalanced situation which grants an advantage to the male leader. As it has been reserved.

> Male politicians ... are not pronounced incapable of being politicians because of gender, if they do not fulfil voter's aspirations. In other words, if women politicians conform to men's political expectations, they are good politicians, because they are good women, but if they do not, they are bad women and consequently also bad politicians.

The issue of gender only becomes an issue for the woman politician; failure for the male politician is rarely attributed to gender. Nevertheless, studies show that "female leaders' style of governance [in India] is certainly not softer, less autocratic or more equal than that of male leaders... women's rule is not necessarily more democratic or less confrontational than that of male leaders..." (ibid: 3). In terms of policy, D'Amico notes that "gender-based expectations are confounded" by examples of women leaders who do not seek peaceful solution to conflict (1995: 25). As a result of these observations, she is faced with the following questions:

> Does this mean that these leaders are not "real women"? Or, that females can't be "women" in the "game of power politics"? Or, does it mean that we need to examine our gender-based expectations more closely?

Thus, Duerst-Lahti and Kelly conclude that Gender perceptions and gender stereotypes so intrude upon assessments of traits and styles that... it is much more productive to view traits and styles as *transgendered...* [meaning] that while it may be seen as appropriate for both women and men to display a particular trait or behaviour, its meaning will not be understood the same.

Therefore, behavioural traits may never embody the same meaning for a woman as they do for a man, and vice versa. Thus, male leadership behaviour will not be interpreted the same as female leadership behaviour, in part due to the institutionalisation of hegemonic masculine behaviour as the behavioural norm. The prospects for confronting the norm are unclear. Institutionalist approaches are diverse in their understanding of the impact of gender on and the inclusion of more women in political institutional structures, especially at the top. Some suggest that there is little difference between men's and women's style and performativity, professing that women leaders imbibe the male organisational norms. This suggests that increasing numbers of women leaders may make little difference to institutional and political culture.

Women's Higher Moral Capital

In contrast, others arguing for the inclusion of more women into national and international political machinery, suggest that the presence of more women may have the effect of changing the style of governance within these institutions. This latter approach known as the *moral capital* argument argues that women are less corrupt than their male counterparts; they are less likely to act opportunistically with self-interest, with the resulting benefits to democratic governance of society. This argument focuses on gender-as-difference, and therefore essentialises behavioural traits. This places constraints on efforts to destabilise existing gender norms and to bring about transformative change in gender relations. However, while the moral capital argument is theoretically problematic to some, the structural and gender bias that exists in many societies means that it is has proved to be a successful strategy for obtaining an initial advantage when attempting to acquire positions of power.

In sum, an individual's ability to lead and his or her corresponding behavioural style of leadership will be anticipated on the basis of gender-biased expectations, both in the form of observation by peers and the wider society, as well as through critical reflection of the leader on their own ability and performance. This will determine the efficacy and style of the individual in their role as leader, particularly in terms of adapting to the "rules of the game". The leader can however use these gender-biased expectations instrumentally to their advantage.

As many studies of leadership note, the position of leader is intrinsically contingent on the position of follower. The leader's position of authority is dependent on the willingness of followers' to grant power to the leader, to be exercised over the followers themselves. Therefore, followers' perception of the leader's legitimacy and authority is important. As women in Indian society have a significant lack of material and structural power relative to men, this is particularly relevant for the study of gender and leadership in India.

Weber's "three types of legitimate authority" is frequently quoted as a classic typology. Legitimate authority, according to Weber can be "traditional", what has always been will remain; "charismatic", based on an individual's appeal and personality; or "rational-legal", recognising the rational, legal authority of the ruler to govern over a subject population. These three categories are not mutually exclusive and each can manifest itself simultaneously to that of another, buttressing power derived from multiple sources of legitimate authority.

The strong liberal democratic discourse in India suggests that the last of these three, "rational-legal" authority, is the most prevalent due the vibrancy of democracy, the centrality of electoral politics in the political system, and high turnout levels of the electorate at polling time. Thus one of the central sources of legitimate authority of the Indian political leader is to win the mandate of the people, as Hart's conception of leadership suggested. Rational-legal authority often overlaps or is placed in juxtaposition to "charismatic" authority, the latter coming a close second in India. Indian politics is replete with successful charismatic politicians, some of whom boast a cult following. This is particularly so for leaders of political parties with a low level of institutionalisation, in which party workers and followers tend to revere the charismatic party leader.

While Weber's is an oft-cited classic typology, and is a good starting point, it does have its limitations.[21] Most notably, Weber's analysis does not explicitly take account of how gender affects sources of legitimate authority. In the Indian case, this has been analysed explicitly in terms of women leaders, and can be said to differ from some Western explanations.[22] There are several interpretations of sources of authority for women in India, and a few contemporary accounts will be discussed here, namely roles of authority within the family, Hindu goddess imagery, and 'performative sustainability'.

Firstly, followers of women leaders in India, as in many places, frequently look to commonly understood roles of authority that women hold within the private sphere of the family. Most often referred to is the mother-figure, as the cultural reproducer of the nation and as the nurturing caretaker.[23] These sources of authority, like any that draw upon socially established gender relations, can be said to embody *gender power*. Duerst-Lahti and Kelly define gender power "as power and power dynamics resulting from the practices of people performing gender within the normative constraints gender modes impose". In the case of women leaders in India, commonly understood gender roles for women are transposed from the private sphere of the household to the public sphere of politics[24], and with them, their sources of authority and social capital.

Woman's symbolic sacrifice for the family is replaced by a symbolic sacrifice for the nation. Thus, as Sunder Rajan asserts, "[t]he acceptable face of leadership is service; it denies [material] power, stress[es] sacrifice, and positions the hierarchy of public duty and private affections to give primacy to the first". Their commonly understood sources of authority take on an altered form, providing them legitimacy in the political sphere. Women leaders in India become *didi* (elder sister), *behenji* (sister), and *amma* (mother). Many women leaders have capitalised on this imagery, such as Indira Gandhi who internalised and promoted her image as *Bharat Mata*[25]. Many have used gender power to imbue themselves with legitimate authority and political capital.

Evidently, by drawing on gender power these women leaders reinforce and legitimise traditional stereotypes. But does the instrumental power-hungry use of gender power for the purposes of augmenting public power and popularity contradict and the very stereotypes these women are endorsing and threaten to undermine their credibility?

This transfer of gender power does not appear *prima facie* to be consistent with Duerst-Lahti and Kelly's elaboration of gender power. They go on to say that "like gender, gender power is dynamic, fluid, and *situationally derived;* it can only be determined by the particular context. "This would suggest that sources of authority derived from within the family can not be transferred to the public sphere. On the contrary, the Indian example would suggest that, while gender power is still recognised as dynamic, symbolic gendered expectations may run deeper than the situational context. Nevertheless, women's political participation may be scuppered, however, by the informal and institutionally male-biased political networks which limit women's ability to convert social capital into political capital.

Power of Hindu Goddess

Secondly, Hindu imagery is commonly invoked in India as a means to explain women's power according to which is potentially awesome and quite different to notions of the "weaker sex" in classic Western philosophy[26]. Goddess imagery mobilised in Hindu symbolism is linked to notions of *shakti* (women's power) and is common in Indian culture and philosophy. *Sita,* as the *pativrata* (model wife), is traditionally worshipped by girls and young women as the method of family institution to prepare and socialise daughters into positions of subservience for marriage. Kali and Durga, on the other hand, are the female goddesses that are feared for their potentially awesome rage summoned to take vengeance against demonic forces.

As Madhu Kishwar asserts, "every woman has this roop, this aspect latent in her, that a woman is both gentle and nurturing, as well as capable of superhuman rage, which can destroy the world and hence needs to be feared". While some argue that Hindu goddess imagery is a demonstration of how religious culture provides agency to women, opponents reject this explanation in favour of an another that uncovers how this imagery is used to reinforce women's subservient position in a patriarchal and oppressive society. Mobilising goddess imagery to explain women's power and authority has the symbolic effect of mystifying women's power and reinforces a distinction between itself and male material power.

Lastly, Weber's typology does not explicitly address the concept of credibility drawn from the performative aspect of leadership as a means of sustaining legitimacy. There are two interrelated aspects relating to performance, that of "efficacy" and that of "performativity". Regarding "efficacy", it can be argued that the institutional ladder route to power is based on the very premise of the rising leader's ability to prove he or she can deliver results while in office.[27] For women leaders, winning a second mandate is a crucial element to becoming recognised and established, due to the perceived risk element to political parties of contesting women candidates and gendered perceptions of leadership ability based on behavioural expectations. However, regarding the "performative" aspect, some accounts of leadership posit that demonstrating efficacy in transactional politics is not a crucial factor to ensuring sustainability of leadership in an ostensibly democratic polity.

Leadership identity and charismatic authority can override notions of accountability and corruption. As Thomas Blom Hansen argues with his notion of 'Politics as Permanent Performance', 'political performativity comprises... the construction of images and spectacles, forms of speech, dress and public behaviour that promotes the identity of a movement or party, defines its members, and promotes its cause or worldview'. This is all part of the 'politics of the spectacle' as a new form of 'politics of presence' in which an 'ability to stage public performances' as well as self-stylisation are crucial in generating 'the illusion of their own power'. An analysis of this new form of politics entails focussing on "the creation of public moods and sentiments, the production of authority" through this new style of politics.

Thus, the performative aspect of leadership demonstrates the potential of a leader's source of legitimacy to change over time, and requires a longitudinal analysis as well as a focus on the perceived and actual performance of the politician's term in office as well as their performativity of leadership. As noted earlier, expectations are likely to be affected by gender-biased judgments of leadership performance.

Overview and Conclusions

Where J. Jayalalithaa[28], Mayawati[29] and Uma Bharti[30] have taken the institutional route, Rabri Devi[31] represents the "proxy" route to power. All had a mentor who supported them when they first entered politics, although Rabri Devi's was more prescriptive towards her leadership performance. All except Mayawati draw upon Hindu goddess imagery as a means to muster legitimacy. Mayawati's exclusion is not surprising given that Dalits in general are less likely to mobilise Hindu imagery. All including Mayawati transpose sources of gender power from within the private family to the public sphere. All except Rabri Devi have renounced the prospect of being a mother and a wife and the same invoke notions of suffering for their service to their followers. All except Rabri Devi possess charismatic authority, some more in their own right, such as Mayawati and Uma Bharti, whereas Jayalalithaa draws some charismatic authority from her predecessor, M.G. Ramachandran. Rabri Devi draws upon Laloo's charismatic authority as his "proxy".

As elected office-holders, all in theory possess strong rational-legal authority, yet in practice this authority may take second place to charismatic authority. Interestingly, Mayawati and Uma Bharti draw authority and legitimacy most from their which is situationally based within their respective movement-based politics. Both are low caste women but caste is a more salient factor for Mayawati as a *Dalit.* Uma Bharti draws legitimacy among *Hindutva* supporters as a *sadhvi* and her credibility as office-holder rather than mobiliser has increased over time. Yet, both movement-based agendas offered little in the way of transformative potential for women; Mayawati's *Dalit* agenda obscures the voice of *Dalit* women, and the *Hindutva* communal agenda espoused by Uma Bharti, although less vociferous now, is potentially violent, threatening and degrading to Muslim women and socially conservative for Hindu women.

All cases refute the moral capital argument, which argues that women will behave less self-interested and with greater moral consideration, though this is true for some more than others. For example, while Jayalalithaa and Mayawati were alleged to have amassed wealth during their tenure through alleged corrupt activities. Rabri Devi has been absolved of past alleged corruption due to gendered conceptions of authority within Indian marriage which, as the justifications underpinning her acquittal suggest, have a legal binding in reality.[32]

Conclusions

The aim of this study was to provide an enriched and alternative account of female political leadership in India. Alternative paths to power, other than dynastic succession, were discussed. Four paths to power were outlined; that of "institutional", cultural transfer, "proxy", and dynastic succession. The first three, as alternative routes to power, were discussed in terms of their gender component. Addressing Thompson's lack of contextual detail in the Indian case, women's political participation in India was contextualised both within the political and social environment of Indian women's participation in politics, from the national movement to the present day. It was concluded that the alliance of the women's movement with the nationalist movement bore few emancipatory outcomes for women's political participation, as the latter was based on a strategy of solidarity by mobilising their commonly accepted subservient role in society to fight colonial domination. This provided an explanation towards understanding the disparity between women's improved legal status and the prevailing liberal political discourse compared with women's continuing poor status in Indian society and why women's political participation had not become more pervasive after Independence.

Female political leadership was contextualised in terms of how the institutional environment by arguing that the changing scene of Indian politics, that of the regionalisation and fragmentation of electoral politics and the party system presented a different platform on and arena in which new political leaders were emerging, which deserved new attention for the role of women leaders in this new formation. While some female leaders have benefited from the changing political scene in terms of bargaining power within alliance formations with national parties, there is little to suggest that the fragmentation and regionalisation of Indian politics has increased the support of women candidates by political parties.

Ultimately, the political parties have not lived up to the rhetorical support for women's participation in party structures. Thus, the changing political system has only worked to catapult a few women into positions of power. Thus, the presence of women in top positions has made little apparent difference to the allotment of tickets to women. In any case it appears to be an essentialised assumption that it would make a difference at all. Female political leadership was further contextualised in terms of how legitimate authority is constructed in India, demonstrating how legitimacy in India is both a culturally-specific phenomenon, such as the mobilisation of Hindu goddess imagery and the transposing of sources of gender power from the private to the public sphere, as well as more general applications of Weber's classic typology. Lastly, underlying essentialised accounts of women's moral capital were challenged in a more general discussion of behavioural styles of leadership. One can conclude that while the moral capital and other similarly essentialised arguments are theoretically problematic and pose problems for destabilising constrictive gender norms, arguments like that of the higher moral capital of women tend to be accepted as a stereotypically gendered perception of leadership style, despite actual performative similarities between men and women. Thus structural gender bias and gendered-biased perceptions and expectations are understood to have a significant impact on assessments of behavioural style and performance. Yet, these sources of gender power can be utilised by leaders, reinforcing and legitimising stereotypes.

All except Rabri Devi have defied conventional behavioural styles of leadership expected by essentialised accounts of female political leadership. However in some cases the interest for more women in governance structures because they are perceived as less corrupt is a misguided but conscious effort and interest in increasing accountability and "good governance" in democratic institutions.

NOTES AND REFERENCES

1. The central focus of this critique of Thompson's work is not to discount his work but to provide a focal point against which alternative accounts of female leadership in India can emerge. Thompson's study is situated within a wider project with Claudia Derichs, consisting of several working chapters as part of an edited series, which together present a diverse view of female leadership in South Asia.
2. While Thompson (2002) includes Indira Gandhi as his Indian example of dynastic succession, his account is not consistent with several authors who emphasise the time gap between Nehru's

death and Indira Gandhi's succession. See Carras (1995), Everett (1993) and Mitra (1988). Thompson and Derichs (2003) include Sonia Gandhi as well as her mother-in-law and acknowledge Sonia is only one of many female political leaders in India today.

3. But, the distinction, attributed to Burns (1978; quoted in Fleschenburg, 2004), may be temporary in that "[t]ransformational leadership can easily be turned into transactional, merely power-securing leadership once in office, as [an] institutionalised career politician" (Fleschenburg, 2004: 5). Nevertheless such a distinction is important to this argument. Contrary to Fleschenburg's (2004) and Thompson's (2002) study of Asian female political leaders, many of the female political leaders in India are primarily of the transactional type displayed by career politicians.
4. It is also relevant to the debate on the importance of the participation of women in times of constitutional change as a critical juncture which can potentially offer an opportunity to transform their position in society (Dobrowolsky and Hart, 2003; Waylen, 2004).
5. The concept of legitimacy will be returned to in a later section.
6. Debate exists over how individuals internalise norms in an institutional setting. The rational, calculus approach emphasises incentives and reward structures by which preferences can be objectively reasoned with; in contrast approaches emphasising internalisation via channels of institutional or organisational culture focus on more subtle, affective, emotional and cultural change.
7. Kudva (2003) for a detailed discussion and study of this phenomenon. See also Rai and Sharma (2000) and Rai (1999) for a more general discussion of women's reservation policy in India.
8. In Hindu imagery, *Sita* is the subservient and suffering devoted wife of Lord Rama. This appeal was particularly powerful as the private sacrifice and subservience was essentially packaged as voluntaristic, mirroring the public male sacrifice in the interest of the nationalist struggle, and thus struck a chord with nationalist, anti-colonial sentiments among Indian women (Majumdar, 2002:

22). See also Bald (2000) for Gandhi's role in mobilising *Sita* during the struggle for Independence.

9. For a comprehensive account of the women's movement, see Omvedt (1993), especially chapters four and nine; also Akerkar (1995), Forbes (1998) and Kumar (1989). See also Pande (2002) on anti-arrack protests and domestic violence.

10. This has the consequence of extracting the radical element from the women's movement and highlights the need for alliance formation in order to create momentum on priority issues (Akerkar, 1995).

11. Mary F. Katzenstein (1981) argues for example that a crucial factor for women's political participation of Indian women was the Congress (I) party's support of giving tickets to women to contest seats. Political party support of women candidates will not be discussed here at length, as this relates more to women's general participation in politics, although it can be argued that it is a determining factor in providing opportunities to women to become career politicians and thus progress up the institutional ladder by proving their capability, ultimately with the potential to become political leaders.

12. The Congress(I) Party is a paradox in this sense. As possibly the most institutionalised party, professing secular ideals, it is surprising that dynastic succession should be the acknowledged route to elite-level leadership.

13. For example, the competing parties of Congress (I) and the Left parties, such as the CPI and CPI(M), will form alliances to avoid contesting against each other and losing seats to their opponents, whereas in other regions where both have more of a stronghold, particularly in Kerala and West Bengal, they will compete against each other and other regional-based parties for seats and vote share.

14. The BJP has used this as a direct strategy for increasing its national support base and "pan-Indian presence" (Blom Hansen and Jaffrelot, 2001: 14)

15 Jayalalithaa's withdrawal of support from the BJP in 1999 which led to the collapse of the government that had been elected by a

marginal victory is another demonstration of the rise in importance of the state-level parties, which has political repercussions for national level politics, especially with regards to the ability of national parties to win elections and to dictate policy once in government.

16. These five women chief ministers were Sheila Dixit (New Delhi), Jayalalithaa (Tamil Nadu), Uma Bharti (Madhya Pradesh), Scindia (Rajasthan), and Rabri Devi (Bihar). As *The Hindu* notes, "it would have been two-thirds of the country, if Mayawati had not worked her way out of office in Uttar Pradesh recently" (2003).
17. However, it is recognised that the study of gender and political leadership and women's participation in world politics has been relatively neglected in political science and particularly international relations—see Cynthia Enloe (1989) who asks "Where are the Women?".
18. For an extreme example of this account, see Singh (2001).
19. It is not uncommon for women leaders to also justify their capabilities or actions according to this line of thinking, as did Indira Gandhi and Sirima Bandaranaike, as discussed earlier (respectively, Sunder Rajan, 1993; Hellmann-Rajanayagman, 2004; see also Indira Gandhi, 1974).
20. For a brief review of the criticisms of *gender-as-difference*, see Mansbridge (2003).
21. A minor limitation concerns applicability. As Blondel notes, it is not apparent whether Weber was trying to formulate a theory of authority of leadership, as clearly *legitimate* authority suggests a dominant but consensual form of authority, rather than authoritarian, dictatorial rule and consequently the analysis is limited (Blondel, 1987: 50-51). For the purpose here, this limitation does not cause substantial problems but must be recognised, especially with regards to dynastic accounts of female leadership that frequently use democratic revolution and the overthrow of dictatorship as their case material.
22. Some branches of Western feminist theory have historically sought to defend the virtues of motherhood as a source of authority; others have fought against the stereotypical images of women as

mothers and wives, questioning the "natural" ability of women as mothers. For a discussion of both positions, and particularly how motherhood has defined women's position in relation to the state, see Pateman (1992).

23. This appears to be a legacy from the nationalist movement, as discussed earlier, which sought to entrench Hindu imagery of the goddess Sita as the devoted wife. Sarojini Naidu, a female leader of the nationalist and women's movement, often used this symbolism in her speeches, as did Mahatma Gandhi. For an excellent account, see Forbes (1982; 1998).

24. As noted earlier, feminist theorists have shown this distinction between public and private *vis-a-vis* what is deemed as "politics" to be deeply flawed. Here, it serves the purpose of demonstrating how gendered perceptions of authority are transferable between different sites of activity, and thus how leadership, its protagonists, and the exercise of authority are affected by gender.

25. Many, however, have claimed that the authoritarian and autocratic period of the Emergency, during which democratic rule was sidelined, has reduced the credibility of Indira Gandhi's claim to the title of *Bharat Mata* (Mother India) (Mitra, 1988; Sunder Rajan, 1993, Carras, 1995).

26. Some commentators assert that Hinduism has appropriated these symbols and imagery from earlier traditions, particularly in the latter part of the twentieth century during the post-Independence "reinvention" of the Hindu nation. See Corbridge (1999) and Corbridge and Harriss (2000) for example.

27. This is certainly the case of Sheila Dixit, Chief Minister of Delhi, who was re-elected in 2003 despite the anti-incumbency factor, and on the back of her many efforts to improve the city's infrastructure (The Hindu, 2003). She has proved herself as a very capable politician, beyond her entry into politics by way of her influential father-in-law.

28. J. Jayalalithaa was the Chief Minister of Tamil Nadu and party chief of the regional All India Anna Dravida Munnetra Kazhagam (AIADMK) party. She also held the office of CM of Tamil Nadu from 1991-1996.

29. Mayawati is currently party chief of the Bahujan Samaj Party and is currently chief minister of Uttar Pradesh State. She has held the office of CM of Uttar Pradesh (UP) during 1995 and 1997, as well as being a member of the UP State Legislative Assembly from 1996-1998.

30. In November 2003, Uma Bharti became the first woman CM of Madhya Pradesh. She has also served as a member of the Lok Sabha for five consecutive terms from 1989-2003. She has held the offices of Union Minister of State (independent charge) for Tourism (1999-2000), Union Cabinet Minister for Youth Affairs and Sports (2000-2002) and Union Cabinet Minister for Coal Mines (2002-2003). She has also served as Vice President of the Madhya Pradesh unit of the BJP.

31. Rabri Devi became the first woman Chief Minister of Bihar in 1997. She has held the post of Chief Minister in Bihar for three successive periods: July 1997-February 1999; March 1999 to March 2000.

32. This is a reference to Rabri Devi's acquittal in relation to CBI charges against Laloo Prasad Yadav in 2000. Rabri failed to prove ownership of specific assets her husband had put in her name and the CBI claimed she had '"aided and abetted" her husband's "illegal earnings"' (*Frontline*, (magazine, 2000a). However, Rabri was later released on bail by a judge's order, who commented that: '"The accused person's offence dates back to when she was a housewife. The Indian tradition has it that the housewife has to work according to the will of the husband." (quoted in *Frontline*, 2000b). The judge's order demonstrates the gendered legal attribution of responsibility in this case in recognising the lack of authority and responsibility of Rabri Devi—including for her own actions—as an Indian housewife in relation to her husband. It also assumes Rabri's subservience rather than complicity.

7

SELF-HELP GROUPS: A STRATEGY FOR WOMEN'S DEVELOPMENT

Introduction

Self-help Groups (SHGs) are playing a major role in rural India today. The group-based model of self-help is widely practised for rural development, poverty alleviation and empowerment of women. Self-help as a strategy for social development places emphasis on self-reliance, human agency and action. It aims to mobilise people, to give them voice and build people's organisations that will overcome barriers to participation and empowerment. Central to the idea of self-help is the formation of groups, concept of a 'community' and the development of egalitarian relationships that will promote people's well-being.

The self-help model in India facilitates institution-building in the form of people's organisations in the form of groups, clusters and federations. The poor, however, seldom organise themselves. It is an assisted self-help process where the State, the financial institutions and the non-governmental organisations (NGOs) play an important role in mobilising and assisting the poor and the needy. While the policies of the external agents of development place emphasis on building institutions to assist the poor and women, the practice-oriented reality has to deal with the structural barriers that people, women and the organisations face. At the level of practice, the outcomes of self-help depend on building mutually beneficial relationships, negotiating power and gaining control.

The examines the main approaches to the building of women's self-help in India, its implications for practice and effect on women's ability to exercise agency. This will be examined through an analysis of the strategies adopted by the various development sectors to promote women's development, and the possibility to change gender and power relations. The chapter is based on fieldwork done in two districts of India during 2003-2004: Sonipat in Haryana and Kolar in Karnataka.

Self-Help and the Group Model for Women

Alternative development thinkers emphasise participation, self-reliance and self-help as basic human rights (Friedman 1992, Gran 1983, Rahman 1993). Development involves changes in the awareness, motivation and behaviour of individuals, in the relations between individuals as well as between groups within a society. These changes can come from within individuals and groups through self-help, and not necessarily from outside. The experiences of self-reliance have led to attempts to build local level organisations like, cooperatives, credit societies, neighbourhood or community development associations, water sharing associations or women's groups. The Neo-liberal paradigm has also incorporated self-reliance as a strategy for building people's entrepreneurial spirits and absorption into the capital market.

People's participation in self-help organisations is not new. In Kenya, local self-help development efforts *-harambee*; in Vietnam, Tontines or Hui with 10 to15 members that are involved in financial activities through cash or kind; and in

Indonesia, self-help efforts through credit unions, fishermen groups, village-based banks, irrigation groups etc. have been in existence. In the areas of urban development and housing, self-help takes the form of neighbourhood groups, tenant groups, slum development committees and so on. In rural development, it is through credit groups, development committees, user groups and so on. Group-oriented efforts in the form of micro-credit groups in different countries of Latin America, Africa and Asia are examples of current self-help efforts. The grameen groups in Bangladesh and the self-help groups (SHGs) in countries like Thailand, Nepal, Sri Lanka and India are forms of micro-credit groups.

Financial Assistance

The SHGs in India are small, informal and homogenous groups of not more than twenty members each. The groups are kept informal to minimise their association with bureaucracy and corruption, unnecessary administrative expenditure and profit constraints. The size of twenty is devised as any group larger than that would need to be registered under the Indian legal system and that brings a whole range of regulatory constraints. After a group is formed, it starts collecting a fixed amount from each member for about six months. During this period, the groups are expected to open a savings account with a financial institution which would like to extend credit. After accumulating a reasonable amount of resources, the group starts lending to its members. As the group members develop the experience of handling resources, understand the value of credit and the importance of repayment and accountability to the group, it can approach the financial institution for term loans. The group becomes jointly liable to the bank for repayment and it is expected to assume responsibility in monitoring the members. This joint liability provides incentives or compels the group to undertake the burden of selection, monitoring and enforcement that would otherwise fall on the lender.

The roots of the SHG model lie partly in indigenous savings systems of India and partly in the group-based model of Grameen Bank in Bangladesh, though it differs from it in several aspects. The Indian experience is distinctive in that the groups are mostly formed by women, they are formed through grassroots mobilisation with the help of NGOs and they are engaged in both poverty alleviation and empowerment activities. Through the selective incentives of benefits in the form of savings and credit (Olson 1965), the SHG model seeks to build collective action and enhance people/women's power. The State and the voluntary sector play an important role in mobilisation through facilitation and linking the groups to credit. The promotional strategies of the external agents can impact on how the participants develop their expectations from the system and what they gain.

The spread of SHGs in India has been phenomenal. It has made dramatic progress from 500 groups in 1992 (Titus 2002) to some 1,618,456 groups that have taken loans from banks. About 24.25 million poor households have gained access to formal banking system through SHG-bank linkage programme and 90% of these groups are women only groups. The NABARD (2006) homepage declares that more than 400 women join the SHG movement every hour and an NGO joins the micro-finance programme every day. There are also agencies which provide bulk funds to the system through NGOs. Thus organisations engaged in micro finance activities in India may be categorised as Wholesalers, NGOs supporting SHG Federations and NGOs directly retailing credit borrowers or groups of borrower. The spread of the SHGs again show that it is highly concentrated in the southern part of the country with very few in the north and the east. Over half a million SHGs have been linked to banks over the years but a handful of States, mostly in South India, account for almost 60% of this figure. Andhra Pradesh has over 42%, Tamil Nadu and Uttar Pradesh have 12% and 11% respectively, and Karnataka has about 9% of the total SHGs.

Thus, the rise of the movement has been very high in the Southern States, and very minor in Haryana and in the North-East.

The widespread formation of the SHGs means that it has also taken the form of a movement for women's social development in India. Self-help groups, as a strategy for women's development, have arisen out of the perceived problem of women's lack of access to resources at both the household and the village level. Women's development has to go beyond the economic and place emphasis on issues relating to equality, autonomy and self-reliance at the individual level and on solidarity of the community (of women) at the group level. As a group-oriented model, SHG is a mechanism for women's development to bring in individual and collective empowerment through improvement in both 'condition' and 'position' of women. Women are organised as collectives towards the overall goal of achieving gender equality as well as sustainable, comprehensive community development (Purushothaman, 1998:80). As women experience powerlessness in and through the interaction of multiple social, political and economic institutions, the self-reliance model for women's development aims to empower them.

Thus, an important aspect of SHGs is the implicit assumption that through participation in the groups, women will gain, generate and acquire power, and improve their 'position' within the family and the society. Psychological empowerment or the inner processes are given importance for the development of self-esteem and self-confidence so that women are able to motivate themselves into action. The SHGs, however, work within an existing socio-cultural structure and there is a need to look at SHGs as an emerging structure of women in a patriarchal society. The SHGs have to be able to address the structural inequalities in which women are located, yet affect the hold of patriarchy in a manner that does not work to the detriment of women unlike other structures that are dominated by patriarchal interest.

Positive Impact

In a study of the role of self-help in Kenya, Thomas found that self-help is politicised, but powerless. It does not alter fundamental power relationships within the political and economic system, but self-help groups have some positive impact. The benefits shared within a group cut across socio-economic lines, thereby promoting both gender and intra-community equity.

Unlike the self-help projects in Kenya, the SHGs in India are primarily micro-credit groups and the direct objective of micro-credit is to improve the 'condition' of women. There is, however, conflicting evidence as to whether micro-credit groups improve the 'position' of women. Social 'position' or status of women is an aspect of positional power that refers to the power or authority assigned to specific positions and roles in a society.

Studies have found positive indicators of the cost effectiveness and economic potential of micro-credit loans, but their positive social impact remained doubtful. Literature review points to conflicting evidence of women's ability to achieve control over decision-making and loans, incidence of increases in violence and dowry and evidence of economic and social empowerment.

The link between access to credit for women and that of transformation in gender and power relations was not found to be automatic. Goetz and Sengupta's study of Bangladeshi women's actual control of the credit received by them from the banks had found that a significant proportion of the loans are actually controlled by male relatives. Mahmud found that the group fund provides an economic base that holds the groups together. The group fund fosters a sense of unity and solidarity since it represents a source of collective bargaining power for women in the marketplace. While it provides a base from which to assert control and autonomy, it is only within a particular configuration of male power relationships in the family or village.

Socioeconomic Empowerment

Rahman found that financial sustainability was taking precedence over women's socio-economic empowerment and women were not acting as autonomous agents in any meaningful sense. The pressure to return loans can increase tension and frustration among household members, produce new forms of dominance over women and increase violence in society. Providing resources to women and encouraging them to maintain control over these resources may provoke violent behaviour in men. Rahman concluded that loans alone, without viable opportunities for women to transform the power relations and create their own spaces in the prevailing power structure, make equitable development and empowerment of women unattainable in the society. Similarly as Mahmud found, micro-credit participation did not improve women's access to material resources nor did it expand women's choice a great deal. Women's participation in the public sphere that could become choice enhancing remained limited, as they were not able to overcome the structural barriers.

In aiming to improve women's rights and status and thereby, responding to not only their practical interests, but also strategic interests, the self-help efforts enter the realm of the Indian women's movement. The Indian women's movement is influenced by various efforts to characterise the specificity of women's oppression and the links with other forms of social oppression. Women are mobilised to protest against domestic violence, legal discrimination, rising prices, prohibition of liquor, rape, dowry, child marriage, female infanticide, sexual abuse, domestic violence, male alcoholism and so on.

In dealing with women's strategic interests, women participate in collective activities through SHGs to address these strategic needs. In the process, it aims to empower women with several forms of power. SHGs are nascent organisations that are supposed to achieve 'power to' (increasing capacity) through NGO facilitation, 'power within' (internal change) through self-empowerment, 'power with' (collective mobilisation) to gain 'power over' (challenge and change subordination). Development for women through SHGs, thus, aims at transformation of power relations so that the disempowered can achieve increased control and choice.

It becomes, therefore, important to analyse the meanings of self-help to the promoters of SHGs, the strategies adopted to assist the SHGs, and the manner in which women exercise agency through SHGs to address powerlessness. It is also pertinent to understand the paradigms through which the external agents look at women's development—from Women in Development (WID) to Gender and Development (GAD).

The Promoters-Assisting Women's Development through SHGs

There are three main sectors promoting the SHGs in India: the voluntary sector including the non-governmental organisations, the government sector and the financial sector.

The SHG system was initiated by NGOs, such as Myrada in the mid-1980s in India. In the Indian voluntary sector, there are two types of NGOs that take the initiative to organise SHGs for linkage with the banks: development NGOs and empowerment NGOs (Rajasekhar 2000). For development NGOs, micro-finance is a core activity, while empowerment NGOs combine their financial role with issue-based struggles. In promoting SHGs, the primary task of the NGOs is to mobilise, form and nurture the groups so that they can reach maturity. They form and train the groups, and assist them through the qualifying process of saving and internal lending. The groups are introduced to a bank to open a savings account, and later to take a loan. The NGO may remain heavily involved, assisting the members to manage their affairs, and possibly promoting higher-level clusters and federations of SHGs, or it may withdraw and work with other groups. Thus, the NGOs play an important role in linking the SHGs to banks.

Prior to the developmental role of today's NGOs, some NGOs had taken up advocacy and begun to emphasise empowerment of local communities and the poor in the 60s and 70s. A wide range of women's issues, such as rape and violence, were taken up as part of their efforts to influence public policies and practices. Empowerment NGOs today mobilise people for such social issues and advocacy. Credit or micro-finance did not start as a core activity even for organisations like Myrada. It was used to supplement other activities aimed at providing sustainable livelihood to the people.

The adoption of group model, like, the SHGs, *mahila mandals* (women's groups) and others for women's development represents a form of women's collective action through which gender specific issues are taken up. These issues are, alcoholism, male violence and dowry deaths, rape and sexual harassment. Direct policy advocacy and developmental works undertaken by NGOs are different from the wider phenomenon of social movements concerning women's issues. But they are inter-related, as policy advocacy can be considered to be one of the many strands of a movement.

The NGO approach theoretically combines both the developmental (WID) and empowerment (GAD) perspectives with the objective of building equitable social relations. NGOs emphasise the social dimensions of poverty and the self-help groups (SHG) are one such medium through which the NGOs work for economic and social empowerment of women. The poverty alleviation paradigm underlies many NGO integrated poverty-targeted community development programmes. Some NGOs act as banking intermediaries, channeling finance to different SHGs, others have formed collectives of several SHGs forming federations and linking them to banks. According to one estimate, NGOs have promoted about 80 per cent of SHGs linked to banks. Others adopt the GAD framework to challenge patriarchal structures. Thus, NGOs range from service-provider, developmental to empowerment-oriented. However, very few in practice follow the feminist empowerment model of organisations like, SEWA and WWF.

Rural Banking

The launching of NABARD's Pilot phase of the SHG-Bank Linkage programme in February 1992 was a landmark development in rural banking with the poor. For financial institutions, such as, the *Banks*, SHGs form the basic constituent unit of the microfinance movement. The SHG model with bank lending to groups of (often) poor women without collateral has become an accepted part of rural finance. Self-help for the banks is understood through the performance of SHGs in savings and credit activities. As the women learn the nuances of financial discipline, bank credit becomes available to the groups to augment their resources for increased lending to members. The objective is to attain financial sustainability through fees charged and interests earned from borrowers of the group fund including interests paid by banks on the money deposited. The activities associated with SHGs are part of an overall arrangement for providing financial services to the poor in a sustainable manner.

It needs to be emphasised that NABARD sees the promotion and bank linking of SHGs not simply as a credit programme but also as an exercise in capacity building for the members of these SHGs. It is assumed that increasing women's knowledge and access to micro-finance services will lead to individual economic empowerment through enabling women's decisions about savings and credit use, enabling women to set up micro-enterprises, and increasing incomes under their control. This in turn is assumed to enable women to initiate broader social and political changes. Within the guise of poverty alleviation and empowerment, the financial sustainability paradigm assumes importance for the banking sector.

Sa-Dhan is an association of Community Development Finance Institutions in India and was founded in 1999. SEWA (Self-Employed Women's Association) and WWF (Working Women's Forum) are movements that deliberately seek to change gender relations within wider society.

For *Government*, self-help is the act of contributing to growth by active involvement of the poor through a process of social mobilisation, encouraging participatory approaches and institutions and empowerment of the poor. It is the opposite of waiting for government to deliver services and has a collective connotation. Three main strategies guide this approach: involvement of NGOs, group-based approach for mobilisation and rights-based approach for women's development.

In the Government of India's discourse, the Sixth Five Year Plan (1979-84, section 11.43) recognised that development programmes aimed at the transformation of rural societies would be meaningless if they do not involve the rural women, but it was only during the Seventh Plan (1984-89) that women's ability to form groups and participate in economic activities was recognised. It was also realised that the role of voluntary organisations would be crucial in organising women and to supplement government efforts. The Eight Five Year Plan (1992-97, Section 15.5.1) went further and recognised that 'women must be enabled to function as equal partners and participants in development and not merely as beneficiaries of various schemes—Social, cultural and administrative constraints to the realisation of women's full potential need to be removed and there has to be greater societal awareness of their contribution to national well-being'.

This approach specifically laid emphasis on building women's agency through the formation of women's groups and participation in income-generating activities. The main strategy adopted wais to facilitate the access of poor women to employment, skill up gradation, training, credit and other support services so that women as a group could take up income generating activities for supplementing their incomes. Assistance was to be given either to individual woman or to those organised into homogenous groups to take up economically viable activities together with the provision of support services and child-care facilities for the women so organised. This approach of welfare and poverty-alleviation within the paradigms of WID culminated in the DWCRA programme.

The discourse at the Government of India level has moved from poverty alleviation to incorporate elements of gender justice from the GAD framework. The Ninth Five Year Plan (1997-2002) is the most vocal about women's empowerment and Government's direct efforts at formation of SHGs. The Plan (section 3.8.27) committed itself to empower women as agents of social change and development, to create an enabling environment for women as equal partners with men, where women can freely exercise their rights both within and outside home and organize women into SHGs marking the beginning of a major process of empowerment. Government, however, plays a passive and indirect role in SHG formation and functioning.

The entry of government into the SHG movement was through the Rashtriya Mahila Kosh which funds NGOs for forming and nurturing SHG. The Plan also placed emphasis on women's concerns from the perspective of gender equity in terms of cognizance to the existing gender inequalities in land inheritance laws and ceiling laws. The equity concerns expressed in the Plan are also reflected in the National Empowerment Policy, 2001 for social empowerment of women. Apart from education, health etc. it recognised the needs of women in difficult circumstances, violence against women, rights for the girl child and gender sensitisation at all levels of governance.

Threefold Strategy

The Tenth Plan aims to continue with the process of empowering women through translating the national policy for empowerment into action with a threefold strategy: economic empowerment, social empowerment and gender justice. Economic empowerment would ensure provision of training, employment and income-generation activities with the ultimate objective of making all potential women economically independent. Social empowerment aims at creating an enabling environment through various affirmative development policies and programmes for development of women besides providing them easy and equal access to all basic minimum services so as to enable them to realise their full potential. Gender justice aims at eliminating all forms of gender discrimination.

The formation, stabilisation, growth and expansion of SHGs take place under the overall philosophy of 'empowerment' of the poor women. Empowerment is understood as one aspect of a multi-dimensional definition of poverty. The assumption is that increasing women's access to micro-finance will enable women to make a greater contribution to household income, either through their own economic activity or equally becoming a channel for loans to household activity. This contribution and subsequent increase in status in the household will in turn give women the support they need to enable women to bring about wider changes in gender inequality in the community.

The policy approaches in practice, however, still have the dominant thrust of either the financial sustainability paradigm or the poverty-alleviation paradigm. Financial sustainability and poverty-alleviation paradigms very easily fit into the WID approach, and can leave the gender aspects to women's own agency. Though gender sensitisation is incorporated for government and bank officials through the GAD paradigm, the process is slow and the embeddedness of women's social reality make it difficult to negotiate existing structural barriers and achieve social transformation. There is a tendency to see gender issues as cultural and hence not subject to outside intervention. This is what prevents the promoters from raising gender awareness issues in the Muslim villages of Kolar or the issue of land rights in Sonipat.

Any prioritisation of women's interests from a feminist paradigm is seen as inherently divisive. This also often brings resistance to the role of the fieldworkers as facilitators of gender equality, when they have to face abuses from the villagers.

The State's role in implementing empowerment enhancing programmes for women and weaker sections of society is often indistinguishable from other poverty alleviation programmes, like, income generation, assets creation and health and education. For government, SHGs also represent an important mechanism through which to deliver subsidy to the weaker sections. As a result, subsidy amount under programmes such as SGSY[14] can be used as a mobilising force for forming SHGs of Scheduled Castes (SC) and Scheduled Tribes (ST) people. In both Kolar and Sonipat, SC groups with poor members got loans easily and it is used as an incentive for others to form groups with them. Some SC members even have the option of changing membership in groups, as they are much sought after by others.

Little Political Space

The practices of development NGOs remain service-oriented, as they can gain access to the women only with male permission. As a result, the development NGOs pay more attention to credit, leaving the issues of gender and women's position to women's own efforts. At the same time, there is very little political space available to NGOs for a feminist engagement with the State at the local level. NGOs act as an ideological partner of the State when giving training to women on legislations that are women-friendly. Empowerment NGOs do work against the State when they mobilise women to demand services from the State or to protest against any harmful State policy, such as, policy on the sale of alcohol. Yet, the State remains the main player. At the local level, networking and coordination among the NGOs with each other is weak in India. This gives the Deputy Commissioner, as the local level representative of the State, the power and authority to arbitrate for NGOs in the case of conflicts and disputes among NGOs or public complaints against NGOs.

Further, the banks' role is confined to sanctioning credit for financially viable schemes. Due to the limited economic opportunities available for rural women, very few non-traditional occupations are available. Thus, local may remain limited to getting some 'free fund' from the government (through subsidy and grants) or even fatigue with too much loans when members realise the futility of taking too many loans for unproductive purposes. This was observed in both Sonipat and Kolar. Gender sensitisation trainings for field officials emphasize the triple role of women, but biases about women's appropriate role in society can come into play or an approach of non-interference in household matters can rule the decisions of the external agents. The distinction between the public and the private is not overcome in the dealings between the women and the bank officials.

Indian Women, SHG Practices and Power

What matters in women's social development is whether women could improve their 'position' and not 'condition' alone; how and at what level SHGs answer to women's strategic needs and not their practical needs alone. In women's development through self-help, social changes should result in a form of social power that gives identity, improves social status and equalises gender relations for women. This section discusses SHG members' experiences in the bank-linkage model to negotiate existing power relationships through the assertion of identity, improvement in status and changes in gender relations.

The emphasis on the SHG-bank linkage in both Sonipat and Kolar meant that most of the practices were based on the dominant material incentive, that is, bank loan. The primary emphasis placed on fulfilling practical needs – through both the mobilisation strategies and the formation of people's expectations – meant that credit was the primary motivation for seventy nine per cent of the women to join the SHGs. This was, no doubt, an important concern for the poor. Few of the older women gave importance to the social aspects of SHGs, and the educated ones acknowledged the utility of trainings.

The practices of participation in the bank-linkage model for an SHG involve different activities and they go through different stages. The required activities of the SHGs can be divided into three processes: regular, occasional and infrequent. Regular processes include meetings, savings, activities related to lending and borrowing. Recording minutes, keeping accounts, opening bank account, and going to bank for deposit of collected amount are some of the regular processes. Occasional processes include trainings and participation in joint activities geared toward fulfilment of practical interests. Trainings and participation in inter-departmental activities organised by the NGO, like, exposure visits, themes camps etc. are occasional processes in which women participate.

Infrequent processes include acts relating to social movements or social change that are oriented to strategic interests. Such activities involve, running for elected offices, peace building efforts in times of conflict, help to distressed member or other villager, overseeing government programmes, fighting against the alcoholism of husbands and other male members in the village and so on. From the point of strategic needs, such socially empowering activities are important, but they are informal and take place infrequently.

Financial Development

These are also the stages through which a group has to travel before it is considered mature. Wilson identifies four stages through which a group has to travel in its path toward financial development – savings, interlending, linkage and sustainability. Corresponding to these, the development process of an SHG's life can be said to go through three stages: *forming, functioning and sustainable.* Groups that have started saving, inter-lending and deal with bank loans can be said to have moved from the forming stage to the functioning stage. Within the formal rules of SHG formation and bank linkage, groups have to accumulate sufficient experience in inter-loaning and account keeping before they are eligible for bank loans.

The functioning groups are the ones that have started inter-lending at the minimum. These groups supposedly help in social development through knowledge of organisational functioning, women's physical and mental well-being and experience in economic as well as non-economic activities. Sustainable groups give wider exposure to women through their links with clusters and federation – the ultimate philosophy of group sustainability.

Though the women interviewed belonged to SHGs in different stages, yet groups in both the areas had some form of group or collective identity. The SHGs form a community that is distinctive by its gender and task. It is also an informal credit-based organisation for the women. Through emphasis on the independent and self-reliant nature of group functioning, the participants negotiate an identity that is separate from their identity as a member of any particular family. The focus on women's rights and awareness of their inner power is an attempt to produce a new subjectivity and identity for the women, which is a form of a politicised woman.

This was not easily achievable within the existing patriarchal social reality of Kolar and Sonipat. A woman's identity in rural India is through her position in either her natal or marital home as daughter, sister, wife, mother and/or mother-in-law. At the societal level, the identity of the individual women is also structured on the basis of her caste, class and family status. This was particularly significant for married women at the village level in Sonipat. During fieldwork, individual woman could be located only as somebody's wife or daughter-in-law.

An independent identity of one's own by a young, married and illiterate woman is not easily achieved unless the woman can negotiate it through her new role in the SHG. As the SHGs NABARD has elaborate rules providing guidelines as to how SHGs can reach the stage of maturity. [16] The women interviewed in Sonipat belonged to either forming (30%) or functioning (70%) groups, whereas most of the women in Kolar belonged to sustainable (94%) groups.

formed were still in their evolving stage in Sonipat, this aspect was not achieved by the women. The few women who had an independent identity were the ones who were also *Anganwadi* (child care) workers. As one member in Sonipat explained, '*we only belong to somebody, we do not learn to be individuals... it takes for us to be mothers-in-law to open our mouths in front of others*'. For women in Kolar belonging to sustainable groups, this had changed through their association with the SHGs. Laxmiamma in Bandakote village very confidently said: *Now-a-days, people identify me as an SHG member.*

Self-Empowerment

In the area of participation, satisfaction and perceived feelings of self-worth can be used as indicators of women's feelings of self-empowerment. Seventy-one per cent women in Sonipat and ninety-one per cent in Kolar expressed some form of satisfaction from their participation in the SHG activities, but it reduced when it came to their perception of increase in social status through participation in the SHGs. In Sonipat, it was 40%; whereas in Kolar, it was 86%. The changes in perception were higher in Kolar due to the higher maturity stage of the SHGs as shown in the table below.

TABLE 1

SHG Stage and Members' Perception

SHG Stage	Feelings of Satisfaction	Feelings of Satisfaction	Increase in Status	Increase in Status
	Sonipat	Kolar	Sonipat	Kolar
Forming	17		8	
Functioning	43	5	26	5
Sustainable		68		64
	60 (71%)	73 (91%)	34 (40%)	69 (86%)

As far as status was concerned, the responses clearly show that women in Kolar had a greater perception of increase in their status than in Sonipat. This was directly related to access to credit and other benefits through SHGs. In the absence of credit, women felt no difference in their status. One woman in Kolar remarked:

"*Our status has not changed as we have got no loan ... without loan, who thinks we have done something? If I can open a shop, they will think I have done something and there will be a future. My husband is very old, he cannot work much and I have nothing*".

This perception was again coloured by the societal norms on women's appropriate role. In Sonipat, the women remarked, "*They see us going from here to there, but get nothing ... some think we are loafers ....*".

In Kolar, access to bank loans and other resources made a visible impact on the status of the group members of the sustainable groups. They were no longer confined to household activities alone. They moved around from village to village, attended meetings and participated in joint activities with other groups. It was an ability to take on more responsibility and more work that added to their visibility and status. Nagaratnamma in Kolar claimed, "*our status has increased. When one works hard, then only one will gain. Now we get help from the men*

... we also get better treatment from the officials—we respect them and they respect us". This was corroborated by another woman who saw her status improved: "*Wherever we go now-a-days, we get lots of respect. Earlier people criticised a lot, but when they saw the benefits coming, nobody says anything now".*

In the relatively less rigid patriarchal system of Kolar[17] and with access to loans, women were able to negotiate relationships to some extent. This had to do with the fact that men and other villagers' attitudes towards the position of women changed as they saw the women's ability to obtain credit from the banks. Chouramma of Kashettipalli village explained:

"Earlier when we used to go out for training for 3-4 days and return, our men will be angry and ask, 'what have you brought? Sometimes other members will fight with us because they thought that the ones who went for training are hiding something. Now people have understood".

Another member elaborated:

"Earlier we had to keep asking our men to let us go to meetings ... now we ask him what to do with the money ... if there is a dispute between the husband and wife, and as a result there is a problem in returning the loan, the wife will not be entitled to the second installment. So, husbands also learn to behave".

Thus, the capacity to negotiate gender and power relations increased with access to loans and gradual changes in gender allocation of work at the household level occurred among the members of sustainable groups.

Women's social recognition increased with the ability to bring in loan. Aspiration for increasing material condition was by itself not bad if women experienced any form of social power as well. There is a belief that as women in the SHGs receive loans, they become empowered. Their confidence, collective acts and mobility outside the house are cited as examples. Access to resources had, no doubt, given the option of independent decision-making to a majority of the women in Kolar. They were able to claim public space through holding meetings in the DWCRA or gram panchayat (village council) buildings. Access to public spaces had opened their participation at village level decision-making. Pappamma in Kolar informed that villagers give them respect as SHG members and they get invited to meetings. Men and other family members willing to provide women with time to attend meetings and trainings when they see their credit expectations fulfilled.

While important, these do not necessarily transform the hierarchical power structures that place women's position below that of the men and give women social power. Male permission remained a crucial factor for participation in SHG activities. Married women in Kolar unanimously said, "*we are here (participating in SHGs) only because our husbands have agreed*". Along with credit, collective activity against alcoholism and male violence was undertaken not only to assert identity, but also as a means to increase status. More than 80% in Kolar participated in some form of collective activity, but less than 40% did so in Sonipat.

Power had been gained temporally when women interacted with the State informally through group activities. Women in Kolar could organise such activities through their interaction with other members at the cluster level meetings. Sometimes, women from several groups in the same village organised such activities as, when demanding a bus service to their village or removal of an alcohol shop. They were, however, aware of the limits of the power generated in women's collective acts against alcoholism, when they said,

"All of us went to the DC's office and demanded the removal of the liquor shop. It was removed, but after six months, it opened again ... it should be at least far away from the village, so that even if our husbands drink .... it wears off by the time they reach home".

The custom of observing *purdah* or *ghungat* is a cultural constraint for the women in Sonipat (Chowdhry 1994:283). Ironically, it is also construed as a symbol of respect for elders. On the question of removal of *ghungat*, it clashed with the older women's expectations of respect from the young. An elderly widow in village Rajlubhogipur, Sonipat explained:

"*What is purdah? It is just covering your face when some elders are around and then forget about it as soon as they are gone. Getting an opportunity to work is more important. There is nothing bad in being bound in a few social customs ... purdah is not such a bad thing*".

Economic Independence

It was the educated young lady who could express that they do not face any problem with the practice of *ghungat*. What was of more importance is economic independence: "*If we could have had a shop in the village, it would have benefited more. Men say that these ladies are just roaming around – they have not achieved anything*".

In both the areas, the constraints of informal practices, lack of information and uncertainty about the future meant that women chose to save money for their daughters' dowry. Within the existing societal framework, that was the only option for a girl to have a 'good' marriage and the bride's family does not have much option in it. Even in the homogenous scheduled caste village of Seetharampura, it depended on the groom's side to take the final decision. The social entrepreneur informed that they could only take steps to reduce dowry, but it was not possible to stop it. Women felt that "*all these talk about stopping dowry is for Nagarajan (the trainer) only ... if a girl does not take dowry on her marriage, she should be prepared to die or to come back to her mother's house*'. From the perspective of both men and women, marriage is the only viable option for girls for her upward mobility, security and stability in life. In this regard, women showed a process of rational decision-making within the existing institutional structure of patriarchal norms and a weak judicial system.

Women's identity, perception of changes in status and gender relations was mostly higher with the higher stages of the SHGs to which they belonged. The ability to reach the higher stage was, however, a result of many interacting factors and not dependent on women's agency alone.

Conclusion

The SHG movement is a micro-finance movement and it is no doubt, the largest in the world, but can it be a (social) movement that can change gender and power relations? A movement is a collective effort to seek change. Social movements generally arise when individuals act collectively, agreeing on a goal and on an ideology. The self-help model incorporates many of the elements of the social movements that seek to create a (political) sphere that is "directly controlled by the community rather than the state, and share the belief that the way in which change is pursued will largely determine the result".

Viewed from the perspective of the contemporary women's movements, SHGs are informal organisations that fall under the 'empowerment' wing of the movement. Through the SHGs, women are coming together for credit and other benefits, and seek to promote self-reliance for themselves and enhance development. They are also a form of directed collective action where women are mobilised with an implied commitment to advance their interests, but within the broader development goals of the nation-state. The successful groups do articulate a belief system of personal power through savings, improving condition, social entrepreneurs who give leadership for improving position, there is a feeling of collective identification and loyalty to the groups; cluster and federation provide the organisational structure through which it is expected to grow to provide support to a wider range of women and work collectively.

Self-help groups (SHGs), in rural areas, have provided an alternative to prevailing gender roles for women at the local level and federations of SHGs can create a movement of women's solidarity. Women's federation in Mulbagal, Kolar has taken a step in this direction. Whether they will provide resistance to patriarchal norms and values is not yet clear.

Most of the SHGs and their activities remain oriented toward becoming good savers and good creditors. As social and socialised beings women's choices are inextricably linked with the family and SHGs as an emerging structure has to still function in a patriarchal society. Family norms and values are often designed by patriarchal preferences and approval or permission as per these preferences remain a crucial factor. The common identity of these SHGs is formed around the issue of working for material benefits. The changes in gender relations were very much benefit-based, susceptible to pressure and women had to justify their action in terms of benefits received. The identity achieved is temporary as many SHGs show a tendency to disintegrate when credit is not forthcoming or members change groups with the expectation of getting benefits.

SHGs are designed to stand on two pillars—credit (condition) and social reform (position). Self-help as practised from the economic perspective of credit management requires entrepreneurship and competitiveness at the individual level. On the one hand, "It is important to help the women "think big." One of our star entrepreneurs is Vijaya Mayuri, a woman who went from making *pappads* to power cables. That is the kind of growth that is possible. Women should be aware of that". The individual entrepreneurial approach can come in conflict with the collective approach required for empowerment. Fulfilling strategic interests require women's solidarity, perception of common interest and sisterhood from a feminist perspective.

The self-help movement incorporates liberal feminism which struggles for equality with men from within the existing the social structure. This again needs sustained enthusiasm from 'social entrepreneurs' and periodic motivation by NGOs to make sure that the feminist aspirations are not compromised. Unless handled carefully, empowerment through self-help groups becomes a double-edged sword as the initial enthusiasm is not sustained among both the members and the villagers, and the real interests of the women are forgotten.

Mayoux suggests that it is only through organisations mobilised for rights that can aspire to achieve genuine form of power for women. This is, however, not easily achievable due to the limited political space available to NGOs (mentioned above) and the differences among women both at the local and regional levels. Self-help signifies local aspirations and grassroots development, but these do not necessarily overcome existing differences. Women have multiple identities based on class, caste, education and other such categories and they are constantly required to negotiate the terrain of these overlapping identities. The diversity within the SHGs is not always acknowledged and divisions of caste and class remain.

Even in homogenous groups, older women's interests can be different from the younger ones. Leadership remains with the educated and relatively better-off who can afford the time to devote in social activities. Difficulty of reconciling practical needs with what are strategic needs can give preference to the former, as when a woman has to decide between getting a daughter married or getting her educated.

What is often overlooked is that, the SHG efforts remain context-bound, localised and dependent on the facilitator. It needs to be recognised that women's needs and interests can be different in different areas of the country. The condition and position of women in different areas and even within the same group are not the same. Kinship and marriage patterns, caste and class differences, differences in the capacity of facilitating organisations would require different approaches to SHG formation and functioning in different areas of the country.

Due to dependency, the SHGs are functioning more as micro-credit groups and not as social empowerment or social action groups for women. Most of the external agents play an instrumental role by being developmental and service-oriented. Burra, Deshmukh & Murthy's study found that where the NGOs or the facilitating organisations organised women around multiple issues by simultaneously expanding several spaces, the impact of empowerment has been higher. Such attempts are through simultaneous dealing of issues, such as, domestic violence (body space), savings and credit and livelihoods (Physical and economic spaces), contesting elections (political space), and fight against caste and tribal atrocities (socio-cultural space). This is, however, a slow and a difficult process.

The SHGs have the possibility of developing groups of organised, assertive and empowered women at the grassroots level. There is truth in understanding that the economic is political, but this can be limited in failing to take account of the existing differences, structural inequalities and the relationships of power at the local level. The SHGs can make women contribute to the economy; it has changed the lives of many in India. Group power has been found to be a potent force in giving collective empowerment and voice to the poor women in rural areas, but has not necessarily empowered them beyond the confines of patriarchy. There is a long way to go before reorientation of power relationships, both in the household and at the societal level, will take place.

NOTES AND REFERENCES

Agarwal, Bina (1988) *Structures of Patriarchy: State, Community and Household in Modernising Asia*. Sed books, London.

Berry, K. (2003) 'Developing Women: The Traffic in Ideas about Women and their Needs in Kangra, India' in Sivaramakrishnan,

K. & Agarwal, Arun (ed.) *Regional Modernities: The Cultural Politics of Development in India.* Stanford University Press, Stanford, California, pp.75-98.

Burkey, S. (1993) *People First: A Guide to Self-Reliant Participatory Rural Development.* Sed Books, London.

Burra, N., Deshmukh-Ranadive, J. & Murthy, R. (2005) (ed.) *Micro-Credit, Poverty and Empowerment: Linking the Triad.* Sage Publications, New Delhi.

Calman, L. J. (1992) *Toward Empowerment: Women and Movement Politics in India.* Westview Press, Boulder, USA.

Carr, M., Chen, M. & Jhabvala, R. (1996) (ed.) *Speaking Out: Women's Economic Empowerment in South Asia.* Intermediate Technology Publications, London.

Chakrabarti, R. (2004) The Indian Microfinance Experience–Accomplishments and Challenges, in Debroy, B. & Khan, A.U. (ed.) *Integrating the Rural Poor into Markets.* Academic Foundation, New Delhi.

Chowdhry, P. (1994) *The Veiled Women: Shifting gender equations in rural Haryana, 1880-1990.* Oxford University Press, Delhi.

Cornwall, A., Harrison, E. & Whitehead, A. (2004) 'Introduction: Repositioning Feminisms in Gender and Development'. *IDS Bulletin*, vol. 35, no. 4, pp. 1-9.

Dube, S.C. (1988) *Modernisation and Development—The Search for Alternative Paradigms.* Sed Books Ltd., London.

Dyson, T. & Moore, M. (1983) Kinship structure, female autonomy and demographic behaviour in India. *Population and Development Review*, 9, 35-60.

Fernandez, A. P. (1994) *The Myrada Experience: Alternate Management Systems for Savings and Credit of the Rural Poor.* MYRADA, Bangalore, India.

Fernando, J. L. (2006) *Microfinance: Perils and Prospects.* Routledge, London.

Fisher, T. & Sriram. M.S. (2002) (ed.) *Beyond Micro-Credit: Putting Development Back into Micro-Finance.* Vistaar Publications, New Delhi.

Friedmann, J. (1992) *Empowerment: The Politics of Alternative Development.* Blackwell, Cambridge, USA.

Gaonkar, R. (2004) 'Role of Self-help groups in Empowerment of Women'. Chapter presented at the ISTR Sixth International Conference, Toronto, Canada.

Goetz, A. M. & Sengupta, R. (1996) 'Who Takes the Credit? Gender, Power, and Control over Loan Use in Rural Credit Programmes in Bangladesh'. *World Development*, vol. 24, no 1, pp. 45-63.

Government of India (1985) *Seventh Five Year Plan, 1985-1990*. The Planning Commission of India, New Delhi.

Government of India (1992) *Eight Five Year Plan, 1992-1997*. The Planning Commission of India, New Delhi.

Government of India (1997) *Ninth Five Year Plan, 1997-2002*. The Planning Commission of India, New Delhi.

Government of India (2001) *National Policy for the Empowerment of Women, 2001*. Department of Women and Child Development, Ministry of Human Resources, New Delhi, India.

Government of India (2002) *Tenth Five Year Plan, 2002-2007*. The Planning Commission of India, New Delhi.

Gran, G. (1983) *Development by People: Citizen Construction of a Just World*. Praeger Publishers, New York.

Hardiman, M. & Midgley, J. (1982) *The Social Dimensions of Development: Social Policy and Planning in the Third World*. J. Wiley, New York.

Harper, M. (2002a) 'Self-help Groups and Grameen Bank Groups: What are the Differences'? in Fisher, T. & Sriram. M.S. *Beyond Micro-Credit: Putting Development Back into Micro-Finance*. Vistaar Publications, New Delhi, pp. 169-198.

Harper, M. (2002b) 'Promotion of Self-Help Groups under the SHG Bank Linkage Programme in India'. Chapter presented at the Seminar on SHG-Bank Linkage Programme, New Delhi, India.

Hoff, K. and Stiglitz, J. E. (1990) 'Introduction: Imperfect Information and Rural Credit Markets – Puzzles and Policy Perspectives'. *The World Bank Economic Review*, Vol. 4, No. 3.

Hunt, J. & Kasynathan, N. (2001) 'Pathways to empowerment? Reflections on microfinance and transformation in gender relations in south Asia', in *Gender and Development*, vol. 9, no. 1, March 2001, pp. 42-52.

Kabeer, N. (1994) *Reversed Realities: Gender Hierarchies in Development Thought.* Verso, London.

Kanitkar, A. (2002) 'Exploring Empowerment and Leadership at the Grassroots: Social Entrepreneurship in the SHG Movement in India', in Fisher, T. & Sriram. M.S. *Beyond Micro-Credit: Putting Development Back into Micro-Finance.* Vistaar Publications, New Delhi, pp. 234-62.

Kannan, R. (2004) 'SHG Movement Aiming at Giving Women Larger Role', in *The Hindu,* March 8, 2004.

Katz, A. H. (1993) *Self-Help in America: A Social Movement Perspective.* Twayne Publishers, New York.

Krause, P. (2004) 'Institutional Framework for Poverty Alleviation in Krishna and Nalgonda Districts of Andhra Pradesh' in Rajasekhar, D. & Biradar, R.R. (ed.) (2004) *Reluctant Partners Coming Together? Interface between People, Government and the NGOs.* Concept Publishing Company, New Delhi, pp. 35-56.

Mackenzie, L. (1992) *On our feet: Taking Steps to Challenge Women's Oppression: A Handbook on Gender and Popular Education Workshops.* Centre for Adult and Continuing Education, University of the Western Cape, Belville, South Africa.

Mahmud, S. (2003) 'Actually how Empowering is Microcredit?' *Development and Change,* vol. 34, no. 4, pp. 577-605.

Mahmud, S. (2002) 'Informal women's groups in rural Bangladesh: operation and outcomes', in Heyer, J., Stewart, F. & Thorp, R. (ed.) *Group Behaviour and Development: Is the Market Destroying Cooperation?* Oxford University Press, Oxford, UK, pp. 209-26.

Mayoux, L. (2001) 'Women's Empowerment Versus Sustainability? Towards a New Paradigm in Micro-finance Programmes', in Lemire, B., Pearson, R., & Campbell, G. (ed.) *Women and Credit; Researching the Past, Refiguring the Future.* Berg, Oxford, pp. 247-69.

Mazumdar, V. (1986) 'Women's Studies in Indian Perspective: Summary' in Raj, M. K. (ed.) *Women's Studies in India: Some Perspectives.* Popular Prakashan, Bombay, pp. 23-33.

Molyneux, M. (1985) 'Mobilisation Without Emancipation? Women's Interests, the State and Revolution in Nicaragua'. *Feminist Studies*, vol. 11, pp. 227-54.

Molyneux, M. (1998) Analysing Women's Movements. *Development and Change*, vol. 29, pp. 219-45.

Monkman, Karen (1998) 'Training women for change and empowerment' in Stromquist, N.

Montgomery, R., Bhattacharya, D. & Hulme, D. (1986) 'Credit for the Poor in Bangladesh: The BRAC Rural Development Programme and the Government Thana Resource Development Employment Programme', in Hulme, D. & Mosley, P. (ed.) Finance Against Poverty. Routledge, London.

Moser, C. (1989) Gender Planning in the Third World: Meeting Practical and Strategic Gender Needs. *World Development*, vol. 17, no. 11, pp. 1799-1825.

Murthy, R. K. (2004) 'Organisational Strategy in India and Diverse Identities of Women: Bridging the Gap'. *Gender and Development*, vol. 12, no 1, May 2004, pp. 10-18.

MYRADA (2001) *The Myrada Experience: A Manual for Capacity Building of Self-help Affinity Groups*. Myrada, Bangalore, India.

NABARD (2005) *Annual Report, 2004-2005*. National Agricultural Bank for Rural Development, Mumbai, India.

Olson, M. (1965). *The Logic of Collective Action: Public Goods and the Theory of Groups*. Harvard University Press, Cambridge, Massachusetts.

Omvedt, G. (2004) 'Women's Movement: Some Ideological Debates' in Chaudhuri, M. (ed.) *Feminism in India*. Kali for Women, New Delhi, India.

Pieterse, J. P. N. (2001) *Development Theory: Deconstructions/ Reconstructions*. Sage, London.

Pitt, M.M., Khandker, S.R. & Cartwright, J. (2003) 'Does Micro-Credit Empower Women? Evidence from Bangladesh'. World Bank Policy Research Working Chapter 2998, Washington. D.C.

Purushothaman, S. (1998) *The Empowerment of Women in India*. Sage Publications, New Delhi.

Rahman, A. (1999) *Women and Microcredit in Rural Bangladesh: Anthropological Study of the Rhetoric and Realities of Grameen Bank Lending.* Westview Press, Boulder, Colorado, USA.

Rahman, Md. A. (1993) *People's Self-Development: Perspectives on Participatory Action Research.* Sed Books, London.

Rajasekhar, D. (2000) 'Non-governmental Organisations in India: Opportunities and Challenges'. Working chapter no. 66, Institute for Social and Economic Change, Bangalore, India.

Rowlands, J. (1999) 'Empowerment Examined', in Eade, D. (ed.) *Development with Women: Selected Essays from Development in Practice.* Oxfam, Oxford, UK, pp.141-150.

Sa-Dhan (2001) *Microfinance Regulation in India.* Sa-Dhan, New Delhi.

Satish, P. (2001) Institutional Alternatives for the Promotion of microfinance: Self-Help Groups in India. *Journal of Microfinance,* vol. 3, no. 2, pp. 49-74.

Sriram, M. S. & Upadhyayula, R. S. (2004) The Transformation of the Microfinance Sector in India: Experiences, Options, and Future. *Journal of Microfinance,* vol. 6, no. 2, Winter 2004, pp. 89-112.

Stamm, L. & Ryff, C. D. (ed.) (1984) *Social Power and Influence of Women.* Westview Press, Colorado.

Thomas, B. (1985) *Politics, Participation, and Poverty: Development through Self-Help in Kenya.* Westview Press, Boulder, USA.

Titus (2002) 'Costs in Micro-finance: What do Urban Self-help Groups Tell Us?' in Fisher, T. & Sriram. M.S. *Beyond Micro-Credit: Putting Development Back into Micro-Finance.* Vistaar Publications, New Delhi, pp. 199.

Uphoff, N,T. & Esman, M. J. (1984) *Local Organisations: Intermediaries in Rural Development.* Cornell University Press, Ithaca, USA.

Walby, S. (1990) *Theorising Patriarchy.* Blackwell, Oxford.

Wilson, K. (2002) 'The New Microfinance: An Essay on the Self-Help Group Movement in India'. *Journal of Microfinance,* vol. 4, no. 2, pp. 217-45.

8

ROLE OF WOMEN IN SMALL-HOLDER RAINFED AND MIXED FARMING IN INDIA

Introduction

In spite of the progress in agriculture, India still faces a big challenge in job creation and maintenance of food security and women's role in farming is still inadequately acknowledged. It is estimated that 78% of India's economically active women are involved in agriculture, 35% as cultivators and 43% as labourers. Due to more male migration, the proportion is higher in rainfed areas, where uncertain rainfall makes mixed crop-livestock farming the predominant system. Crop production is irregular and livestock more important in household survival strategies.

Across the poor farming communities care of animals is the women's domain, but not in the well off families. In the case of Pastoralists women as well as men look after the animals. Several studies have documented that the women have a considerable knowledge in areas such as feed resources for large as well as small animals, but there is a great need for redesigning training and extension interventions to suit the women's requirements. It means they should be practical, short-term, use audio-visual material and be located at the right time of the day (afternoon) and close to the women's homes. Employment of women training and extension officers would increase the efficiency of the work. A pre-condition for good training is that research generates information of relevance to the women.

Agriculture Scenario of India

While India has achieved rapid and commendable progress in agriculture, we face a challenging task of maintaining food security and providing employment for future generations. A report from the Indian Council of Agriculture indicated that to meet food grain demand by year 2002 we needed to add 30-35 million tonnes of food grains, over the annual production of about 192 million tonnes. Annual population growth is estimated at 1.8%. Meeting the demand of food security and employment in the short as well as the long term is challenging in view of some constraints and emerging developments. India has limited irrigation potential and about 70% of the cultivated area are rainfed, and land holding per family is decreasing.

With increasing purchasing power of the middle income group, the demand for food will change in quantitative as well as qualitative terms. The demand for livestock products is expected to increase along with demand for fruits and vegetables. There is an increase in export of agriculture produce, as a result of liberalisation and it is influencing agriculture production. At the same time, there is a realisation of the adverse effects of over exploitation of resources as indicated by rapid increase in soil salinity, lowering of ground water levels, soil erosion, increasing incidences of chemical residues in food products etc.

Agriculture is not only the main source of employment, income and food for over 70% of the population, but it is also the main 'culture' for rural families. It is reported that 78% of economically active women are involved in agriculture of which 35% are cultivators and 43% work as agriculture labour. The extent of women involvement in agriculture is even higher in rainfed—semi arid—arid and underdeveloped areas. Migration of men, in search of work, is very high from underdeveloped and resource poor areas. And it is the women who bear the burden of agriculture besides looking after the family. Involvement of women in agriculture is inversely related to socioeconomic conditions of the family, development in the area and scale and type of operations.

In undeveloped tribal areas, where most of the agriculture is rainfed, the women have to shoulder responsibility from production management to marketing of produce (crop and livestock). While in irrigated and developed areas where cash crops are dominant, the women have only marginal involvement. A major concern in India is improvement of agriculture production from rainfed–semiarid and arid areas, which contribute substantially to coarse grain, pulses, oil seed and livestock production.

Uncertain Crop Production

Mixed crop-livestock farming and mixed cropping have been adopted by the farmers, from rainfed areas, through generations of experience. Crop production is uncertain in such areas and mixed farming is a way of averting risks. Amongst crops cereals and pulses are usually mixed in view of divergent water requirements and stages of maturity. Livestock are less influenced by rain failure, compared to crops and are invaluable in sustaining family income during drought.

Amongst livestock a mix of large and small animals are usually maintained. Milk production contributes a major share of livestock production and is only next to rice with regard to contribution to agriculture production. Thus, it is common to see a cow or buffalo along with goat and backyard poultry, in a tribal family. Studies of BAIF carried out in semi-arid and arid areas, of North Gujarat and West Rajasthan, indicate that livestock contribute 45% to 52% of family income. It is the women who look after livestock and backyard poultry and thus play a major role in sustainable production and food security for the family, through optimal use of local resources.

Women and Agriculture

There is increasing realisation of the critical role of women in agriculture and of the fact that empowerment of women is necessary for bringing about sustainable development at a faster pace. However, much need to be done to ensure that women get direct benefit particularly those from underdeveloped areas and underprivileged communities. The farming systems are more complex in resource poor, rainfed areas and socio-economic factors influence production systems. Illiteracy, lack of awareness, low level of skills, suppression, lack of appropriate technology, extension and training programmes are the main factors which need be tackled for empowerment of women.

Analyses of various agriculture development programmes in India show that the impact on crop–livestock production is much smaller, in many cases only marginal, in rain fed and semiarid arid areas. However, it is these areas which make the major contribution towards production of coarse cereals, oil seed, cotton and livestock. Bringing about substantial improvement in agriculture production in these areas is a challenge for research, development and extension workers—and calls for a different approach.

The chapter is based on studies carried out for more than a decade in a few underdeveloped pockets of the western states of India. The initial studies were aimed at a gender analysis of crop-livestock production systems and in view of the important role of women, detailed and participatory studies to understand the women's experiences, perceptions, knowledge and innovativeness were subsequently carried out. Observations were also gathered on the women's experiences and suggestions on available services, including training, extension and development support.

Features of Mixed Farming

Some of the characteristics of the farming systems, which prevail in rainfed, semi-arid and arid areas are worthy of notice for developing future intervention strategies.

It is noticed that women farmers are well aware of local resources as well as constraints including difficulties in marketing. However, awareness is poor about new developments like improved dry land farming techniques and varieties suitable for unfavourable soil and moisture conditions. This is probably due to lack of communication and virtual absence of extension programmes, which would directly benefit women.

Features of Mixed Farming in Rainfed Areas

1. Assured subsistence is high priority with the farmers.
2. Mixed cropping and livestock common for risk coverage.
3. The production systems are low external input types developed to fully utilise local resources – including human resources and to recycle all products.
4. Crop varieties, rotation and mix; provide grain and enough straw to meet human and animal needs.
5. Livestock are maintained with multi-purpose objectives.
6. There is a sizeable population of small animals in semi-arid and arid areas since these are easy to manage and to sell.
7. Selection of crops and crop varieties as well as that of livestock is based on their adaptability to local conditions as observed through generations.
8. Use of high yielding varieties of crops or livestock and of chemical fertilisers and pesticides is minimal (only by those having good resources).

9. Storage of produce for family use has priority and only surplus, if any, is sold.

Variation in Involvement of Women in Crop and Livestock Production

In the western states of India, there is considerable variation in involvement of women in crop and livestock production between regions as well as within a region. The variation is due to the nature of the production system as well as social and economic factors. It is observed that women from higher socioeconomic strata are not involved directly in handling of crop or livestock, while those from underprivileged societies like tribals have to manage production as well as marketing. However, amongst the farming community it is the animals, which are considered the main responsibility of the women. Amongst pastoralists the work is equally shared since livestock production is the main source of occupation and income for them.

In some regions, the cultural tradition restrict the women from being involved in outdoor jobs like marketing. Thus, within livestock management, feeding and cleaning or milking operations are done by women while sale and purchase are handled by men and thus the income is in the hands of the men.

However, this behavioural pattern and cultural constraints vary between regions and social groups. Thus in most parts of Gujarat and Maharashtra States in Western India women do participate in outside jobs. The restrictions are much less amongst the socio-economic backward and also communities like tribals and pastoralists.

Women in Crop Production

The involvement of women in crop production also varies according to the type of crop and cropping system and the socioeconomic status of the family. There is a need to distinguish between involvement of women as agriculture labour and involvement in operations of their own farm. Thus women from poor families work as agriculture labour, irrespective of the community to which they belong. Estimates indicate that about 35% of rural women work as agriculture labour.

It is noticed that women handle labour intensive operations needing more care and time. Women, hired as farm labour invariably do transplantation of paddy and weeding operations, amongst various crops. In some areas there is a traditional practice amongst small farmers to take up these operations on a collective basis. Thus whenever there is paddy transplantation women from neighbouring farms would gather and help each other. It was also noticed that contrary to the general belief, women from small farmer families and particularly from rainfed backward areas actively participate in operations like field preparations, sowing, fertiliser applications, besides harvesting of crops which is predominantly the women's job. However, involvement of women from families of rich and big farmers (those with irrigation and cash crops) is only marginal, partly because of mechanisation. It is quite uncommon to see women handling machines (tractors and threshers, etc.). Women mostly manage small-scale vegetable and fruit production, kitchen gardens, for home consumption.

Discussions and participatory exercises with women indicate that they are quite knowledgeable about certain aspects of crop production, but awareness of new developments is very poor. Women were found to be the first to notice pest and disease attack, they were also well informed about soil water resources as well as crops and fruit trees suitable for their respective areas. It was noticed that the information dissemination process such as agricultural and livestock extension does not properly cover the women, even in areas where the training and visit extension programmes are implemented. Moreover, the extension messages and information on new developments are not provided in a language the women easily understand. The women also pointed out that they handle most of the painstaking and back breaking jobs and provision of suitable tools may reduce their drudgery. However, the positive aspect of this system is that women from poor families are able to gather weeds and crop by-products for feeding their animals at no cost.

Involvement of Women in Large Animal Production

Since the last decade or so, the contribution of women in dairy production is getting due recognition. It is realised that women handle most of the critical jobs like feeding, milking, care of newborn and administration of medicine. However, there is variation in involvement of women between socioeconomic groups and regions, as indicated earlier. In tribal, low rainfall, semi-arid and arid areas much of the work with regard to animal management has to be looked after by women due to migration of males for work. However, in many cases the income from dairy animals does not remain in the hands of women and neither does the decision regarding sale and purchase. However, due to the move to develop women's diary cooperatives in many states in India women have better control over sale of milk and use of income from it.

Another positive development is recognition of women as members of dairy cooperative societies, so that the price of milk supplied to the society can be paid to the women directly. Till a few years ago, women were not made registered members of the dairy cooperative society (the registration was in the name of the husband and thus he collected the money for milk produced and supplied by the women). While the contribution of women to the animals' management is recognised, the experiences of women regarding animal production and diseases and their perceptions are ignored. Observations related to these aspects are summarised below:

1. Women are well aware of each animal's behaviour and production characteristics.

2. Women are knowledgeable about local feed resources and are able to identify beneficial grasses, weeds and fodder trees for feeding of dairy animals.
3. Women know the feeding behaviour of each animal and prepare feed mixtures accordingly.
4. For rural women the contribution of dairy cows and buffaloes towards family nutrition and fuel needs is as important as milk for sale.
5. Preferences for animals by the women are based on temperament of the animal, its adaptability and quality of milk besides the quantity produced.
6. In the majority of the cases, the management of the animal is treated as a traditional responsibility and there is a lack of awareness about the potential of this production system to become a major source of income.

There is now some realisation about the knowledge possessed by women and the need to improve their knowledge, skills and awareness. Some organisations, particularly NGOs, are making an attempt to develop teams of women para-extension workers who could be effective in providing information and improve the skills of women.

Women in Goat and Poultry Production

Studies show that goat keeping and backyard poultry production are inversely related to socio-economic status and are largely women's domains. The majority of poor, underprivileged and landless families in rainfed and under-developed areas own goats and or backyard poultry. These are again good examples of low external input production systems and recycling of material.

Goat keeping is totally managed by women and children except for the pastoralists, who keep large flocks of goat. However, the sale and purchase of animals is carried out by men in most cases, except in tribal communities where marketing is also handled by women. With the substantial increase in meat prices in India, goats have become a good source of income, although marketing of goats is not properly organised and is totally in the hands of middlemen. Much of selling of goats in rural areas is to meet contingencies. Hence, goats are usually looked upon as an asset that is easy to convert into cash and an animal, which can be conveniently handled and managed at low cost.

Although goats are mostly grazed, the studies indicate that contrary to common belief the majority of the farmers provide some locally available, supplementary feed. Goat production has not received any support through various development schemes and was always considered detrimental to the environment. However, the livestock census indicates a sharp rise in the number of small ruminants, particularly goats. Goats are slaughtered in largest numbers and kid mortality is high, but still their population is increasing which is indicative of the small farmers' preferences for this animal. The experiences of a few goat development projects in India are encouraging and the outcome indicates there are possibilities for substantial increases in small farmer income and of changing feeding and management practices to make it more environmentally friendly. This has become possible mostly due to the rise in prices of goat meat and the practice of paying according to body weight and body condition. With better prices, the practice of semi-stall feeding and provision of supplementary feed is becoming feasible. In some areas, there is a market for goat milk although it is generally mixed with cow and buffalo milk and sold to dairies.

Studies indicate that 40% to 50% of the income from goats is through milk in such areas and 30% to 35% from sale of animals. The manure from goats is also a significant source of income contributing 15% to 20% of the earnings. It was noticed that there is a difference in the perception of men and women regarding the usefulness of the goat and productivity constraints.

Some of these points are summarised below:

1. Women give high marks for the utility of the goat as a source of low cost milk production on occasions when guests have to be entertained.
2. A goat is easy to manage and needs only marginal inputs.
3. A goat is easy to convert into cash to meet contingencies.
4. Women are not in favour of increasing the number of goats per household in view of the management difficulties.
5. The priority intervention according to the women is against mortality and sickness in kids that record 25% to 30% mortality.

The traditional backyard poultry production is common in interior rural areas and particularly with underprivileged communities. With tribal families it is a common practice to maintain backyard poultry. The women manage poultry production and the sub-system is another good example of low input production, based on recycling of household and farm wastes. Although recently some studies have been conducted of backyard poultry production, in general, the sub-system has been neglected and considered unworthy of study. However, the backyard poultry system has been well studied in countries like Indonesia, Bangladesh, Nigeria and Sri Lanka and ways of improving its productivity are being tried. Very few studies have been or are conducted in India, but those that have been done indicate that backyard poultry is a source of low cost, high quality food for the family and small cash for women through sale of birds and eggs.

Holistic Perspective

The growth of commercial poultry production in India is a fine example of a high rate of growth in a sector without much government assistance. However, from a development perspective there are some negative aspects. The commercial poultry production benefits a very small number of persons and, like any other commercial agriculture venture, the women are marginalised. The third most important aspect is high dependence of commercial poultry production on external inputs. Studies of rural women indicate that they look at backyard poultry from a holistic perspective. Most women were not interested in expanding poultry production and using improved breeds. The women were very clear in indicating that they prefer the local breeds and to keep the size of the flocks within a certain size limit, for reasons, which were logical.

Some of these aspects are summarised below:

Rural Women's Perceptions and Preferences with Regard to Poultry Production

1. The major interest of women in backyard poultry is as a source of small cash and nutritious food for the family at low cost.
2. Women are not interested in increasing the number of birds due to management difficulties and the need for external inputs it would require.
3. The local breeds are preferred since they are easy to manage. They are able to protect themselves from predators, but the most important reason is that local birds and eggs are sold at a premium.
4. Backyard poultry offers entertainment of important guests and functions.
5. Women consider diseases in chicks the major problem in poultry keeping.

It was noticed that the majority of the families from western India were interested in selling birds. Some families undertake production of chicken and sell them to people, who plan to rear the birds. Families of semi-urban and urban areas showed interest in improved breeds and commercial scale production. Discussions with women from interior rural and underdeveloped areas indicate specific priorities for development support. The majority of the families mentioned a need for control of diseases, which cause high mortality in chicken. Newcastle disease is the most common cause and although this disease is controllable there is a lack of vaccination programmes. Improvement in feeding and housing would also control losses and increase productivity. Organising marketing of eggs and birds through a network of women groups is another aspect worthy of consideration. There is a need for undertaking applied research with the aim to develop appropriate approaches for improving backyard poultry production that can develop into a system which would benefit women directly.

Improved backyard poultry and goat production would not only improve income of women but would also contribute to family nutrition. These offer opportunities to directly benefit women from underprivileged families in a sustainable manner and hence special attention is recommended to these sub-systems. There is need to develop women para-extension workers who can organise health control programmes for goats and chicken with guidance from veterinarians. Skill training for health control would be needed. Formation of women's groups for sale of milk, animals, eggs and birds need be organised.

Training and Extension

While there is a realisation of the major role played by women in crop and livestock production not much has been done to modify the approach and contents of training and extension programmes. The major change that has occurred in the livestock sector is the participation of women in training programmes. Studies carried out with women to understand their views and suggestions about training indicate that the conventional approach to training has to be radically changed.

The major aspects to which attention needs to be paid in planning of training programmes for women are summarised below.

Women's Perceptions and Suggestions on Training

1. Women basically dislike long lectures and can effectively learn while doing; hence the programme should be practical.
2. Women prefer discussing problems that they currently face.
3. The women suggested short-term training covering few subjects.
4. They suggested training or meetings to take place in the afternoon, when they are relatively free.
5. Illiteracy is very high amongst rural women and long notes are of limited use. Audio-visual material should be used to the maximum extent.
6. Use of local dialects is strongly recommended.

Involvement of women training and extension officers would increase effectiveness of the programme. In addition to the above aspects the discussions with the women revealed a need to produce training and extension material, as well as messages appropriate for local conditions. Centrally prepared material and messages, based on institutional research, are many times not appropriate. Much of the training and extension material is prepared in developed areas and show high producing animals or crops. While the rural women patiently observe the presentation such material usually gives wrong messages. Social factors should also be given due treatment, in view of the social structures in rural society.

For effective programmes and participation of the women, it is necessary to have as much homogeneity as possible in the groups chosen for training or extension meetings. Factors like socio-economic status, age etc. have a bearing on interaction

TABLE 1

Examples of women's knowledge of animal feed

No	Feed Material	Type of Animal	Benefits Claimed
1.	Cotton Seed and Cotton seed cake	Cows and buffaloes	Improvement in fat percentage and milk yield
2.	Pods and Seeds of Acacia & Prosopis species of trees.	Cow, buffalo, goat	Improvements in milk yield fat percentage and induce heat.
3.	Tinospora Cordifolia (creeper)	Cows, buffaloes, goat	Improvement in milk production.
4.	Leaves of Alangium, Bassia latifolia, Butea monosperma trees	Cows, buffaloes, goat	Improvement in milk production
5.	Azadirachta indica (a tree)	Mainly goat	During participatory studies involving women on goat keeping, conducted by the Indian development NGO BAIF, the women identified 17 to 20 different species of grasses, shrubs and trees useful to feed goats.

(Table Contd...)

During the studies it was observed that the women follow the system of partitioning of the feed, with a view to make the best use of the available resources. Thus better producing animals, the pregnant or working animals are given the most nutritious feed or most nutritious parts of the available fodder, a system which is a good example of optimisation of resources. Moreover, each animal is provided a mix of ingredients or is offered soaked or cooked food based upon its liking.	
It is suggested that while developing or testing a technology, particularly for livestock, it would be most desirable to involve the women in such trials. During trials with Urea Treatment of cereal straws, in one of the projects in Western India, it was seen that the women were able to develop an appropriate system for uniform application of urea solution. In the absence of measuring equipment and sprayers to contain the urea solution they were able to find a simple method using locally available drums and oilcans for measuring and spraying the solution. It was also observed that the women had a good knowledge about medicinal plants that are useful for people as well as for animals. In rural areas the use of traditional medicine is quite common and some of the medicinal plants are regularly used for treatment of minor ailments.	
Thus the traditional knowledge and practices of women can be further developed and used for improving productivity in a sustainable manner through an appropriate programme of research, training and extension.	

among and active participation of the women. Since the women learn best through discussions and by doing things on their own, it is best to use a participatory and interactive approach in training and extension. A special effort should be made to promote interaction and provide opportunities for practical work.

Knowledge and Innovativeness of Women

The various studies, training and extension programmes carried out during the last decade clearly indicated that women have important knowledge on many subjects and are innovative. Their efforts at optimal utilisation of time, labour and local natural resources need to be properly studied, understood and appreciated.

It was seen, during studies on feeding of livestock, that women had knowledge about various local feed resources. They could identify a variety of grasses, bushes, creepers and trees that are good livestock feed. They also identified fodder species, which are useful for different animals. Table 1 summarises these observations.

NOTES AND REFERENCES

FAO (1983). *Women in Agriculture Co-operatives, WCCARD follow-up programmes.* FAO, Rome.

FAO (1990). *Women and Livestock Production Asia and South Pacific,* RAPA, FAO, Bangkok.

FAO (1991). *Most farmers in India are Women.* New Delhi: FAO.

Paris, T.R. (1995). "Gender Analysis in Crop Animal Research". In IRRI discussion paper series No.6. Proc. of an Intl. Workshop on Crop Animal Interaction held at Khon Khan, Thailand, 27 Sept. to 1st Oct. 1993: 501-22.

Poats, S.V., M. Schmink and A. Spring. (1988). "Linking FSRE and Gender an Introduction", in S.V Poats, M. Schmink and A. Spring (eds.), *Gender Issues in Farming Systems Research and Extension.* London: West View Press: 9-18.

Rangnekar, D.V. (1995). "Research Methodology for Crop Animal Systems in Semiarid Regions of India". In IIRI discussion paper series No. 6. Proc. of an Intl. Workshop on Crop Animal interaction held at Khon Kaen Thailand, 27 Sept. to 1st Oct. 1993: 501-22.

Rangnekar, D.V. & S.D. Rangnekar (1996). "Traditional poultry production system—a need for fresh look from rural development perspective". Proc. XXth World's Poultry Congress, New Delhi. 2-5 Sept. 1996.

Rangnekar, S.D. (1992). "Women in Livestock Production in Rural India". In Proc. Of 6th AAAP Animal Science Congress held at Bangkok, Thailand: 271-85.

Rangnekar, S.D. and D.V. Rangnekar (1992). "Involvement of Women and Children in Goat keeping in some villages of Gujarat and Rajasthan". In Proc. Of the 5th International Conf. On Goats held at New Delhi, India.

Rangnekar, S.D. (1997). "Income enhancement and value addition by crop livestock integration, extending benefit directly to women". Proceedings of the National workshop on the technological Empowerment of women in Agriculture held in December 1997 at M.S. Swaminathan Research Foundation, Chennai, India, pp. V-1 to V-7.

Rangnekar, S.D. (1996). "Role of women in traditional poultry production system in India". *Proc. XXth World's Poultry Congress*, New Delhi. 2-5 Sept. 1996.

Rangnekar, S.D. (1997). "Participatory studies with women on Ethnoveterinary practices for livestock health management", *Proc. Of International Conference on Ethnoveterinary Medicine*, held at Pune, India. Nov. 4-6 1997.

Spio, K (1997). "The role of women's in rural society", *Journal of rural development* 16(3): 497-513.

Swaminathan, M.S. (1996). *Role of education and research in enhancing income of rural women in sustainable agriculture: towards food security.* Ed. M.S. Swaminathan, New Delhi: Koran Publishers pat. Ltd.: 143-78.

9

RURAL WOMEN AND FOOD SECURITY

Introduction

Regardless of the level of development achieved by the respective economies, women play a pivotal role in agriculture and in rural development in most countries of the Asia-Pacific region. Evidently, there are serious constraints which militate against the promotion of an effective role for women in development in those societies which were bound by age-old traditions and beliefs. Patriarchal modes and practices motivated by cultures and/or interpretations of religious sanctions and illiteracy hinder women's freedom to opt for various choices to assert greater mobility in social interactions. Resulting from these situations, women's contribution to agriculture and other sectors in the economy remain concealed and unaccounted for in monitoring economic performance measurement. Consequently, they are generally invisible in plans and programmes. They were, in fact, discriminated against by stereotypes which restrict them to a reproductive role, and denied access to resources which could eventually enhance their social and economic contribution to the society.

In terms of the ratio of membership of women in agricultural cooperatives, the percentage is rather low, but they have a strong influence on them – through the heads of the households. Certain obvious barriers restrict their direct and formal entry in agricultural cooperatives. Even in countries like Japan, the ratio of women membership in agricultural cooperative is extremely low. Only very few women serve on the Boards of Directors. Their simple and clear perception is that the administrative and decision-making domain rests with the men and women do not wish to overburden themselves with financial responsibilities in case something goes wrong with the cooperative. They, of course, contribute significantly in farm operations. However, the women are very active in Women's Associations of Agricultural Cooperatives which organise their activities around the life and style of farm household members.

In developing countries, among the poor, rural women are the poorest and more vulnerable. Empirical evidences suggest that women in rural areas are more adversely affected by poverty than men. The incidence of poverty among rural women is on the rise in most of the developing countries. The issues of gender bias and equity point to the double burden women have to bear - that on being poor and being a woman. Further strategies and programmes for development had largely overlooked the question of gender equity. Projects aiming to reduce poverty view the poor rural women as the recipient of benefits of development, instead of active participant and still poor rural women have the least access to basic needs such as food, health and education.

Hunger and Poverty

Hunger, which usually follows food shortages, is caused by a complex set of events and circumstances [social, economic and political factors] that differ depending on the place and time. Although hunger has been a part of human experience for centuries and a dominant feature of life in many low-income countries, the causes of hunger and starvation are not very well understood. Our understanding of the main causes of hunger and starvation has been hampered by myths and misconceptions about the interplay between hunger and population growth, land use, farm size, technology, trade, environment and other factors.

Poverty cannot be defined simply in terms of lacking access to sufficient food. It is also closely associated with a person's lack of access to productive assets, services and markets. Without access to these, it is unlikely that production and income-earning capacities can be improved on a sustainable basis. Rural poverty is related to food insecurity, access to assets, services and markets: income-earning opportunities; and the organisational and institutional means for achieving those ends.

Throughout the history and in many societies, inequalities of women and men were part and parcel of an accepted male-dominated culture. It is a complex historical process, which requires detailed study before one can conceive of a viable strategy to improve and sustain the status of women in society. One of the basic factors causing unequal share of women in development relates to the division of labour between the sexes. This division of labour has been justified on the basis of the childbearing function of women and this is biologically important for survival. Consequently, distribution of tasks and responsibilities between men and women in a given society has mainly restricted women to the domestic sphere. Mass poverty and general backwardness has further aggravated the inequalities.

While the women's childbearing and child-rearing functions are respected in many countries, there has been very little recognition of women's actual or potential contribution to the economic, social and cultural states. The role of women within the family combined with high level of unemployment and under-employment of the population in general, has led to the unequal state of priority to men in matters of employment. It is understandable that women cannot be expected to join the army, for instance, as foot soldiers but Israel's well-known and rightfully feared *sabrahs* or women commandos, have shattered the myth of man's physical superiority and thus priority for most jobs.

Discrimination and Underdevelopment

It is relevant to consider some aspects of the marginalisation of the status of women in the world by having a look at the figures which are based on the documents of the United Nations. Some of the findings are:

- **Unemployment Rate:** Male unemployment rate decreased by 11% from 1984 to 1988 while that of women, unemploy-ment rate increased by 0.5% during the same period;
- **Women in the Informal Sector:** Without legal protection or security, women depend on informal trade for their survival. In Third World countries, a high percentage of food vendors were women: in Nigeria 94%, Thailand 80%, and 63% in the Philippines;
- **Inequality in Pay:** All over the world women earn only two-thirds of men's pay and earn less than three-quarters of the wages of men doing similar jobs. Women form a third of the world's official labour force, but are concentrated in the lowest-paid jobs and are more vulnerable to unemployment than men;
- **Domestic Work:** Women do almost all the world's domestic work and coupled with their additional work in the productive spheres—this means most women work a double day. Unpaid domestic work is regarded as women's work. Though it is vital work, it is invisible work, unpaid, undervalued and unrecognised. Yet, the women's contribution to society in this regard is enormous;
- **Agriculture:** Women grow about half of the world's food, but own hardly any land, have difficulty in

obtaining credit and are overlooked by agricultural advisors and projects. In Africa, three-quarters of the agricultural work is done by women while in Asia, Latin America and the Middle-East, women comprise half of the agricultural labour force;

— **Health:** Women provide more health care than all health services combined and have been major beneficiaries of a new global shift in priorities towards prevention of disease and promotion of good health;

— **Education:** Women continue to outnumber men among the world's illiterates by about 3:2 ratio, but school enrollment boom is closing the education gap between boys and girls;

— **Political Affairs:** Due to poorer education, lack of confidence and greater workload, women are still under-represented in the decision-making bodies of their countries.

The effects of the long-term cumulative process of discrimination against women have been accentuated by underdevelopment. Graphically, while women represent nearly half of the world's adult population and one-third of the total labour force, they labour nearly two-thirds of the total working hours but receive only one-tenth of world income and own less than one per cent of property. The story of overworked women in the rural areas of the developing and underdeveloped countries of the world is too well known. The type of agricultural activities generally expected of women is highly labour-intensive and the rural women generally do not enjoy the benefits of new technologies. Their wages are generally less because it is assumed that the efficiency of women's labour is poor compared to that of men. Regarding ownership of land, women do not enjoy equal rights, particularly in the developing countries where most of the production, processing, storage and preparation of food is carried out by the women.

These account for 50% of the total labour required for food production. Many of these tasks are performed by children, especially the girls. Besides helping the menfolk in many farm operations, women have to shoulder the entire responsibilities for household chores. Bringing water from far-off wells and rivers and gathering fuel wood from forests are also part of their daily duties. Such enormous waste of human energy is unnecessary in this technological age.

Gender Division of Labour in Agriculture

The particular tasks done on farms by men and women have certain common patterns. In general, men undertake the heavy physical labour of land preparation and jobs which are specific to distant locations, such as livestock herding, while women carry out the repetitious, time-consuming tasks like weeding and those which are located close to home, such as care of the kitchen garden. In most cultures, the spraying of pesticides is considered a male task, as women are aware of the danger to their unborn children of exposure to chemicals. Women do a major part of the planting and weeding of crops.

Care of livestock is shared, with men looking after the larger animals and women the smaller ones. Marketing is often seen as a female task, although men are most likely to negotiate the sale of crops. Some jobs are gender neutral. The introduction of a new tool may cause a particular job to be re-assigned to the opposite sex and men tend to assume tasks that become mechanised.

The impact on women of the modernisation of agriculture is both complex and contradictory. Women have often been excluded from agrarian reform and training programmes in new agricultural methods. Where both men and women have equal access to modern methods and inputs there is no evidence that either sex is more efficient than the other. Technological changes in post-harvest processing may even deprive women of a traditional income-earning task.

Women and Food Security Issues

Not only do women produce and process agricultural products but they are also responsible for much of the trade in these and other goods in many parts of the third world. In many parts of the world, women continue to play an important role as rural information sources and providers of food to urban areas. This may involve food from the sea as well as from the land. Although women rarely work as fisherpeople they are often involved in net-making and the preparation and sale of the catch.

Women's roles and status all over the world are generally determined by social institutions and norms, religious ideologies, eco-systems and by class positions. The Indian social systems exhibit such grave disparities. Indian women are not a homogeneous group. Their traditional roles are not identical in all strata of society. Norms and taboos governing their roles and behaviours within and outside the family, the structure of family organisations and social practices and the positions accorded to women in a community differ considerably across regions, cultures and levels of socioeconomic development.

It is needless to emphasise on the significant contribution of women to agricultural production and household food security. In the process of production, handling and preparation of food, women play a multiple role throughout the sequence. They are said to be "feeding the world". Do women really feed the world? Let us consider the evidence. On a global scale, women produce more than half of all the food that is grown. In sub-Sahara Africa and the Caribbean, they produce up to 80% of basic foodstuffs. In Asia, they provide from 50 to 90% of the labour for rice cultivation.

And in Southeast Asia and the Pacific as well as Latin America, women's home gardens represent some of the most complex agricultural systems known. In countries in transition, the percentage of rural women working in agriculture ranges from about a third in Bosnia and Herzegovina to more than half in Poland. Across much of the developing world, rural women provide most of the labour for farming, from soil preparation to harvest. After the harvest, they are almost entirely responsible for operations such as storage, handling, stocking, marketing and processing.

Women in rural areas generally bear primary responsibility for the nutrition of their children, from gestation through weaning and throughout the critical period of growth. In addition, they are the principal food producers and preparers for the rest of the family.

Despite their contributions to food security, women tend to be invisible actors in development. All too often, their work is not recorded in statistics or mentioned in reports. As a result, their contribution is poorly understood and often underestimated. There are many reasons for this. Work in the household is often considered to be part of a woman's duties as wife and mother, rather than an occupation to be accounted for in both the household and the national economy. Outside the household, a great deal of rural women labour—whether regular or seasonal – goes unpaid and is, therefore, rarely taken into account in official statistics.

In most countries, women do not own the land they cultivate. Discriminatory laws and practices for inheritance of and access and ownership to land are still widespread. Land that women do own tends to consist of smaller, less valuable plots that are also frequently overlooked in statistics. Furthermore, women are usually responsible for the food crops destined for immediate consumption by the household, that is, for subsistence crops rather than cash crops. Also, when data is collected for national statistics, gender is often ignored or the data is biased in the sense that it is collected only from males, who are assumed to be the heads of households.

These handicaps have contributed to an increasing "faminisation" of poverty. Since the 1970s, the number of women living below the poverty line has increased by 50%, in comparison with 30% for their male counterparts. Women may feed the world today, but, given this formidable lists of obstacles placed in their path, will they be able to produce the additional food needed for a world population expected to grow by three billion in 2030?

During the FAO-sponsored World Food summit of 1996, world leaders from 186 countries adopted the Rome Declaration on World Food Security and a Plan of Action. These international agreements specified that the role of women in agriculture and food security must be emphasised, in order to create the enabling political, social and economic environment required for the eradication of hunger and poverty.

Under Commitment-I of the World Food Summit Plan of Action agenda, governments committed themselves to:

— Support and implement commitments made at the 4th World Conference on Women that a gender perspective is mainstreamed in all policies;

— Promote women's full and equal participation in the economy... including secure and equal access to and control over credit, land and water;

— Ensure that institutions provide equal access for women;

— Provide equal gender opportunities for education and training in food production, processing and marketing;

— Tailor extension and technical services to women producers and increase the number of women advisors and agents;

— Improve the collection, dissemination and use of gender-disaggregated data [which distinguishes between males and females];

— Focus research efforts on the division of labour and on income access and control within the household; and

— Gather information on women's traditional knowledge fisheries, forestry and natural resources management and skills in agriculture.

FAO's Plan of Action for Women in Development ensures that gender issues are considered in its development work. Objectives include giving women equal access to and control of land and other productive resources, increasing their participation in decision-making and policy-making, reducing the workloads of women and enhancing their opportunities for paid employment and income.

Gender Equality and Sharing of Opportunities

The Universal Declaration of Human Rights (UDHR) recognised several dimensions of human rights for all people. Some are tangible and quantifiable, such as access to education, health and a decent standard of living and ability to take part in the government of the country. Others are intangible, such as freedom, dignity, and security of person and participation in the cultural life of the community.

The goals of gender equality differ from one country to another, depending on the social, cultural and economic contexts. So, in the struggle for equality, different countries may set different priorities, ranging from more education for girls, to better maternal health, to equal pay for equal work, to more seats in parliament, to removal of dissemination in employment, to protection against violence in the home, to changes in family law, to having men take more responsibility for family life.

Equality is not a technocratic goal – it is a wholesale political commitment. Achieving it, requires a long-term process in which all cultural, social, political and economic norms undergo fundamental change. The UNDP Human Development Report-1995 outlines a vision for the 21st century that should build a world order that:

— Embraces full equality of opportunity between women and men as a fundamental concept;
— Eliminates the prevailing disparities between men and women and creates an enabling environment for the full flowering of the productive and creative potential of both sexes;
— Promotes more sharing of work and experience between women and men in the workplace as well as in the household;
— Regarding women as essential agents of change and development and opens many more doors to women to participate more equally in economic and political opportunities;
— Values the work and contribution of women in all fields on par with those of men, solely on merit, without making any distinction;
— Puts people—both women and men—clearly processes, at the centre of all development

The UNDP Report-1995 also states that the GDI [Gender-related Development Index] ranking can be different in different situations, as is shown by the following conclusions of a recent survey:

— No society treats its women on equal footing as well as its men. Substantial progress on gender equality has been made in only a few societies;
— Gender equality does not depend on the income level of a society. What it requires is a firm political commitment, not enormous financial wealth;

— Significant progress has been achieved over the past two decades, though there is still a long way to go. Not a single country has slipped back in the march towards greater gender equality at higher levels of capabilities, though the pace of progress has been extremely uneven and slow.

Much progress remains to be made in gender equality in almost every country. And in equality of choice in economic and political participation, industrial countries are not necessarily taking the lead. The areas showing the least progress are parliamentary representation and percentage share of administrators and managers. The clear policy message from this simple exercise is this: "In most countries, industrial or developing, women are not yet allowed into the corridors of economic and political power. In exercising real power or decision-making authority, women are a distinct minority throughout the world."

Women in Agriculture

Women play an indispensable role in farming and in improving the quality of life in rural areas. However, their contributions often remain unsung due to some social barriers and gender bias. Even government programmes often fail to focus on women in agriculture. This undermines the potential benefits from programmes, especially those related to food production, household income improvements, nutrition, literacy, poverty alleviation and population control.

Equitable access for rural women to educational facilities would certainly improve their performance and liberate them from their marginalised status in the society. Other areas where women's potential could be effectively harnessed are agricultural extension, farming systems development, land reform and rural welfare. Landmark improvements have been recorded in such cases as the extension of institutional credit and domestic water supplies where women's potential have been consciously tapped.

Socioeconomic goals of productivity, equity and environmental, stability are closely woven around the agriculture sector policies and new dimensions in programmes implemented are already emerging as new values. Regardless of the level of development achieved by the respective economies, women play a pivotal role in agriculture and in rural development in most countries of the Asia-Pacific Region. Asia-Pacific region had witnessed spectacular development in crop yields which even surpassed the population growth rate in the past decade. However, pockets of hunger remain when landless or small farm rural population lack economic access to food because of a lack of remunerative non-farm employment in rural areas, where 80% of Asia-Pacific's 400 million poor live.

It has also been suggested that with the acceleration of crop-diversification programmes and the transformation of agriculture to commercial production levels, women's lot had been even further worsened by the addition of new burdens which they have to shoulder in order to realise profits in farm operations.

Rural Poverty

Rural women who are obliged to attend to all the household chores, children's welfare, nutrition and family cohesion along with farm work, are desperately driven to adopt a survival strategy to save the family food security from total collapse. Rural poverty has increased in the region particularly for farmers as priority has been accorded to the industrial and service sectors: this is both the cause and an effect of rural-urban migration leading to the "feminisation of farming". Thus, the numbers and the proportion of rural women among the absolutely poor and destitute, currently around 60%, is expected to increase to 65 to 70% by the year 2000.

In spite of social, political and economic constraints, women farmers have proved extremely resourceful and hardworking in their attempt to ensure household food security. Social constraints place barriers around their access to scientific and technological information. Lack of collateral denies them access to agricultural credit. Culture or traditions accord membership of cooperatives only to heads of households – usually a man. Many rural women, even in highly mechanised farming systems such as the Republic of Korea and Japan would have agriculture for work in other sectors if choices were available.

After some decades of development, global problems and issues concerning environment, women in development, and poverty have reappeared. All these have emerged in rural communities and threatening their sustainability. Rural communities with norms developed for managing resources are important for the stability of community life. Gender-oriented rural development programmes which focus on role of women to guarantee the stability of life provide a sound basis for integrated development of the quality of life.

In progressive economies like Japan, rural women have shown anxieties over several concerns affecting their livelihood. Some of the priority items include measures for success in agricultural enterprises, expansion of periodic farming resulting in reduced holidays, the need to reduce agricultural work, changes in awareness of rural societies and reduction in the work connected with caring for elderly people. In order to redress these problems, five tasks have been identified for promotion which will result in making rural living more pleasant and comfortable. These tasks include:

(i) Creating awareness of changes and measures pursued to change the status of women by their active participation in agricultural and fisheries cooperatives;

(ii) Improving working conditions and environment;

(iii) Appreciating the positive aspects of living in rural areas and creating environment which will contribute towards better rural life; a conducive;

(iv) Acquiring skills to diversify areas of involvement by women supporting women in entrepreneurial roles; and

(v) Adopt a structured approach to execute the vision to improve rural conditions.

Rural Women in Agricultural Cooperatives

Women are represented in various forms and in various types of cooperatives in the region. In most of the South-Asian countries, women membership in mixed membership cooperatives is generally lower as compared with those from other countries in the region. In societies where culture restricts women's membership in cooperatives, women-only cooperatives proliferate. It is in women-only cooperatives that women feel freer and less restricted in their participation in cooperatives.

In South Asia, women comprise just 7.5% as compared with men (92.5%) of the total membership. In Malaysia, it is around 30.6%. In many of the Asian countries women's membership is low [ranging from 2 to 10.5%] in agricultural cooperatives. This reflects the age-old stereotype that men are the farmers and not the women, and the title of the farm property should be in the name of the man. This situation automatically prohibits women to be the members. Out of a total of 450,000 cooperatives with a total membership of 204.5 million in India, there were 8,171 women-only cooperatives with a total membership of 693,000. It is also known that the women-only cooperatives e.g., cooperative banks, consumer stores, fruits and vegetable vendors, have done exceedingly well and provided a whole range of services to their members.

In India, with a view to involve women in the process of decision-making in local self-government bodies including cooperatives, a 33% representation has been instituted and in a number of states all boards of directors have women serving on them. There has also been a discussion to have a similar representation in state and national legislatures as well.

The highest number of women in cooperatives in the region comes from the credit and consumer sectors. In Japan the membership of women in agricultural cooperatives and in decision-making organs is low. No discriminatory provisions preventing women's participation in agricultural cooperatives are contained in the Agricultural Cooperative Law nor in the bylaws of the agricultural cooperatives. In the majority of the bylaws, membership is based either on land-ownership or work on the farm for more than 90 days a year. Despite this, women membership has not increased mainly due to the fact that most cooperatives have a membership policy that allows only one member per household, based on the idea that a household is the minimum unit for production.

In addition, it is customary that women follow their husbands in the village life and decision-making. Women themselves do not want to cause troubles by challenging such a tradition. Therefore, men became the majority of directors and delegates and women quietly accepted the situation. However, the concept of plural membership from households is being encouraged.

There are still some prevailing laws which place barriers for women's participation in agricultural cooperatives and/or farmers' associations, like land ownership and head of the household. In many societies, the very women who need to organise to cooperate and prosper, lack the time for participation due to multiple work demands. Cooperatives being people-centered movement had recognised these limitations place on women by the society and economic institutions. Experiments made in different parts of the world clearly indicate that women's participation in cooperatives and other local government bodies not only provides them an opportunity to articulate their problems but it also helps them to be an active partner in decision-making process.

The relationship between women and their cooperatives in the context of gender integeration can be summarised as under:

— A cooperative being a social development agency should play an active role in advocating for gender equality;

— Since women have been active in development work, they should play central role in development;

— The cooperative can be a venue to improve women's social status and economic conditions; and

— thus, cooperatives should promote women's empowerment by integrating gender concerns and formulating a strategy that would address gender issues.

In terms of the ratio of membership of women in agricultural cooperatives, the percentage is rather low, but they have a strong influence on them – through the heads of the household. Certain obvious barriers restrict their direct and formal entry in agricultural cooperatives. Agricultural cooperatives, in present times, everywhere have come under dark clouds due to heavy competitions and pressures of open market economy systems. They are now expected to meet the challenges which they had never anticipated before. Their business methods remain traditional and they expect government support in the form of protection and subsidies. These are no longer available and will not be available in the near future. In several countries, agricultural cooperatives have either folded up or are under massive reorganisation. The challenges faced by agricultural cooperatives can be enumerated as under:

— Need to improve professional management skills of those who provide advisory or guidance services to cooperatives and of the managers and some key members of primary level cooperatives;

— Establishment of a marketing intelligence system within the Cooperative Movement to enable the farmer-producers follow market trends and plan their production and marketing strategies;

— Assured supply of farm inputs [quality seeds, chemical fertiliser, farm chemicals, credit and extension services];

— Establishment of business federations through cooperative clusters to undertake primary agro-processing marketing of local products and to cover financial requirements;

— Be aware of quality controls and standardisation of farm products to be able to compete effectively in the open market;

— Participate in efforts to conserve natural resources which directly and indirectly, influence farm production and rural employment;

— Need for providing information to the farmers and farmers' organisations on the implications of restructuring, globalisation and World Trade Organisation WTO agreements.

Constraints faced by Rural Farm Women

Based on the experiences of farm extension workers, field advisors and rural farm women in the Asia-Pacific Region, the following are the general constraints faced by them:

— High illiteracy rates and poor living conditions among rural women;

— Lack of leadership and inadequate participation in the organisational and economic affairs of their agricultural cooperatives;

— Absence of property inheritance rights, restriction on acquiring membership of agricultural cooperatives consequently being deprived of farm credit etc.;

— Inadequate health care services in rural areas;

— Inadequate water supply for household and farm operations;

- — Lack of appropriate agricultural technology aimed at reducing the physical burden of farm women;
- — Inadequate access to credit and agricultural inputs and other services;
- — Lack of female farm extension workers;
- — Lack of marketing facilities and opportunities;
- — Traditional, religious, social and cultural obstacles;
- — Less participation in decision-making – even within the household;
- — Male migration/urban drift which increases pressure on women;
- — Lack of opportunities to improve socioeconomic status of farm women;
- — Lack of skills and attitudes in leadership and management development; and
- — Lack of secretariat supporting functions for women's organisations and allocation of funds for them in cooperative organisations.

Facilitation Role of the ICA and its Development Partners

Since the establishment of the ICA Regional Office in New Delhi in 1960, efforts have consistently been made to initiate and promote programmes aimed at emancipation of women and their involvement in the organisational and business activities of cooperatives. This has been done through a long chain of seminars, discussions, conferences and technical assistance programmes which have been carried out with the collaboration of its Member-Organisations and development partners. In the agricultural cooperatives sector some of the most recent initiatives have been as follows:

- — A series of technical meetings and conferences were held which had taken note of the recommendations of

UN and other international conferences and initiatives on women in cooperative development;

- A series of specialised training courses for rural women leaders in agricultural cooperatives, on an yearly basis, with the financial support of the Government of Japan and in collaboration with the JA-Zenchu and the IDACA;
- Three top level Asian and African Conferences on Farm Women Leaders in Agriculture and Agricultural Cooperatives during 1997 and 1998 in collaboration with the JA-Zenchu, AARRO and the IDACA and with the full technical support of the Government of Japan in the Ministry of Agriculture, Forestry and Fisheries-MAFF;
- Development of training manuals and other supporting materials for the use of women leaders to develop women's associations and help increase women's participation in agricultural cooperatives.

Issues Involved

In the background of the above discussion and in view of the constraints faced by women with regard to their participation in agricultural cooperatives, the following issues need to be tackled by the concerned authorities and cooperative institutions:

- Identification of an appropriate mechanism which could provide development opportunities to women in rural areas;
- Encouraging cooperatives to have special programmes and tasks for women to perform in the organisational and business affairs. It has been observed that in many of the countries of the Region more women are being taken in to undertake administrative and functional activities–they make very good, reliable and honest

cashiers, sales girls, inventory controllers, secretaries, public relations officers and member contact persons;

— Review, revision and reformation of cooperative legislation and government policies which facilitate and encourage women to become members of cooperatives and participate in decision-making processes. Cooperative institutions and their federations may take the lead on their own to institute programmes for the participation of women in cooperatives. Voluntary initiatives by cooperatives themselves do not necessarily to be qualified by government approvals. Cooperatives should lobby with their governments to replace or suitably amend the restrictive laws;

— Accord due credibility to the achievements of women in agricultural cooperative development through publicity, exchange of visits, participation in meetings and conferences. Women need a platform through which they could justify their participation in cooperative action;

— Replication of successful experiences. The work done by the Women's Associations of Japanese agricultural cooperatives and Han Groups has produced good results for the community and business of their cooperatives. Such experiences need a thorough study. They have a lot of good things to offer;

— Development of Plans of Action at all levels. Women's cooperative organisations at primary levels should try to federate themselves into higher federations or association so that their 'bargaining power' is strengthened. The cooperatives and women's associations should develop realistic plans of action to be followed for three-five years;

— Cooperatives to initiate education, training and extension programmes for women through vocational and literacy programmes [these also include home improvement activities e.g., cooking classes, handcrafts, social interactions, environment related activities etc.];

— Creating conditions for women to market their products through outlets established by agricultural cooperatives. [Agricultural cooperatives in Japan set apart a space in their shopping areas exclusively for the Women's Associations and even for the individual farmers to sell their products, including organising Morning Markets etc.

Conclusion

Women have been the focus of attention of all international and national development programmes. Efforts have been directed at empowering them in all fields of activity. Special programmes have been instituted to improve their social and economic status through provision of education, employment, health-care and involvement in social and economic institutions, including cooperatives.

Cooperative institutions and especially the agricultural cooperatives are the agencies which hold enormous potential for the development of women, and more particularly the rural women. Rural women are actively involved in the process of food production, processing and marketing. They often lack the legal status which prohibits them to have access to credit, education and technology. Cooperative institutions can help accelerate the process of development and participation of women in their organisational and business activities. Institutions like the International Cooperative Alliance (ICA) and the Institute for the Development of Agricultural Cooperation in Asia-Japan (IDACA) together with the support of other international organisations and national level institutions can develop and sponsor programmes which are aimed at improving the lot of rural women. In the past some efforts have been made through which member—organisations, cooperative and agricultural departments all over Asia and Africa have been requested to make special programmes for rural women and set aside budgets for their implementation. In some cases, some good responses have been received.

While it is generally agreed that education is central to women's development the participation of girls in the national educational system continues to lag well behind that of boys at every level. Among the factors that are believed to contribute to this gap are women's self-perpetuating negative social status, economic constraints and male-oriented biases in the design and delivery of primary and secondary education. These limitations have meant that millions of women have not received formal education and that millions more are deprived of the opportunity for more than token participation. Women, however, retain a strong orientation to self-help and group cooperation. They look to their own resources and to other women when faced with a problem of opportunity. This perhaps is the key factor on which women's development programme could be developed. This is their greatest asset. They have kept folk art, family bonds, religious traditions, cultural heritage alive, thriving and vibrant. They have played significant role in food security efforts and rural and small industrial sectors.

What was Wrong with Previous Approaches to Alleviate Poverty

Some of the reasons for failures in the past were:

- a low level of participation by the poor. Rural poor are often denied a voice in the formulation and even in the execution of a poverty programme;
- Programmes have tended to rely on grants and subsidies as the main tools for serving the poor;
- Too little attention has been given to strengthening the

capacities of the poor, to enhancing their power to meaningfully in policy formulation and in the marketplace; negotiating participate

— Most poverty alleviation programmes have had a single vector of intervention and have failed to confront the multi-dimensionality of poverty. Priorities usually have been set from 'the outside', thus being supply-driven rather than demand-driven and unable to respond to the particular needs and potentials of the poor.

Basic Requirements for Poverty Alleviation

Poverty alleviation is facilitated by:

— Increased access to productive assets for the poor such as land and water, credit and education, extension and public health services;

— The active participation of the poor and their representative bodies in decision-making. They must be provided with an enabling environment that encourages collective self-help action, personal investments and accumulation. Programmes need to be designed on a demand-driven basis rather than be imposed from the outside;

— Government institutions and the incentives that make them accountable to the general public should be reformed. They must become more responsive to the needs of the poor. Decentralisation and privatisation of government services and administration can assist in that process, and the NGO and private sectors have a crucial role to play. Transaction costs must be kept low;

— The building of sustainable capacities for poverty alleviation requires a well-defined and long-term development approach.

NOTES AND REFERENCES

Cooperative Leadership Training for Women – Report of the Regional Seminar held in Malaysia in December 1997. Issued by the ICA Regional Office for Asia and the Pacific, New Delhi.

Cooperatives and Poverty Reduction – Enhancing Social and Economic Imperatives by Daman Prakash, ICA ROAP, New Delh.

Food Security Issues, WTO and Agricultural Cooperatives by Daman Prakash, International Cooperative Alliance Regional Office for Asia-Pacific, New Delhi.

Gender-Sensitivity Training for Cooperators – A Trainer's Manual. Issued by NATCCO—the National Confederation of Cooperatives—Philippines.

Paradigm Shift in the Management of Agricultural Cooperatives in Asia by Daman Prakash and GC Shrotriya. Published jointly by the ICA Regional Office, and IFFCO, New Delhi.

Rural Development and Women—Lessons from the Field. Issued by the International Labour Organisation (ILO), Geneva, Switzerland.

The Contribution of Cooperatives to Social Development – The Cooperatives as Social Actor by Daman Prakash, ICA ROAP, New Delhi.

Women in Decision-Making in Cooperatives. Issued jointly by the International Cooperative Alliance Regional Office, New Delhi, and the Asian Women in Cooperative Development Forum-Philippines.

Women in Rural Development – A Report. Issued by the Afro-Asian Rural Reconstruction Organisation (AARRO), New Delhi, India.

Women Farm Leaders of Agricultural Cooperatives – Third Asian Conference Report and its Documentation. Edited and compiled by Daman Prakash. Tokyo, Japan. 1998.

Women in Agriculture and Rural Development by Maithili Vishwanathan. Published by Rupa Books Private Limited, New Delhi.

Women's Health and Human Rights. Published by the World Health Organisation (WHO) Geneva.

10

RURAL WOMEN AND WATERSHED DEVELOPMENT

Experiences of Action for Social Advancement

Action for Social Advancement (ASA), has over ten years experience developing rural livelihood security amongst the predominantly Bhil tribal communities in western Madhya Pradesh and eastern Gujarat. It delivers an integrated package of interventions into a community, based on an intensive process of natural resource development and local institutional development. Bhil tribal women play the role of supporter, responsible for numerous household and agricultural-related activities that generally carry low status. Natural resource management has traditionally not been their responsibility.

However, they are responsible for a number of household-level socioeconomic decisions. ASA's experience of promoting women's participation in watershed development is mixed: practical needs can be met and strategic space can be created directly within the watershed development process (eg. attendance on Watershed Development Committees). However that does not guarantee that women will be able or willing to take that space up. The most successful vehicle for promoting women's empowerment at the village level comes in the form of SHGs set up for micro-finance purposes. This is the case in ASA's project area, where strong groups exist and are supported by a SHG Federation. The challenge for ASA now is how to use these strong women-led, women-promoting institutions outside their micro-finance remit to influence the process of village development. This chapter summarises the main activities undertaken by ASA in its approach to women's empowerment and the key lessons learned from implementing each of these activities.

Background to ASA

Action for Social Advancement (ASA) has been working for over 10 years on rural livelihood security of the predominantly tribal communities living in western Madhya Pradesh and eastern Gujarat (districts of Jhabua, Ratlam, Barwani, Khargone, Ujjain in M.P. and Dahod and Godhra in Gujarat).

ASA's typical project area is characterised by large Bhil and Bhilala tribal populations, who depend on a degraded natural resource base and out-of-date agricultural technologies, which results in poor land productivity (5-8 times lower than state average), high food insecurity and poor livelihood security. Migration levels are high, literacy rates remain low and exploitative loaning by money-lenders is the norm.

• *In-situ* soil and moisture conservation	• Agricultural extension and development
• Water resources development (construction of small and large harvesting structures, irrigation management)	• Common property resource management
	• Human and institutional resources development, together with
• Strategic plantations	• Micro-finance activities.

Taking cognisance of the fact that rural livelihoods are intrinsically linked with the local environs, ASA's basic strategy has been to identify the key environmental problem underlying people's livelihood insecurity and tackle it head on. Its watershed development programme, following a "watershed plus" approach, consists of:

ASA believes that integrating value addition and income generating measures into the watershed development approach from the design and planning stages, results in a better and more sustained impact and less conflict during the implementation process.

Women in ASA's Project Area

The baseline PRAs undertaken in ASA's project villages conclude that tribal women's lives are characterised by low literacy, a lack of access to fuelwood, diminishing access to water, and a heavy workload of reproductive and productive household duties. Her life remains that of a supporter to her husband, with her tasks carrying low status – including food preparation; water and fuel collection; cleaning; lifting cow dung; washing, pounding and grinding corn; fodder and NTFP collection; as well as agricultural activities like field preparation, sowing, weeding, harvesting and threshing. She is an essential resource for animal and child care and family health. Women also play a vital part in managing the cropping pattern which takes care of maximising food and fodder availability while minimising production risks.

In relation to watershed development, gender inequality exists in the following manner:

- Fewer women than men participate and their involvement in planning and decision-making is marginal;
- In most activities, women are neither able to exert control over the implementation process nor gain control over direct benefits;

- Managerial skills and decision-making authority remain "men's prerogative" – the men's domain.

ASA's Approach for Inclusion of Women

(i) Collected sufficient, relevant and correct baseline data on women

(ii) Decided what is feasible in the local context

(iii) Created practical space for women to participate

(iv) Created strategic space for women to participate

(v) Raised awareness amongst both men and women community on inclusion of women.

This may seem basic, but it is critical that correct and relevant information on women is collected during the baseline assessment. Guidelines on what to collect and how to collect it should be developed beforehand. When beginning activities in a village, ASA undertakes a PRA to collect data from which the village action plan is developed. The data on women includes: typical division of labour, a typical day in a women's life, the role of women in decision-making at the household level (rights, role, responsibilities), and the problems and restraints to development of women in the village. With this information, one can identify women's practical and strategic needs, which inform the design of a gender implementation strategy.

Lessons Learned

The data collected and the process through which it was collected provided ASA with a solid understanding of women's roles and responsibilities. Data collectors and reporters must be take care to undertake this exercise thoroughly and not extrapolate the same data across a large number of villages, thereby missing out on potential important variations in women's situation.

Decided what is Feasible in the Local Context

From project outset, one must decide what can realistically be achieved in terms of women's empowerment, given the project resources, timeframe and local community dynamics. This decision must be based on a thorough assessment of the local women's situation in terms of participation in community affairs and barriers to participation. It must then be boiled down into a set of inputs that will result in set of outputs, outcomes and impacts, over a specified timeframe.

ASA set out the following as achievable objectives of empowerment in its watershed programme:

1. Raise awareness amongst women of the role they can play in decision-making (including awareness on why their opinion is important).
2. Raise awareness amongst men as to the role of women and why their inclusion is important.
3. Create practical space for women to participate: ie. by reducing time spent in meeting practical needs (eg. collection of drinking water, firewood); by making a policy to encourage women's participation in training programmes; by working on financial empowerment. This will also engender feelings of trust in women about the project.
4. Create strategic space for women to participate: (whether sustainable or not) – through mandatory inclusion of women on Watershed Development Committees (WDCs), formation of women-only Watershed Development Committees and Self-Help Groups (SHGs) and prioritisation of those.

Lessons Learned

Whilst ASA has always outlined key objectives related to women's empowerment under watershed development, it has not framed these within an overall gender strategy, and has ultimately not identified the realistic impact that can be achieved. This impact might be enabling women to participate on an equal footing with men in the decision-making process regarding watershed management. Having this frame plus an overall goal to work towards, that is closely monitored throughout implementation, may have deepened the impact ASA has had, bringing gender mainstreaming in as a central focus to its programme.

A separate example illustrates this point:

As part of a separate Participatory Irrigation Management (PIM) project, ASA developed a systematic gender-orientated strategy to promote active involvement of women in community affairs related to canal restoration and maintenance. The objectives of the strategy were: (a) to create an environment more responsive and sensitive to women's needs; (b) to ensure equal access to participation and decision-making; and (c) to ensure equal access for women to their fundamental legal and social rights.

A two-pronged intervention strategy was developed, part one being capacity building of women and part two (equally important)—gender sensitisation of the male population. As a result of the strategy, ASA achieved a number of policy changes including provision of voting rights to the spouses of Water User Association members, mandatory inclusion of one female member in the management committee, and formation of women sub-committees. The next step forward will be getting 33% reservation for women on the management committee. The impact of this strategy so far has included the exercise of voting rights during election of Water Users Associations.

However, ASA's objectives for women's empowerment in watershed development have always been realistic, and based on the assumptions that it is a long term goal and that not all activities aimed at women will be successful. In this context, often the process is as important as the results.

Created Practical Space for Women to Participate

A project must enable women to participate. It must therefore address their most immediate practical needs, as the tasks required to fulfil them are typically time-intensive and often a barrier to regular and sustained participation.

ASA's approach to meeting practical needs of tribal women include:

- Ensuring that watershed development activities provided solutions to women's critical needs/duties related to water, fuelwood and fodder.
- Making it mandatory for 50% of participants on all training courses and exposure visits under watershed development to be women.
- Providing for financial needs of women through establishment of SHGs, and enabling women to access and avail of low interest credit.

Lessons Learned

Without addressing these needs, it is very difficult for women to participate. Addressing such needs not only frees up women's time, but as importantly, shows women that the project is relevant to and interested in her. This forms a solid basis for a mutual relationship of trust.

Having a policy is one issue yet enforcing it is another, particularly when there are practical constraints. Sometimes, pressure on field staff to meet training targets means that policies get overlooked. This happened for a while at ASA, where the 50% women participants rule was not enforced. Also creating the space for women to use their newly enhanced/developed skills is critical.

Created Strategic Space for Women to Participate

A project must create strategic space that is acceptable both to women and the wider community. Experience has shown that tribal women (whilst having a significant role in household level socioeconomic decision-making) are hesitant or are otherwise socially restricted to be vocal in public fora where major village decisions are taken, eg. a Gram Sabha. In Bhil society, this is often because villages are composed of tight-knit kin groups where every person is a member of a woman's in-laws. She must therefore observe a certain code of conduct towards them in meetings.

In this tribal society, small kinship groups which are socially and economically homogenous already exist. These groups are based upon existing cooperative social units with social and economic exchange and networks of mutual assistance. Past experience of ASA suggested that participation in planning and decision-making is achieved through working in small hamlet-based groups. The implementation of activities through such groups has worked out to be the best strategy for developing skills, confidence and new management capabilities.

The question for ASA, therefore, became, "Which CBO?" In deciding this, comes the acceptance that:

(a) there will certain CBOs which are more acceptable to women and to wider society, and to which women more readily will be part of.

(b) the space created for women in CBOs by a project won't necessarily be sustainable. However, one outcome is to leave behind examples of participation that will be remembered and which may be built upon again in the future.

ASA worked to create institutional space by:

- Ensuring that each Watershed Development Committee (WDC) had a minimum of 35-40% women members (the women themselves being members of SHGs).
- Organising women into women-only SHGs, to gradually but steadily capacitate them so that ultimately, they can participate in the development process. Similarly by giving priority to the formation of women-only groups. ASA's experience in these communities shows that with

increasing access to credit and improvement in ability to articulate concerns and views, women's participation with regard to common development issues including natural resources, increases.

- In villages where only women-only groups exist, discouraging men's groups from forming, since experience shows that male groups tend to dominate and give little scope for women's groups to surface as decision-making fora.
- Making provision for grooming of female village-level workers (10th Standard pass) within the project team.

Lessons Learned

In reality, participation of women on WDCs has not been successful, primarily due to a lack of sustained effort and follow-up on the part of ASA, itself due the paucity of funds for capacity building. NRM remains very much the male domain in this society. It must be remembered that creation of institutional space is a long term activity, and will not become a sustainable space over night. Yet, as previously mentioned, the process of creating this space and its short-lived existence is also important.

On the other hand, SHGs have proven to be a successful institution for mobilising women in the project area and creating a formal women-led community organisation. On an average, each member is availing Rs. 5000 of credit, primarily used to purchase agricultural inputs and implements, itself an indication of women's role in household decision-making. Most of ASA's SHGs are now members of a Federation, which provides loaning funds and makes strategic decisions on their behalf. The issue that ASA now faces is how to use these strong, women's community-based organisations beyond micro-finance activities. They have not yet been mobilised to participate in watershed development activities, but are taking the lead in ASA's Water Aid-funded drinking water and sanitation project that is currently on pilot.

Often, it is the small activities that can have a significant impact. ASA's policy of grooming 10th Standard pass local village girls as project workers was a great success, firstly in terms of quality of work completed and secondly, acceptance of their new role within the local communities themselves. Often, they were found to be inspirational characters amongst the local female communities.

Raised Awareness Amongst Male Community on Inclusion of Women

Social norms and opinions of male family members often restrict a woman from participating in development activities. There is occasion to discuss with the male community why women need to be included, and at times, prioritised.

For example, in one village ASA's worker had already completed the necessary groundwork to set up a women's SHG. When the worker arrived in the village to hold the first meeting, men rather than women had turned up, ready with the initial deposit. The worker had to discourage the men and make a fresh proposal with the women's names. Not only was effort needed to convince the women but also effort was required to explain to the willing men why they could not set-up a group. ASA workers convinced the men by telling them:

- That women have less chance to interact than men outside the villages, therefore, it is necessary to give them the chance to come forward.
- As women are in the village more than men, women's attendance at the SHG meetings should be better, which is more propitious for the household.

Impact of ASA's Watershed Development Programme on Women's Empowerment

Practical Needs

- Water resources development has provided women access to a permanent source of water that they can use to bathe, clean clothes and wash. However, drought has affected the effectiveness of this programme.

- The regeneration of common and forest land in some villages has led to an increase in fodder availability, tree species and non-timber forest products – the collection of which is usually a woman's responsibility.
- Women are now able to access credit and save through the SHGs – both significant advancements in terms of their empowerment. This also reduces their exploitation by money-lenders. However their ability to capitalise on this opportunity depends on other issues such as changing social/cultural norms.

Strategic Needs

- Training and capacity building has built women's confidence and increased women's ability to participate. However, women in the project area are generally quite restricted in their own capacity. The issue of low literacy has not been tackled and is a limiting factor to development.
- Using SHGs as a new platform for formal community organisation amongst women has generally been successful. Their link-up to WDCs by representation in the Committee has not worked as a
- Method for creating sustainable space for participation. ASA must now look to see how to widen the SHG's remit and get the body involved in village development, as the representative of women's needs and rights.
- Social and cultural norms still very much influence the participation of women in watershed development decisions. However ASA's policies – such as the representation of each SHG on the WDC, women-only SHGs and training and exposure visits going some way to influence these norms. Efforts to increase awareness of the Panchayat and rights is also an important step.

To summarise, key lessons for ASA in terms on women's empowerment through watershed development are:

- Flexibility in project design and patience in implementation are vital for encouraging women to participate. One might have to undertake activities not viewed as core to a project—e.g. micro-finance SHGs in a watershed development project – but which have proven time and again to be the most successful vehicle for promoting women's participation in village development.
- Creating space for women to participate is the first step; getting women to take up this space and use it is the second and more difficult step. This is a long term activity, and might not be realised in the project timeframe.
- Expected outcomes and impacts related to women's empowerment must be clearly defined from outset and based on a thorough understanding of what is achievable in the local community, in the given timeframe.
- Often small activities can have a significant impact on empowerment.

In general, watershed programmes had been purely land-based development programmes and there had been only a marginal scope for involving women and landless poor. Though women can play a vital role in CPR development by and large they had not been directly involved in the same. In fact, it is women who attend to collection of fuel wood, fodder, non wood forest produce etc., in rural areas, but their choices or opinions have been often ignored. Though women are being involved in JFM programmes, their involvement in watershed management had been limited mainly due to limitations such as lack of land ownership (entitlements), credit and capabilities, low literacy, lack of productive skills and suitable technologies etc.

How Women can be Involved?

The natural resources which are directly concerned with rural poor women are drinking water, fuelwood and fodder. The needs of these women with specific reference to available natural resources have to be identified. The objectives of the watershed project should be framed based on the needs of women. Based on the requirement, exclusively women user groups can be formed or proper representation should be there in the user groups and watershed committees. Women should be involved in planning and implementation of watershed activities at all stages.

What Actions can be Proposed to bring Gender Equity?

- Formation of women SHGs and net working them into user groups or watershed committees.
- Increasing access to resources, ownership of assets created.
- Imparting leadership skills to resourceful women and new skill development.
- Equal wages and opportunities.
- Sensitising the women with respect to health education, nutrition, literacy, girl child education and social evils like dowry, child marriages, violence etc.
- Livelihoods, employment and linkages with banks.
- Participation in community development programmes.

Activities

- Drinking water can be taken up as entry point activity. It can be augmenting the existing source or creating a new source or attending to fluoride problem etc.
- Soil moisture conservation measures like soil bunding, field bunding, raising agro forestry species on the bunds, rock fill dams, check dams can be taken up by women user groups.
- Raising plantations in the common lands and avenue plantation can be taken up.
- Horticulture, Vermiculture and green manuring.
- On-farm crop demonstrations of improved agronomic practices involving women farmers.

- Raising green fodder for cattle and teaching scientific feeding practices.
- Adopting smokeless *chullahs* or sanctioning cooking gas connections as done under 'Deepam' scheme in Andhra Pradesh.
- Taking up various livelihood activities like tailoring, basket-making, mat weaving, dairy, poultry etc.

Other Issues

- *Literacy:* Enrolling the women in adult literacy programmes and encouraging them to send their children to schools and seeing that dropsout are made to rejoin in the school.
- *Health and Sanitation:* Utilising the services of a health organizer in bringing awareness among women regarding nutrition/malnutrition, communicable diseases, family planning and personal hygiene. The women have to be encouraged to go for individual sanitary latrines.

  Women SHGs can play a vital role in attending to the above issues.
- *Communication of information:* Information regarding the latest technologies in Agriculture, Horticulture, Animal Husbandry etc., should be communicated to the women SHGs.
- *Training Programmes:*Skill enhancement programmes and other training programmes on natural resources management, livelihood aspects and leadership aspects should be imparted to women.
- Encouraging women with entrepreneurial capabilities and bringing out collective strength of women.
- Government and interested NGOs have to play a vital role in the form of financial assistance, facilitating bank linkages, imparting training programmes, inducing transparency and accountability etc.

Expected Outcome

Women have to play a vital role in identification, prioritisation and execution of all works through participatory approach involving all sections of people like women, men, farmers, landless and wage labour in the village. The collective social action will definitely result in empowering the women, improved wage employment, improved agricultural productivity, enhancement of sustainable livelihoods, improved education, health and family planning, adoption of non-conventional energy resources to reduce drudgery etc.

If the watershed programmes are implemented with concern and sincerity, the women can be involved at all stages of implementation and the monetary and non-monetary returns will be significant.

NOTES AND REFERENCES

Franzmann, Majella. 2000. *Women and Religion.* Oxford: Oxford University Press.

Kelkar, G. 1991. *Violence Against Women In India: Perspectives and Strategies.* Bangkok: Asian Institute of Technology

Rosaldo, M. 1974. "Introduction", in *Women, Culture and Society.* in Michelle Rosaldo and L. Lamphere (eds.), *Women, Culture and Society.* Stanford: Stanford University Press.

Scott, John Wallach. 1988. *Gender and the Politics of the History.* New York: Columbia University Press.

The United Nations. 1975. *Conference on Women in Mexico City.* New York: United Nations.

UN. 1995. *The Convention on the Elimination of All Forms of Discriminations against Women.* New York: United Nations.

11

DEVELOPMENT OF TRIBAL WOMEN

The status of any social group is determined by its levels of health-nutrition, literacy-education and standard of living. The tribal women, as women in all social groups, are more illiterate than men. The low educational status is reflected in their lower literacy rate, lower enrollment rate and their presence in the school. United Nations has defined the status of women as the "conjunction of position a women occupies as a worker, student, wife, mother—of the power and prestige attached to these positions, and of the right and duties she is expected to exercise".

"To what extent, do women, compared with men, have excess to knowledge, to economic resources and to political power, and to what degree of personal autonomy do these resources permit in the process of decision-making and choice at crucial points in the lifecycle?". Women make up only 6% of India's workforce and the numbers get skewed as you go up the corporate ladder. Only 4% women are at the senior management level and almost none in a leadership role. Status of women is generally measured using three indicators— education, employment status and intra-household decision-making power.

In general, women with higher education tend to have a better position (WHO, 1989). In some cases, however, education alone may not be sufficient to enhance status unless it engages employment as well (Hogan et al., 1999). In addition women's ability to communicate with and convince their spouses or other members of the family indicates their decision-making autonomy. Women with great decision-making power are supposed to have a higher status in the household.

In India, women are discriminated due to several historical, religious and other reasons. A girl child is suppressed from the movement she is born in terms of personal development. She is made to undergo the feelings of being inferior and feeble. She is denied the prospects for personal expression.

There are various hypotheses about why women have relatively high or low status. The common premise is that women status is high when they contribute substantially to primary subsistence activities. Women position is low in the societies where food getting is entirely men's job like hunting, herding or intensive agriculture. In the historical times, when warfare was essential, men were more esteemed than women. Likewise in the centralised political systems, men had high status. Men in most societies contribute more to primary subsistence activities, as women have infant and child care responsibilities. However, women contribute substantially to primary subsistence activities that depend heavily on gathering and horticulture and in which men are away on labour or pastoral duties while subsistence work has to be done. When primary and secondary subsistence activities are counted, women work more than men.

Male and female and other genders are culturally constructed categories, associated with culturally defined expected patterns of thought and behaviour that are subjected to hierarchical distinctions, advantages and disabilities. In India, the low status of women derives from a lack of control over material or social resources and from a lack of choice in the unfolding of one's destiny. This started with men maintaining their monopoly over the use of ox-drawn plough used for breaking the dry, hard packed soils. Men achieved this monopoly for essentially the same reasons that they achieved over the weapons of hunting and warfare. Their potent bodily strengths enabled them to be more efficient than women. However, a single measure cannot be used to assess the status of women; rather a multi-dimensional cluster of variables is required to indicate the status. Status is not a fixed rigid concept, it changes overtime. Women occupy different positions in the social structure as they pass through the lifecycle, and the very basis upon which the community ascribes power, privilege and prestige also changes.

Tribal Womenfolk

Tribal societies have been by and large characterised as egalitarian societies especially in relation to the hierarchical character of caste society. However, it cannot be said of women status. Status of women varies in different societies. All societies offer its children the presence of two genders and related roles, according to kinship, sexuality, work, marriage and age. It also supplies the broad guidelines for undertaking these roles through a body of attitudes, specifications, metaphors and myths. In the present study, an effort has been to describe the status of women in four different ecological regions, with different socioeconomic conditions and cultural backgrounds. The women, which form part of this study are from: (a) Ladakh, a high altitude area, 3500- 4500 metres; (b) High valleys of North Sikkim, 3000 metres; (c) Bharmour tehsil, Chamba district, Himachal Pradesh, a middle altitude area, 1340 metres; and (d) Kotra and Jhadol tehsils of Udaipur district, Rajasthan.

As suggested by the altitudes, these areas have different ecologies and consequently diverse economies. The Ladakhi Bodh women and Bhutia women of Lachen and Lachung in North Sikkim profess Buddhism while Gaddi women of Bharmour in Chamba district own up Hinduism, and the religious sphere of Bhil women of Rajasthan represent different spirits, gods, goddesses, deities, worship, fear, awe, reverence etc. The Bhils believe in witchcraft, once identified, the witches (always women) meet a severe treatment.

If we see Ladakhi, Bhutia, Gaddi or Bhil women in regard to their educational achievements, legal and political rights, employment opportunities and demographic characteristics, these women do not have high status. Majority of the tribal women in the study area have never attended school; therefore for those who have completed their primary education, it will make a positive difference in their status. Work status of women in these areas is broad and it includes all forms of women's labour force participation: formal as well as informal work, work inside and outside the home, and work for payment in cash or kind or no earnings.

In these traditional tribal communities, the women have an important role to play. Gender principles are central to the organisation of traditional communities. Gender and the division of labour that depends on its recognition, are decisive elements giving these societies stability and cohesiveness. Emphasis on gender, a relational concept provides opportunities for looking at full range of social and cultural institutions, which reproduce gender hierarchies and gender-based inequalities. The cultural interpretation of gender is central to the identity and status of women that entails web of relationships. The conceptual framework to analyse women's status comprise the seven roles women play in life and work: parental, conjugal, domestic, kin, occupational, community and as an individual. In order to appraise the social status of women in these diverse ecological areas, the findings have been divided into subsequent categories: (a) a girl /daughter/ a unmarried woman; (b) a married woman; (c) a widow; (d) divorcee; and (e) a barren woman. Apart from the social status, women role in the social sphere; her political domain; religious sphere; economic activities; and decision-making have been discussed.

LADAKH

Ladakh is a mountainous district situated in the eastern part of the Kashmir valley. Ladakh is a cold desert, both southerly and westerly winds prevail in summer and winter making climate of Ladakh extremely dry and cold. The high-altitude, harsh natural environment of Ladakh is characterised by extreme cold and dryness, high radiation, strong winds, low precipitation, low humidity; and desert like extensive barren landscape, rugged topography, steep and vertical glaciated slopes, minimal forest cover and mineral resources, few pastures at high elevations; and settlements in narrow oases like valleys having limited arable land and limited water for irrigation. The region is extremely poor in conventional energy sources (fossils, fuels and wood) and has almost no industrially exploitable resources

According to survey, the people of Ladakh are a mixture of Mongolian and Aryan races. 52 per cent of the Ladakhis are Buddhists while 44.6 per cent follow Islam. Their main occupation is agriculture and they grow mainly barley and wheat. A few of them grow vegetables and fruits as well. Buddhism does not recognise any caste system but some differentiation is made on the basis of social and occupational considerations. Ladakh region has a unique social pattern, which functions as strong social groupings.

Among Ladakhis, the household *(grong)* serves as one of the primary corporate groups of society. People are recognised by their house name *(grong-ning)*. Economic relations of labour, production and subsistence are arranged in the household. Other corporate groups are *phas-phun* and *bcu-chogs* (group of ten). Families in common patriline or common lineage form a kind of group, mostly 4 to 10 in number, who worship a common *phas- lha(* common family god) that mutually help each other in many activities, but chiefly in agricultural operations. *Phas-pun* is an association of households engaged in mutual assistance and collective rituals at times of birth, marriage and death.

Barter System

The dominance of religion in the daily life of Bodhs helped in preserving the traditional values. There was a little change in the operative technology, almost no surplus production. The inter-regional trade was limited to barter with grain, butter, wool, salt being the main exchange commodities. Regional isolation helped to retain the traditional socioeconomic system till the winds of change swept in. Till a few decades ago, fraternal polyandry, primogenitor and monasticism were part of a traditional culture among the Bodhs to overcome economic and demographic problems.

Now-a-days, the patterns of marriage among Bodhs represent a broad variety of alliances representing flexibility with which they react to periods of relative affluence and periods of shortage. During the time of shortage, Bodhs follow the 'monomarital' or one marriage on one estate principle. Polyandrous and polygamous alliances are often based on monogamous marriages in which additional partners may enter informally, especially in the fraternal or sororal type. Even the number of monks and nuns is decreasing.

An economic system such as the Bodhs requiring hands for farming, herding, collecting fuel and fodder, trading, etc. would limit the number of monks primarily by economic necessity. The earlier inheritance pattern (wherein only the eldest son inherited the estate) and limited job opportunities may have encouraged the monastic institution. Now-a-days, of course, the monastic order has to compete with administrative jobs or jobs offered by Indian army. Now, with the opening of the region and the demand of development, new sources of income and jobs have been created which totally or at least partially depend on tourism).

NORTH SIKKIM

Sikkim, a small mountainous state in the eastern Himalayas with an area of 7096 square kilometres, has witnessed great changes in its political structure, social structure, economic life and cultural values during past hundred years. The process of change was quickened by currents from four different directions, resulting in a multiform ethnic mix. It lies between 27° and 28° N latitude and 88° and 89° E. Sikkim has been strongly influenced by the Tibet in its religious and cultural life. Sikkim may be among India's smallest states, but its biodiversity, topographical and ethnic diversity belie its size. The state is divided into four districts—North, South, East and West.

Before its assimilation into the Indian Union, Sikkim was an independent kingdom ruled by a hereditary *Maharaja,* who was assisted by large landowners, the *kajis,* in the administration of the state. The *Maharajah* was a Buddhist and Buddhism flourished greatly because of the encouragement to the Lamas and the setting up of the monasteries.

The Bhutias are of Tibetan origin. They are about 14 per cent of total population and a scheduled tribe. The Bhutias, who took refuge in Sikkim after the schism in 15th and 16th century, are now spread out in all districts of Sikkim. However, the Bhutias in the north Sikkim, inhabiting the two river valleys of Lachen and Lachung, situated on the banks of the tributaries of the Tista-Lachenchu and Lachungchu respectively at the height of 3,000 metres are called Ha-Pa.

The Bhutias of North Sikkim are a poly-androus tribe of agro-pastoral transhumants who migrate in the high altitude valleys of North Sikkim. These areas are especially 'reserved' ones where the right to settle or own land is not permitted to strangers, irrespective of their ethnic origin. The villages in the Lachen are compact. The houses are clustered but not adjoining. These houses are occupied from February to May, as for the rest of the rest of the year they migrate with their families and animals in search of fodder and firewood to higher and. lower altitudes along the tributaries of Lachen chu. Lachung is a small town with scattered settlements. There is an army cantonment for the border protection. Previously, these areas were closed to outsiders. A person had to obtain a permit from the government official to visit these areas. However, now these areas have been opened on 20th December 2000 for foreign and domestic tourists.

The Lachen and Lachung area has a special status with regard to land settlement, revenue and local administration. Lachen and Lachung have their own traditional local government encompassing *Dzumsha* (village council) and *Phipun* (headman) that resolve all subjects under discussion. There are nearly 50households under one *Dzumsha.* They have an elected *Zilla Panchayat Samiti* representative as well. They have two elected heads -senior *Phipun* and junior *Phipun,* and an elected member called *Gyapen,* who acts as secretary. *A Dzumsha* election takes place annually. The method of election is through popular voting by adults in favour or against the candidature. However, the women, though they have their say in the decision making process and the election of the *Phipun* and the *Gyapen,* they cannot contest the elections. The *Dzumsha* of north Sikkim has been given full protection by government of India. The provisions of the 1965 *Panchayat* Act are not extended to this area (Bhasin, 1993).

The situation of Bhutias is unlike that of other ethnic minorities and it does not conform to the usual pattern of integration into larger economic and political systems. Political events beyond their control have led to the transformation of their traditional economic system, forcing them to reorient it. Variations in the economic strategies of the Lachenpas and Lachungpas emerge from several factors, showing interrelations of ecology, technology and social organisation.

Although no reserve was created for them as was the case with the Lepchas, they did have some degree of seclusion reinforced by political and ecological factors. Before the closure of the border, the Bhutias combined pastoralism with the trading, but after 1962, their economy received a setback and under went a number of changes; they were obliged to work as labourers and to look out for alternative occupations. In their ecological milieu, it is found that sharing scores over the value of competition. In spite of these changes, Bhutias as transhumants have been able to retain their separate identity in their cultural and social life (Bhasin, 1989).

BHARMOUR, HIMACHAL PRADESH

The Bharmour tehsil in district Chamba , Himachal Pradesh lies approximately between the north latitude 32°-11' and 32°-41' and the east longitude 76°-22' and 76° and 53'. The lowest altitude is about 1340 metres and the highest about 5900 metres above sea level.

The Bharmour tehsil is remarkably mountain-ous; level and flat pieces of land are an exception. Cultivation ranges, approximately, between 1400 metres and 3700 metres. Slopes are steep and for irrigation they depend on rainfall. The demarcated forests occur between 1850 metres and 2450 metres.

The sheep and goat breeders and graziers Gaddis of Bharmour in Chamba district, Himachal Pradesh, in the Mid Himalayan Zone are transhumant, who spend summer in their permanent homes in Bharmour and cultivate their lands. In winter, which is characterised by heavy snowfall, they migrate to lower hills with their sheep and goat. Gaddis is a caste term in Bharmour, however, the local inhabitants draw a distinction between the four classes: (1) The Brahmans;(2) The Gaddis, Rajputs (formed by the union of Rajputs, Khatris, Thakurs or Ranas over several hundred years; (3) The Sipis; and (4) The Reharas, Kolis, *Lohars* (blacksmiths), *Badhies* (carpenters) and Halis etc.

They lack adequate education facilities, means of communication, productive and irrigated land, medical facilities, mechanised cultivation and big irrigated holdings. Agriculture production is reduced by the shorter season, low temperature, high altitude and smallness of the land holdings. To compensate for the agriculture deficit Gaddis raise large flocks of sheep and goat. The lush mountainous meadows and grazing grounds in the area facilitate the raising of sheep and goat. Accumulation of snow in winter months prevents the year round sustenance of large flocks. The socio-cultural system of Gaddis is influenced by transhumance as they are dispersed in winter and concentrated in summer. This alternating pattern of dispersal and assembling makes for certain fluidity in interpersonal relations. Gaddis are Hindus, both in their origin and their social organisation. Gaddis of Bharmour have been given the status of a scheduled tribe by the Government of India for the sake of development in view of their social and economic backwardness (Bhasin, 1988).

SOUTHERN RAJASTHAN

The state of Rajasthan is situated in the northwestern part of the Indian Union (23°30 'and 30° 11' North Latitude and 69° 29' and 78° 17' East Longitude). It came into existence by the union of 22 princely states and the integration of the former state of Ajmer and Merwara. Great vagaries of temperature characterise the climate of Rajasthan. Winter is very cold and hot during summer is intense and scorching. The Scheduled Tribes form 12.44 per cent of the total population of Rajasthan. Bhils constitutes the third largest tribal group of India. They live at the borders of Rajasthan, Gujarat, Maharashtra and Madhya Pradesh, in the forests of Vindhya and Satpura hills. Until he 19th century, Bhils practiced shifting cultivation. With the advent of British rule, they were forced to settle down and a Bhil Agency was established to help them. Presently, the Bhils are settled cultivator and agriculture is their main occupation.

Bhil villages that form part of this study are from Jhadol and Kotra tehsils of Udaipur district in southern Rajasthan.

Jhadol and Kotra are backward tehsils having all the three backward productive sectors (agriculture, general industries and small-scale industries). Significant portion of their geographical area is under forest and uncultivable land leaving a small per centage for cultivation. Physioclimatic conditions have led to poor economic and social infra structural facilities. Lack of infra structural facilities hinder the growth of Productive sectors. Forest, land and human labour are principal economic resources of the Bhils. The Bhils undertake various economic activities. They have covered a long journey from subsistence economy to a competitive economy, from isolation to involvement in the local mainstream and from lawlessness to a law-abiding community. The traditional animistic religious beliefs of the Bhils have been largely influenced and modified by the impact of Hindu sects (Bhasin, 2005).

Before starting a discussion or any generalisation of the status of women in these areas, it is important to know the factors that help in interpreting the status that they enjoy in their own family.

GIRL CHILD

Tribes too have son preference but do not discriminate against girls by female infanticide or sex determination tests. Boys and girls do not have similar inheritance laws. Tribal girls do not inherit land, except in matrilineal societies or under special circumstances. Nonetheless they are not abused, hated, or subjected to strict social norms. Girls are free to participate in social events, dancing and other recreational programmes. There is no dowry on marriage.

Among tribes, the father of the bridegroom pays a bride price to the father of the girl. Widowed or divorced women are free to marry again. As incidence of child labour is high among the tribes, girls are no exception. Girls care for younger siblings, perform household jobs and work in the fields along with their brothers. This leaves no time for education of girls; consequently there is gender gap in education. Both boys and girls are equally exposed to hazards, infections and undernourishments. Infant and child mortality among tribal is high due to poverty and its related malnutrition for both boys and girls. However, all household members are heavily involved in agriculture and subsistence tasks, and that all family members contribute long hours each day to the household economy.

Among Bhutias of Sikkim and Bodhs of Ladakh, there is no hard and fast division of labour between the sexes, although the heavier works are done mostly by men. There is practically no such distinction as men's work and women's work. Both men and women run small businesses and shops, women also work as porters. In Bharmour and Rajasthan, though different socio-cultural condition prevail, the women take part in all economic activities including labour.

(a) *Work as a Child:* Among tribes under study girls are not considered as burden because of their economic value. In all the four societies, girls participate in all types of work at home and agricultural activities along with their mothers. The girls are trained to be good housewives and motherhood, together with behavioural pattern that are consistent with obedience, being ladylike and as expected passive. While boys are trained in the fields or pastures under the supervision of their fathers or in the educational institutions, the girls are trained at homes under the strict supervision of their mothers. They are taught to take care of their homes and household work. They act as pseudo-parents and look after their siblings. If they have spare time in spite of all these activities and obtain permission from their parents then they may go to school.

(b) *Freedom in Selection of Life Partners*: The ideal, the arranged marriage between an unrelated pre-pubertal boy and girl, both coming from different villages holds good for all the four communities. However, as pre-pubertal marriages are prohibited, girls and boys do come in contact and want to have their say in selection of the partners. The girl choice is also considered but the boy has to fulfil the other conditions. Among Bhutias of Sikkim and Bodhs of Ladakh, child marriage and the dowry systems are unknown. As the bride price is important among these tribals, if one cannot pay, he has to work for the girl's family for a specified time decided by the village council or he or his family has to arrange a bride for the girl's brother or cousin.

(c) *Pregnancy before Marriage:* In the four societies under study the response regarding the case of a girl who becomes pregnant before marriage was analogous. If it happens then the matter is brought in the village council and either the boy has to marry the girl or has to pay the compensation to her family. The child is born in her natal family and it does not have an effect on her marriage prospects in any way.

(d) *Education:* The education is a fundamental right that provides opportunities for socioeconomic uplift. The girl child is deliberately denied and the future oppotunity of the toal development. The reasons associated with not educating girl child are financial constraints, early marriages, submissiveness, motherhood, and parental perception of education on women's worldview. Girls have no say on the topic of education. It is entirely parents' decision. Regarding their aspiration to educate their daughters, the parents in the four communities had different response. More than half of them wanted to send their daughters to schools but others thought it was useless. In absence of hired labour the girls, work at home and fields is of utmost importance and all considered the fact that eventually the girls have to get married and start their families. Where parents are enthusiastic about educating their daughters, they enroll their daughters in schools but rarely allow them to complete their schooling. The girls study up to primary or middle level and get married. Sometimes, girls are withdrawn from school after three years to work, with preference for education given to boy s. There is major gender disparity, in terms of more limited educational opportunities available for Gaddi and Bhil girls. Bhutia and Bodh girls probably have benefited most from increased access to educational facilities.

(e) *Beneficiary of the Father's Property:* The concept of patriarchy prevails in all the four societies, yet views regarding inheritance were different among the four groups. The inheritance of household property is determined by customary laws. Previously among Bodhs of Ladakh, primogeniture was the norm, whereby the eldest son inherited all property except the ornaments of the mother used to go to eldest daughter. This has been changed after the introduction of the laws pertaining to abolition of big land estates, and individual rights. Presently, all siblings have equal share in the family property. In the absence of any male sibling, the Ladakhi girl is the sole inheritor, and may enter in to a type of marriage by negotiation known as *magpa,* where the husband who has no property rights takes up residence with her.

Bhutias households follow a patriarchal family system, with the adult male as the head of the household. Bhutias are generally polyandrous, a practice still in existence. Among Bhutias of Sikkim, possession of animals, fields, grazing rights, household effects as well as the house itself belongs to the father or male head of the household. Ownership of material property devolves jointly on a set of blood brothers. Land tenure is always registered in the name of the male head oh the household. Women have no legal right to family property. Upon the death of the male head of the household, women retain usufruct rights to the family holdings and continue to live there until their death. However, women and girls are given gifts and assets including livestock, utensils, ornaments, land (if the household is wealthy), and other goods, which may be taken with them after marriage. This practice is known as *pew a.* If there are no sons, adoption of a close relative or any body from the village is permitted with the consent *of the Dzumsha.*

Gaddi and Bhil girls have no ligal rights over the property. Even in the absence of sons, they have no right to claim the property.

Married Women

Tribal women in India contribute positively to the local economy and participate along with men in subsistence activities. In reality, women do more work than men. They participate in all agricultural activities and other sectors of indigenous cottage industries. They share major responsibilities in the production process. In addition, they have to manage household chores, which is a stupendous task. Child rearing is also the responsibility of the women.

Woman's Work: Married women in the study area carry out all types of work at home as well as outside that are demand of mixed agro-pastoral economy. Apart from looking after the house, children and cattle major portion of the agriculture is done by women who do weeding, hoeing, harvesting and threshing. Among Gaddis and Bhils women also work as labourers, Gaddis in the houses of landlords in Kangra and Bhils at construction sites or as field or forest labour. Bhutia and Bodh women apart from performing their household duties, take on small business, run shops or work as porters, as and when need arise. Role of women is not only of importance in economic activities, but her role in non-economic activities is equally important.

Marriage, Divorce and Household Harmony: The ideal is the arranged marriage; however other types are prevalent in the four communities in the study area and equally valid. She should remain married to the boy for the life but it is not always so. In the study area monogamous, polygamous and polyandrous marriages are prevalent. There may be a premature death, marital discord or infertility that threatens family continuation. It was gathered from the ethnographic data that all the four communities were ready with way out to overcome these. The women are rarely abandoned. Ladakhi Bodhs and Siklanese Bhutias are polyandrous and the premature death of one husband does not affect her social standing. Even in case of infertility, she is not deserted though another wife is brought into the family. Child marriage and the dowry system are unknown among Bodhs and Bhutias. Bhutia daughters have no rights of inheritance to their fathers' properties, even when they are no sons. Bhutia women who marry outside of their ethnic group forfeit their rights to any personal and *pew a* property.

Among Gaddis and Bhils, it is socially expected and considered as desirable that subsequent to the death of her husband a woman should marry her brother-in-law, but in actual practice the woman has the final say and she may refuse alliance with such a man. Widow Bhil women have option *of natra,* where they have choice to marry any other person, who has to pay compenoation to the deceased's family.

Marriage, according to Buddhism, is essentially a mundane affair, something of a social contract with right of divorce. Among Bodhs and Bhutias, parents of the boy arrange marriages but wishes of both sides are respected. Bride price is paid in cash and kind. The negotiations are conducted and betrothal concluded by boy's maternal uncle or paternal uncle sent by the suitor's father. He fixes a bride-price with the father of the affianced bride, who later instead of returning only an insignificant present, sends back almost the equivalent of what he received The bride-price does not represent the purchase price of the wife. The parents of the girl give her clothes, ornaments and other household items.

At the wedding, bride's mother demands *zo-rintho or ome-rin* (price of milk) from the parents of the bridegroom. The amount of such demand and compensation is however meager and customary. In case of marital discord among Bodhs and Bhutia, a woman is free to divorce her husband. In most of divorce cases the bride price is returned. In case of remarriage, the groom to be would pay to first husband if she comes from there or to her father if she comes from her parental house. All these matters are discussed at length and settlements are reached after number of meetings. Among Gaddis, marriage is a religious sacrament; however there is provision for divorce with mutual consent. Dowry system, in its true traditional sense, is not prevalent among Gaddis.

However, at time of marriage certain essential items are given to the girl as gifts by her parents. There is no custom, which might be termed reversed dowry system entailing some payment by the parents of the bridegroom to the parents of the bride. In some cases, especially in those where there is a doubt that girl may not be treated well by her husband and his family, some ornaments are demanded as a kind of security from the bridegroom's parents, and these are retained until the parents of the girl are satisfied that the girl is being treated well and has settled down. When there is a marriage by exchange, in which brother and sister in the family may marry a sister and brother belonging to another family, no bride price is paid.

In the case of widow remarriage, if she does not want to marry her brother-in-law, some compensation is paid by her new husband to her ex-husband's family in accordance with the possibility of her bearing children again, as well as her age.

Moreover, the man has to bear the cost of the marriage much more heavily than the women. Also a girl's father has little responsibility for making a monetary outlay for his daughter by compulsion although he often does give a substantial gift to his daughter at the time of marriage. If a father wants to avoid that too, he can permit his daughter to elope. Similarly *ghar-jawantari,* a typical form of marriage where the boy has to work as a domestic servant in the house of his would be father-in-law for a specified time (Bhasin, 1988).

The custom of (bride price) is prevalent among Bhils as well because here also the father considers a girl as an asset as she contributes a lot to the family economy and it facilitates marriage expenditure. By tradition Bhils are polygynous. Marriage among Bhils is not a sacrament. For a Bhil, both male and female getting married is a mark of adulthood and maturity. If the bride price is high, then he looks for other options. A Bhil must have a wife and he does obtain one either through a negotiated marriage (by exchange) or through *natra* or by elopement (Bhasin, 2005).

Divorcee/Widow Women

Among Bodhs and Bhutias, because of automatic levirate, once married a women has a social security. Traditionally among these groups, fraternal polyandry was practiced and in such polyandrous social structure, women are never insecure. If the eldest husband dies she remains the wife of the brother/brothers. Young widows are rare in these societies. If a younger brother wants to opt out of this arrangement and wants to marry another girl, the girl's father has to pay the compensation in the form of a head and a thigh of yak, *chaang* (millet beer) and cash payment. Among Gaddis and Bhils too the custom of levirate prevails.

Amongst Gaddis and Bhils, a wife is the possession of the family, especially entrusted to the husband. In case her husband dies, it, however, does not effect the alliance, as she is supposed to marry her younger brother-in-law *(dewar vatta)*. If she wants to marry some one outside the family, he has to pay the bride price to her husband's family. It is socially accepted and considered as desirable that subsequent to the death of her husband a woman should marry her brother-in-law.

However it is at the discretion of the widow if she wants to go into the affiliation. Among Gaddis, in case of the birth of a child after the husband's death irrespective of the time gap, the child if it be born in the husband's house, *chaukhandu(born* within the four walls), has full inheritance rights. Woman is responsible for the continuity of patrilineage. As replacement of women is not easy in Gaddi society because of demographic reasons, rights of sexuality are ignored, but right on the womb is there. In case, the child is born after a gap after husband's death and away from husband's house, the child gets a share of property from the woman's father or brother, and in case of remarriage the child is entitled to inheritance rights from her new husband. In the later case the amount of the property is settled before the woman agrees to remarry.

It was seen in the field areas that divorce and remarriage is permissible among all the four groups and the bride price is given back at the time of separation. As among Gaddis there is no clearly defined bride price, there are a few conditions under which marital status is ambiguous. A promiscuous woman who stays with a lot of men, and if she bears a child *(hallar* or bastard) and genitor may not be willing to accept it as legitimately his, the child is accepted by girl's parents. There is also a question when a woman leaves one man for another without obtaining a divorce. The first man may object and demand a substantial compensation that the second cannot pay. Under such circumstances, the caste council is likely to support the claim of the first man but public sentiment usually is that nothing can be done to force the girl to return to him. The divorcee or widow women among these communities have similar rights and duties as other married women have. The position of women in these environments is related to her economic importance. Women are not viewed as life partners in the usual accepted sense, but also as economically indispensable copartners in the subsistence economy. Her labour is sufficiently in demand. In all the four groups, there are no fixed rules for barren women. However one thing is sure that a new wife is brought to the family. Barren women are generally not abandoned, as their labour is even now valued. Though they may not have many rights however have loads of duties.

Women's Role in Economic Sphere

In the traditional societies which lack market system, the business of everyday living is usually carried on gender division of labour (Illich, 1982). In the study area, the division of labour is mainly between herding and agriculture. In all other tasks concerned with life in the village, such as crafts, house building, watermills and work on boundary walls, there is division between men's work and women's work. Among Gaddis and Bhutias the men are shepherds and women grow crops for food. It is equally valid for Bhils and Bodhs, there too men are out on different duties and women grow crops for food. However, the boundaries are not so clearly marked, as there is overlapping and deviations from the rule. There are as well cases where the rule is inflexible and times when change is possible.

Major portion of agriculture is done by women who do weeding, hoeing, planting, harvesting and thrashing except ploughing (which are done by men) in the fields adjacent to houses or far off fields. The other activities of women include looking after the house, children and cattle. Food processing and cooking is women's job. It is the women who with the assistance of children are largely responsible for the cattle, water fuel and fodder. This permits them considerable time away from home and the village. When they are away from home, they are free to talk to whom so ever they please, male or female, of any caste or creed. As a consequence, communication among women and between men and women is as high as it is among men.

Tribal women are very strong and courageous in the handling of environmental imperatives as can be demonstrated in the trekking and work pattern under the severe limitations of the harsh environment. Several studies dealing with pastoral societies indicate that the position of women in such societies is not very high because the actual care of the livestock and handling of economic affairs is entirely a male domain. However, among Gaddis and Bhutias, though women do not directly help in handling of livestock, they do look after their husbands during migrations. They cook for them and carry loads.

Women's Role in Social Sphere

Role of tribal women in the study area is not only of importance in the economic activities, but her role in non-economic activities is equally important. Formation and continuity of family hearth and home is the domain of the women. Women's role as wives, mothers, and organisers and as basic foundation of other dimensions of social life is of extreme importance. Among Gaddis, as men are out for pastoral duties, the socialisation of children automatically becomes mother's business, in the early years of life at least. The Gaddi family assumes mother centeredness with the children and some important decisions falling to the sphere of women's intervention. The role of women in childbirth, funerals and fairs and festivals is an important part of village life. In the tribal areas, women are carriers of traditional information in absence of written records. They are crucial actors in the preservation and dissemination of such knowledge. They are not only competent food producers and house makers but are also the transmitters of rich local oral traditions.

Women's Role in Political Sphere

The role of women's empowerment for a just society was highlighted in the Beijing Conference (1995). In all the four societies under study, women power does not extend to societal or political spheres. The economic power of the women in the household is not translated in to corresponding community authority. They are not ignored at household level but are not given due credit and importance at official level. Women supremacy is restricted within the family domain and does not extend to social or political spheres. It is interesting to note that although by convention every village Panchayat has a female member, the lady never bothers to attend the meeting or to take any active interest in the proceedings of Panchayat. Sikkim has a tradition of collective decision-making by communities through the institution of *Dzumsha*. However, traditional institutions do not witness a significant role for women and *Dzumsha* is constituted of males only. In the absence of a male member, a female can represent her family unit.

If a male head is absent from *Dzumsha* meeting, he is fined, however if represented by female head, she is liable to pay half the amount for her absence. This shows that women have a secondary importance in public affairs and community decision-making. Women are generally bypassed and marginalised either they lack the requisite skills, or because women's heavy and unending domestic responsibilities makes attending meetings and participating in decision making difficult. It always happens that men take over the more profitable activities.

Women's Role in Religious Sphere

All the four societies under study show male dominance in ritual sphere. Three prominent religions—Buddhism, Hinduism and Traditional that are professed by the tribal under study operate with tenets that are restrictive of women's participation in their rituals. Gender is a significant slip up in Buddhist societies, as in Hindu or Islamic ones. Buddhist monastic practices reinstate the social heirarchies that the Budha had disparaged. Nuns and their nunneries are completely ignored. Nuns remains subject to the authority and scrutiny of monks throughout a religous life that is theoretically devoted to rise above gender and other social hierarchies.

In Buddhist communities, monasticism is as structured around a gender division of labour and the dualities of sex as are the lay communities. Nuns are distinguished from female renunciates who live at home and do not perform any public rituals. Buddhist women can never become monks or be ordained due to the ideology of purity and pollution. Among Bodhs of Ladakh, the lay and monastic realms are not alternating, as the monks play a central role in politico-economic processes.

In Ladakh, Buddhist monasheries are wealthy, as the monasteries are biggest land owning agencies and act as treasury. The lay patronage which sustains Buddhist monasticism is the Buddhist idea of learning merit. Conversely Buddhist nuns face many hardships first in establishing and afterwards maintaining these nunneries. To become a nun, women reject her faminity and maternity and dedicate her to spiritual life in nunnery to learn rituals and Buddhist surmons, even then she is not free of her economic responsibilities towards the family and the village. She performs her agricultural duties on the family farms and monastic estates. Families allows their daughters to join nunneries in order to earn merit and at the same time make sure the assurance of their productive services. Buddhist nuns play an important arbitrating role between the monastery and the laity by performing ritual services and serving monks and society, thereby earning merit for their families and communities while continuing to perform labour in the fields. Both nuns and monks take vows to abstain from worldly pursuits, but nuns endup working as domestic help. The Buddhist way of life and making merit can neither assure a livelihood for nuns nor provide funds for their periodic rituals while assuring the same for the monks and their *gompas.*

Despite the fact that nuns earn wide ranging merit for the entire community, it does not assure then patronage, as they do not perform practical *tantric,* instrumental and propitratory rituals like monks. Among the Nyingme Buddhist of Sikkim, the monks like other householders perform both ritual services and productive labour on the family farms in order to sustain themselves, as their monasteries cannot support them financially. Yet, unlike the Buddhist nuns of Ladakh, the householder Lamas of Sikkim marry, beget children, and inherit property, engage in trade, and enjoy considerable status and power in their families and communities. Ascetic monks have higher status and spiritual authority as compared to householder lamas in Sikkim, yet gender hierarchies persists as celibate nuns in Sikkim are ranked below any ordained household Lamas.

The religious organisation of Buddhist societies gives an idea about the gender inequality that denies status and independence to Buddhist nuns and perpetnally subordinate and marginalise them.

Women are never appointed as priests, and are skillfully manipulated against themselves. Both sexes participate in ceremonies, but men shoulder major responsibilities. Men mainly play musical instruments. Women do take part in dancing but their movements are different from men. Bodhs. and Bhutias place great emphasis on coercive rights of exorcising and destroying demons. Both the communities have trained male and female specialists for exorcising demons. Bodhs have *lha-ma* (female) and *lha-pa* (male) and Bhutias have *pau* (male) and *nejohum* (female) who play part in exorcising rights. Bodhs and Bhutias nunneries are geographically separated from the *Gompas* (monastery) and nuns do not perform rituals and funeral rights for the people. They are present only during festivals and certain ceremonies as spectators or at the time of earning merit for oneself. Bhutias even make difference between male and female funeral pyres. In the case of female and male funeral pyres, eight and seven tiers of firewood are laid respectively for consuming the body into flames. Bhutias explain this discrimination in a way that women are one degree below men in the society. To compensate this lower status of women, her pyre is raised higher.

Among Gaddis and Bhils as well men control ritual realm. Women participate in dancing and singing. In the rituals of Gaddi *Chela* or Bhil *Bhopa,* Gaddi and Bhil women merely participate as spectators. There are no female counterparts of Gaddi *Chela* or Bhil *Bhopa.*

Male Domination

As the religious sphere is most dominating among tribals it constitutes a major field for male domination. The women are deprived of public authority. Religion legitimises gender hierarchy. The subordination of women in religious activities and their denial of access to positions of religious leadership has been a powerful tool in most world religions in supporting the patriarchal order and the exclusion of women, from the public form. The religious sphere is a major field for male dominance, and a strategy to deprive women of public authority. There are a few innovations in religious sphere, and hence these changes must exist within a traditional, ritual and textual structure. Religious institutions are resistance to gender equality. In structure, an explicitly male religious framework contains the tribal societies. Though the secular institutions strive to eradicate inequality but it was seen that women of these areas were lagging behind in all fields.

Even the economic power of the women in the household is not translated into a corresponding community authority. They are not ignored at household level but are not given due credit and importance alongside. However, female labour is central to all economic activities among tribals. Women perform waged and non-waged, productive and unproductive labour. The workload that is associated with these activities most unlikely does not give women any time to indulge in community affairs.

Women play an important role in their household economy. They work in most operations of all sectors of the local economy and for longer hours each day than men. In addition to the domestic and reproductive activities associated with household maintenance, they also collect and gather free goods especially fuel, fodder and water. Tribal women operate effectively in most economic and social institutions, participating in both local and migrant labour activities. Women's autonomy in terms of decision-making is highly constrained among tribals. They have little access to, and exercise limited control over resources; and few are free from threat and violence at the hands of their husbands. Working for wages is not necessarily an indicator of autonomy. The wage earning tribal women cannot make the decision to work on their own, nor do they have control over their earnings. The marriage pattern and family ties ensure that women are not cut off from family support.

In these areas, women have their own perceptions of gender equality that cannot be easily quantified by standard indicators *Women's Perceptions on the Subject of Husband's Contribution in Work at Home.* About fifty per cent women in the study area replied in affirmative. Husbands should and do help in cooking and bringing water. There is practically no task, other than minding small children, which does not require cooperation of both sexes. The work done by women is constant, diverse and often arduous. The work of men tends to be seasonal. In the men's light working season, they may help in the work at home.

Prohibitions during Pregnancy and Menstruation. There are no restrictions during pregnancy between Bodh and Bhutia women, while among Gaddis and Bhil women there is restriction on keeping fast. After the childbirth, among Bodhs and Bhutias, the mother observes a period of pollution, when she is confined to the house for a certain period, usually lasting 30 days. Even outsiders cannot eat food or drink water from the house where childbirth has taken place, as a house is defiled by the childbirth *(bangthip).* It is a socially imposed *zemches.* They also cannot appear before the shrines of family and village gods. Among Gaddis there are no such restrictions, as sometimes deliveries take place during migrations. Bhils observe prohibitions during menstruation. They do not worship, cook food and bring water. All the women justified the restrictions considering them impure.

Ownership of Jewellary after Marriage. More or less all the women considered it as their right to own jewellary.

Permission of Remarriage of a Divorced Woman. All women agreed on the point that like men, women should also have the prospect to remarry. The four societies under study do have provision for remarriage of a divorcee or a widow. The equality of sexes can be seen in the attitudes and practices concerning marriage and divorce in the four groups.

Women's Talk: Tribal women talk about their homes, children and emotions; while men talk about work, innovations, ideas and politics. Tribal women in the study area are separated by language. They speak local language; Hindi is mostly understood and spoken by men. Now-a-days children who go to school can also understand and speak Hindi. Education is generally conceived by tribals as a means of upward social mobility for men. The women's mobility on social ladder is through marriage to a person who is likely to be socially mobile. They think it does not effect women social, position whether she is educated or uneducated. Thus mostly boys are sent to school. This discrimination against girls is not because of her lack of intelligence or ability to learn, it is only that it is not going to help her in the traditional lifestyle. The problem of conversing with women is that all questions have to be asked through men and getting the answers by men. Men translate, take things for granted, and mould their answers to suit their occasion.

Concept of Women's Space. Among tribals in the study area the concept of women's space is where only women may sit, work or enter freely at any time is relatively informal and flexible and depends on the separation of activities that result from the sexual division of labour. It is a characteristics feature of traditional societies to set apart, or see a distinction in physical space, which is used by men women. In the study area, there are no such private or intimate spaces for women, though men have public space to hold meetings, settle disputes, and discuss political and farming issues. There is at least one such space in each of the settlements, either under a tree or in the open space. Women do not have a similar, formal sitting space. The water mill is another space, which interchangeably becomes men's or women's. However as there are several water mills in each settlement, if women ate at one, it tends to be only women and children, but there are no fixed rules. When women occupy public spaces like water source, water spring, field etc.,. men usually do not join them. The women interact with each other, not with their men as couples.

In the study area, the interaction between individual men and women varies according to kinship relation and relative age, which ranges from relaxed informality to extreme avoidance, marked by women covering their head and men averting their glances. Men who are not kin, especially elders do not come closer to an area where a group of women is sitting. By these standards, the tribals also maintain the integrity of the gender divide.

The courtyards are mainly women's space (except during threshing when men and women work together in the courtyard). All food processing is done here. Washing of clothes, spinning of wool, embroidery, providing bath to children etc is all carried out here. The kitchen is a woman' domain.

The grazing grounds in and around the village, near water source are areas where old women, young girls and small boys sit with babies, to mind cattle and sheep and goat. In the transhumant societies of Gaddis and Bhutias, both summer and winter pasture contains the elements of time and space when compared to village economy. That is to say, the pastures are spatially removed and are at different altitudes. Being seasonally used, they bring the concept of time. They provide gender differences in the utilisation of resources and tool such as animals as opposed to field crops, male instead of female labour. The tribal women in the study area have been denied roles associated with masculinity as a result of ideology of the family and kinship, which identifies paternal roles with authoritative roles. Few women who have succeeded in acquiring some positions in communal life have found that their competence or their executive methods are frequently challenged or ridiculed.

Equal Rights to Men and Women. Tribal women in the study area recognise the fact that they have been discriminated against in education, income, consumption, status and access to power; they have a worse health record than men; they suffer from social, cultural and legal discrimination and often from violence. They are discriminated on grounds of equity (which refers to equality of opportunities and choices) and efficiency. There is need for quantitative measurement, for a complete set of cultural and rights indicators to assess women's rights.

Labour Work. Earlier, when a woman was working on her farm or collecting minor forest produce from the forest for her family, she felt belonged to it. However with the change in scenario, when she has to do the labour work, she has to collect forest produce for the other agencies, her economic role becomes different. They feel as they are working as unskilled labourers, it does not help in improving their position. Providing skilled training to women may help in elevating their status. Tribal women insist on a need based plan for providing work on year round basis, in line with the multiple occupational pattern of their work.

Violence against Women. Few tribal women are free from threat and violence at the hands of their husbands. Violence often becomes a tool to socialise family members according to prescribed norms of behaviour with an overall perspective of male dominance and control. Kelkar situates violence against women 'in the socioeconomic and political context of power relations' and it should include 'exploitation, discrimination, upholding of unequal economic and social structures, the creation of an atmosphere of terror, threat or reprisal and forms of religio-cultural and political violence (Kelkar, 1991). However, the violence in the form of female foeticide and infanticide suffered by women of other castes and communities it seems is not present among tribals.

Voting Rights. Tribal women take pleasure in their voting rights and about 85 per cent of women in the study area exercised their right. Most of them follow the advice of their husbands or some of them are under pressure to accept the wishes of their husbands.

Reproductive Rights. Women in the study areas have no personal opinion on the women's movement in the other parts of the world on the reproductive health issue as a part of women' reproductive rights. They are not comfortable with the idea of women regulating their own fertility. Though they do manage to have abortion with crude methods but men tackle major issues of planning the family. However, the women's reproductive health problems are originated in gender inequalities, control of power and resources.

Utilisation of Health Services. Utilisation of health and maternal health services is influenced by the characteristics of the health delivery system such as the availability, quality and the cost of the services. However, it does not necessarily means that if medical services are operational in an area all women are expected to avail the facility. It may be true that, even under the same conditions of availability, the response is different. Other factors such as social structure and status of women are equally important.

In the study areas women could not take the decision on their own about going to health centres. It was not only peer pressure but lack of education was the deciding factor.

Argument

Tribal speak little of statuses and roles when talking about their social life. What they do talk of are the skills for managing the environment for making a living. They also talk of marriage, married life, children, and their socialisation within a community of relationships.

The Indian family has many forms and different structures. These have direct bearing on the status of women, not only in terms of the number and quality of relationships to which they have to adapt and the distribution of functions and roles, but also with regard to the allocation of resources. In the study area nuclear, joint, polygamous nuclear, polygamous joint, polyandrous nuclear, polyandrous joint and extended types of families are present.

The beliefs and ideas held by locals have a vital influence on the lives of the men, women and children. For one thing, it reinforces the gender division of work, place, tools and language. According to religious beliefs, women are considered impure, that is why they are not allowed to use plough and interact with supernatural beings directly. The present position and condition of the tribal women is not an accidental affair. It has evolved because of the operation of several forces in the past. The economic cycle and division of labour in the tribal areas has given an important role to the women. This economic role has undoubtedly affected the social position of women, who have social freedom that is quite remarkable in its scope.

There is cultural similarity among the different tribal groups in the respective areas under study, as the women from different areas have the similar economic roles to play, necessitated by the demands of environment to grow food for their own consumption. The economic value and worth of women therefore as (a) an independent and necessary unit of economic activity without which the given economic system will not survive, (b) as complementary to the men as work force, in the organised functioning of the whole economic system.

Role of women is not only of importance in economic activities, but her role in non-economic activities is equally important. Women's role as wives, mothers, organisers and as the basic foundation of other dimensions of social life is of utmost importance. The tribal women in these areas occupy an economically significant place that is reflected in the generally high position and the importance that they have. The socioeconomic equality of sexes can be observed in the attitudes and practices concerning marriage, divorce and household harmony. The tribal women work very hard, in some cases even more than the men. However these women are not backward. They have power in their own sphere, no men tell them what to do. They are responsible for their own share of work and share the benefits of their own work as long as the unit of production and consumption remains the home. Their own perception and that of their men, is that women share major share of socio-economic activities and consequently they are respected, well thought of and think well of themselves. The concept of patriarchy, which prevails in subsistence societies, conveys respect rather than envy between the genders.

Despite the fact that tribal women live their lives as dependents throughout their lifecycle: as daughters, sisters, and wives; or as mothers of sons, they have far more power and independence than modern sub-urban housewives. A woman always has it in her power to leave her husband if she is angry, dissatisfied or unhappy. She has great freedom of movement as children, if any, remain with the husband Her labour is sufficiently in demand so that she can move not only back to her natal family but also to a sister's husband's house or a more distant kinsmen's house She can stay there till such times as she returns to her husband's house or finds a new one. There is no great need for her to return to the natal village although this is the usual practice.

Whenever a man in these regions acts on an assumption that his authority will be accepted simply because he is a man and fails to take into account the wishes or feelings of his wife, sister or daughter, he often gets himself into trouble. There is no way for a man to force women' compliance with his wishes. Her economic ability and consequent social position has resulted in special institutional privileges that are bestowed on the women. In spite of having freedom they seldom have a voice in the political sphere. They are not ignored at household level, but are not given due credit and importance in political and religious subjects. They are like invisible hands shaping and maintaining the structure of society.

Women, a majority of the world's population, receive only a small share of developmental opportunities. They are often excluded from education or from better jobs; from political systems or from adequate health care. Even as doors to education and health opportunities have opened speedily for women, the entry to religious and political fields is still not effortless. In the countries for which relevant data are available, the female human development index is only 60% that of males.

Even in the economic field, if they are working outside the household, they have an unequal situation in the labour market. They are treated unequally under social welfare systems that affect their status and power in the family. Women receive a small share of credit from formal banking institu-tions, as they have no collateral to offer. Women normally receive a much lower average wage than men. They are paid less than men for equal work. According to Human Development Report, (1995), the average female wage is only three-fourth of the male wage in the non-agricultural sector in 55 countries that have no comparable data; all regions record a higher rate of unemployment among women than men; in the developing countries, women still constitute less than a seventh of administrators and managers; and women still occupy only 10% of parliamentary seats and only 6% of the cabinet positions.

Before the 1980s, it was assumed that all women shared a common subjugation, and reasons for their oppression were open to explanation. However multiculturalism and identity politics overcame this consensus and set the debate about differences. Full range of social and cultural institutions, which reproduce gender hierarchies and gender-based inequalities include legal equality and excess to education and health.

In the tribal areas under study the economic cycle and division of labour in the area has given an important role to the women. Environmental resource management illustrates that sustainability, especially in fragile ecosystems of Ladakh and Sikkim, is better achieved by knowledge, skills and techniques of local people, which include mostly women. This does not necessarily means that women are generally more ecofriendly; it is just that division of labour has given an important role to the women. Women's participation in the economic activity is important for their personal advancement and their status in the society. Work participation is influenced by a combination of number of social, economic, cultural and demographic factors. This economic role has undoubtedly affected the social position of women, who have social freedom that is quite remarkable in its scope. There is cultural similarity among the different groups in the study area, as the women from different tribes have the same economic roles to play, necessitated by the demands of environment to grow food for their own consumption. The economic value and worth of women therefore as (a) independent and necessary unit of economy without which the given economic system will not survive, (b) complementary to the men as work force, in organised functioning of the whole economic system. Women exhibit ingenuity, creativity and initiative in solving their daily problems of sustenance and survival and often demonstrate organisational skills as revealed during labour exchange (mutual aid groups) and communal service ventures.

These social networks are important for the local economies. This cultural acceptance of the fact of their raised status gives them a voice in household affairs that is almost equal to their husbands. The economic power of the women in the household is not translated into a corresponding community authority. The male head, which is custodian of property, manages the family finance. Selections of the bridegroom for the daughter or sister, acquisition or disposal of property are all domains of the male members or eldest male. In spite of a substantial contribution in the subsistence economy, a women's right is not recognised in the transmission of landed property and this makes her dependent upon men. The socio-economic equality of sexes can only be seen in the attitudes and practices concerning marriage, divorce and household harmony.

The present study corroborates the premise that women status is high when they contribute substantially to primary subsistence activities. Although they lack control of material and social resources, their contribution to subsistence economy give them important and irreversible position. It may be concluded as it is observed that ecology and environmental factors existing in tribal areas under study have given these women a special economic power, and an elevated status. However, there are certain domains in which men continue to dominate, as is culturally required. Moreover, community still is in the hands of men. There is kind of duality observable here. Men dominate in public, in social and religious affairs, and continue to play the role of the head of the family and breadwinner, women enjoy a greater say in their family life, they have a greater deal of social freedom and several of their actions are condoned/tolerated (Bhasin, 1991). This confirms with Ortnel and Rosalindo 's thesis in one way that in spite of the public/domestic dichotomy the ecological/economic division interferes further modification in women's position. Here one may say that the public/domestic dichotomy is not the only criterion for determining women's status in society.

Male Domination

All the tribal societies in the study area are patriarchal in which men dominate in public sector. However, in their own world women have a freedom, and a self-expression. They can only be understood on their own terms. With the onset of development programmes economic changes are taking place but tribal women remain traditional in their dress, language, tools and resources, because they grow food crops rather than cash crops. Significant changes have taken place in the two decades separating the United Nations Conferences on women in Mexico City and the meeting in Beijing.

Modernisation is bringing changes, which affect men and women differently. Modernisation brought by outside agencies is set in a male-biased ideology, women are seen as inherently 'incapable'; the new techniques are aimed at men by men. Male values are also reflected in the view that development is solely dependent on technological and economic advances. Such values exploit both the environment and vulnerable groups such as women (Hewitt, 1989: 351): The thought that women are being treated shabbily, women centered programmes for developments were evolved which tended to overlook the importance of man-woman relations. Inadequate planning and implementation as well as culture resistance gave rise to more gender disparities. The association between cultures, economic organisations and different patterns of women's labour force participation ought to be implicit. Though efforts have been made in almost all countries to improve the status of women but it is still an unequal world.

NOTES AND REFERENCES

Bhasin, V. 1988. *Himalayan Ecology, Transhumance and Social Organisation. Gaddis of Himachal Pradesh.* Delhi: Kamla-Raj Enterprises.

Bhasin, V. 1989. *Ecology, Culture and Change: Tribals of Sikkim.* Delhi: Inter-India Publications.

Bhasin, V. 1991. "Status of women in the Himalayas: A case of Gaddis." *J. Hum. Ecol.,* 2(2): 107-116.

Bhasin, V. 1993. "Social dimensions of politics: The case of tribal democracy in Sikkim." J. *Hum. Ecol.,* 4(1): 63-78.

Settlements and Health. Delhi: Kamla-Raj Enterprises.

Bhasin, V. 2005. *Medical Anthropology: Tribals of Rajasthan.* Delhi: Kamla-Raj Enterprises,

de Schilppe, P. 1956. *Shifting Cultivation in Africa: The Zande System of Agriculture.* London: Routledge and Kegan-Paul.

Franzmann, Majella. 2000. *Women and Religion.* Oxford: Oxford University Press.

Hewitt, Farida. 1989. "Woman's work, woman's place: A gendered lifeword of a high mountain community in northern Pakistan." *Mountain Research and Development,* 9: 335-52 (1989).

Hogan, D.P., B. Berhanu and A. Hailermarium. 1999. "Household organization, women's autonomy and contraceptive behaviour in southern Ethopia." *Studies in Family Planning,* 30(4): 302-14.

Illich, I. 1982. *Gender.* New York: Pantheon Books. Jones, K. B. 1993. *Compassionate Authority: Democracy and the Representation of Women.* London: Routtedge.

Kelkar, G. 1991. *Violence Against Women In India: Perspectives and Strategies.* Bangkok: Asian Institute of Technology

Ladurie, Le Roy. 1979. *Montveion: The Promised Land of Error.* New York: Vintage Books.

Ortnel, Sherry. 1974. "Is female to male as nature is to culture", in Michelle Rosaldo and L. Lamphere (eds.), *Women, Culture and Society.* Stanford: Stanford University Press.

Rosaldo, M. 1974. "Introduction", in *Women, Culture and Society.* in Michelle Rosaldo and L. Lamphere (eds.), *Women, Culture and Society.* Stanford: Stanford University Press.

Scott, John Wallach. 1988. *Gender and the Politics of the History.* New York: Columbia University Press.

Sered, Susan S. 1994. *Priestess, Mother, and Sacred Sister.* Oxford: Oxford University Press (OUP), Oxford.

The United Nations. 1975. *Conference on Women in Mexico City.* New York: United Nations.

UN. 1995. *The Convention on the Elimination of All Forms of Discriminations against Women.* New York: United Nations.

UN. 1995b. *The Beijing Declaration and Platform for Action.* New York: United Nations.

WHO. 1989. *Preventing Maternal Deaths.* Geneva: World Health Organisation.

12

AN OVERVIEW OF GENDER AND DEVELOPMENT

The tendency of the West to search for a generalised model of Indian thought and character has lead to misrepresentations of the peoples and societies of India. The belief that investigations into South Asian can be based upon a single discernable "fact" of Indian character diminishes the history and broad cultural expanse of the region. The meaning of gender and the experience of women in the South Indian region of Kerala on the Malabar Coast differs from the experience of women in other regions of India. Also within Kerala, religious affiliations, caste status, and location impact the social status and experience of women. Constructions of sexuality and gender within the southern region of Kerala are different from those of more northern and central regions of Kerala. Within the region of Kerala, sexuality is linked to household prosperity, as evidenced through the marriage rituals of the nation.

Theory

Anthropological inquiries into the meaning of gender in India resulted in the realisation that gender categories are constructed differently throughout this nation than in the western world. The word gender in the scholarly community has become a politically correct synonym for the study of women. Gender, however, does not refer simply to the study of women, but to the manner in which male and female differences are socially constructed. In antroplogical studies, there has been a general move away in anthropological studies from attempts to formulate universal categories of gender. The criteria for analyzing gendered categories and social status vary cross-culturally.

Western concept of gender tend to group humans into two distinct static categories based upon the physical appearance of genitalia. However, this construction is not universal. South Asian gender definitions emphasize the different essences or humours attributed to men and women as opposed to the overt physical emphasis of the western world. Humours are present more or less strongly in every food or body tissue. Humours include hotness (as associated with fire) phlegm, bile, ether, gross body, subtle body.. Women are seen to possess different proportions of these humours than men. These humours are combined through the process of mixing. Mixing occurs most frequently in bodies that are more open and less closed off to the intrusion of other elements and humours.

It is better to be more closed, for this limits the effects of pollution upon the body. Women are posses the humour of hotness, more so than men, and they are also defined as more open. It is this combination of essences that is linked to their reproductive ability. These essences, however, are not static categories but change over the course of a life-time thereby changing an individual's status as a gendered being. Despite the acknowledgment of that gender is constructed differently in South Asia than in the West, there has been little analysis of the variations in gender definitions within South Asia.

In Indian culture, according to anthropological gender scholars the experience of women within gender definitions has generated a universal picture of the Indian woman. The portrait of the Indian woman is typically based on the experience of upper-class women in more Northern regions of India. Noted scholars of gender in South Asia like Susan Wadley, Sarah Lamb, Anne Gold, and Gloria Raheja focussed their studies in the North and utilised high-caste women as their primary source of information. Their work is typically used as a framework for the study of gender and more specifically women in South Asia. While a broad framework for gender studies within India would be useful outlining the typical experience of women it would based upon the assumption that there is a "typical" female experience. Such beliefs undermine the capacity of women to manipulate their circumstances as well as the wide ranging differences in the experience of women.

Object of Sexual Attraction

A variety of theoretical models have been utilised as lenses through which to view the study of gender in India. Wadley, positions the meaning of gender in India within a paradigm of order and disorder. Women as a gender must be controlled because of their capacity to create disorder within society. Influenced by Sanskrit texts, many Brahmans feel that women lack wisdom and are born with many demerits. However, women also have great power. They have power both to give life as well as a great capacity for destruction. Women's resistance has the power to disrupt the patriarchal order of the society. The power of women is strongly linked to sexuality. Women, as objects of sexual attraction that are attributed a much higher capacity and desire for sexual relations than men, have the power to influence and dissuade men from a higher purpose. Inappropriate sexual relations can create dire consequences for men. Therefore, to perpetuate order and merit within society it is necessary to reign and control the power of women through restrictions on her sexuality.

This model shows that women are not simply silent victims of an oppressive gender system, but are afforded a certain amount of power in society. Their power is derived from their capacity to resist the prescribed social order of Brahmanical traditions and patriarchal hierarchy. Such constructions of gender and sexuality as potential disruptions to a patriarchal framework become problematic when applied to groups without such a strict patriachacal framework. In Kerala, the social hierarchy is not formed upon strict patriachalal schemes. Many castes are in fact matrilineal, in which women become binding forces within society. Women play a pivotal role in creating social order, not simply disrupting it.

Nature of Women

Sarah Lamb, in her study of ageing in Bengal, also holds that gender meanings and women's status are deeply rooted within her position as a sexual being; her status however, is a fluid category that changes with age. The nature of women is perceived as more open and hot than men; as such they are more vulnerable to pollution during their married years. Women, however, are not simply defined by their gender as women, but also by their age. What it means to be female changes over time, as the body of a woman changes over time.

During her reproductive years, women are particularly vulnerable to pollution and must therefore be protected and often confined in Brahman families. As women age however, their bodies "cool" and "dry". In part because of these humoural changes as they age, women are granted more freedom within the community. A woman's status in Bengal is directly linked to her position within the reproductive cycle, and is tied to the bodily changes of puberty, menstruation and menopause. Once a woman has passed her sexually active years, she no longer has to be regulated to a great extent. In essence, she becomes more like a man and does not need to be protected from pollution.

A women's capacity for creating disorder is linked in large part to their reproductive capacity and her nature as a sexualised being. A woman derives power, both creative and destructive from her reproductive capacity. As such, it is during this time that she faces regulations governing her sexual behaviour. The status of women, however is not a strict gender formation, but a fluid category which alters with age as well as caste status. The changes in gender status throughout age are strongly linked to changes in her reproductive capacity and depiction as a sexualised being.

The nation of India represents extreme diversity with regard to language geography, social class and religion. Despite these differences many anthropologists have tried to study India as a holistic entity. The history and cultural geography of Kerala, represent a unique and divergent representation, yet anthropologists such as Dumont and Yalman affirm the cultural uniformity of India and believe the castes of Kerala and the kinship ties of that region can be analysed in Pan-Indian framework.

Kerala: God's Own Country

The state of Kerala occupies a 38,864 sq km stretch of land on the southwest corner of Southern India. It is bordered by the Arabian Sea on the West and the Western Ghats on the East. The state was formed in 1956 from the merger of many smaller states. Tranvacore dominated the Southern part of present day Kerala, whereas Calicut dominated the Northern reaches. Kerala has a tropical maritime climate that is characterised by little fluxuation in the temperature throughout the year. The land of Kerala is lush and green compared with the more arid climate of Northern India. The geographic distinctiveness of Kerala has served to isolate this region from the rest of the country. Malayam, the most recently developed Dravidian language, is the predominant language of the region. The majority of Kerala subscribe to the Hindu religion. However, this region also has strong Christian and Muslim minorities. The major castes in the region are the Namboodiri Brahmans, the Nayars and the Ezhavas or Tiyyars as they are known in Northern India. At the bottom of the caste hierarchy are the Pulayas and the Parayas.

The long stretch of sea coast has played an important role in shaping the history of Kerala. Foreign trade exerted a decisive influence on the region, and has created a more cosmopolitan society than the rest of India. However, the location of Kerala as well as the pepper cultivation made it a key location for conducting colonial conquests (Menon 1979:53). While Kerala has been relatively isolated from the rest of India, foreign trade and colonial occupation influenced the social structure and cultural practices of the region.

History

Civilisation began in Kerala with the realm of the Chera around the beginning of the Christian era. Women at this time in history were afforded professional freedom, and a minimal amount of sexual regulation. In conjunction with this sexual freedom, female imagery played an important role in female worship. Women were associated with power through fertility, but this power did not necessitate extensive regulation. From the fifth century onward, Sanskritisation began to affect Keralese society. Male Gods began to replace female goddesses, although Bhagavati remained an important figure. In the fifteenth century, Kerala had increasing contact with European traders such as the Portuguese and the Dutch. This contact had wide ranging implications for Keralese society, creating a culture that was more cosmopolitan than the rest of the Indian sub-continent.

The history of Kerala unfolded in a different manner than the rest of South Asia creating social heterogeneity in the region. Their earliest cultural traditions provide women autonomy and power within the society. The status of women in this area depreciated as foreign influences began to penetrate the region. Sanskrit, Hinduism and European society gave women a lower position in sociality and imposed stronger regulations upon the freedom of women than did more traditional practices. While Hindu influence in the form of Sanscritisation, and the inclucation of western values during the colonial era had far reaching affects on the culture, they did not entirely replace pre-existing social hierarchies which gave women an important status (Saradomi 1996: 148). The social history of the region, which valued women in religions ritual, in professional status, and in providing personal freedoms continues to exert influence on modern day Kerala.

Marriage Rituals

Marriage rituals, particularly those of the dominant Nayar caste of Kerala have been extensively studied by anthropologists. While these ceremonies are no longer practiced, they have been well documented and widely interpreted, particularly due to the obvious differences in marriage patterns of the Nayars to the rest of South Asia as well as to the Namboodiri Brahmans of the region. Such rituals are strongly linked to the sexuality of the female participants, and illustrated cultural beliefs regarding sexuality.

The Nayars have three major marriage/rite of passage ceremonies which are related mainly to the female gender: the tali tying ceremony, the tirandukalyanam, and the sambandham rite. The tali tying rite took place before the onset of puberty. During this ceremony, the girl was married to a man, preferably a Namboodri Brahman, and ritual defloration took place. The ritual husband had no further duties to the girl after the completion of this ritual, although she had to observe a period of death impurity upon the death of her ritual husband. The tali ceremony was a female centered ritual which emphasised fertility and household prosperity. The tirandukalyanam ceremony was the puberty ceremony; during this ceremony femaleness is celebrated as women occupy the parts of the household typically inhabited by men. The third ritual the sambandham ritual is one in which men play a role, and while the tali tying is no longer in practice the sambandham continues to be important. The sambandham ritual is less auspicious than the tali, and puberty rites. This ritual marks the union of the bride and groom. The marriage, however, was not necessarily a permanent arrangement.

In his 1961 study of Nayar marriage rituals, Dumont positions this ritual within a pan-Indian context.. Dumont depicts the traditions as stemming from a basic Indian framework. He feels that the particular nature of the Nayar marriage ritual is primarily as a compliment to the severely orthodox practice of the Namboodri Brahmins. The purpose of the Sambandham marriages of the Nayars is to protect the caste purity and the strict rules of primogeniture within the Brahman caste. Dumont classifies three main types of marriage (1) primary, (2) legitimate secondary, 3) illegitimate secondary. Primary marriages are virgins' marriages, which are auspicious events. Secondary marriages, however, are less prestigious events. Dumont states that the tali tying right of the Nayar represents a primary marriage, whereas sambandham to the Nayars are secondary marriage. The Brahmins, however, view these marriages as a form of concubinage for the offspring do not possess inheritance rights. In this way, the Namboodri Brahmans can engage in sexual acts without jeopardizing their family property, and caste regulations.

This view, however, ignores the history of Kerala and caste development in this region. Before the influx of Hindus in 1000 AD women enjoyed a certain amount of sexual freedom in what is present day Kerala. Sanskrit speaking people entered the regions and many settled into communities of Brahmins, called gamma. It was at this time that the Brahmans and Hindu religion asserted considerable influence over the character of the region. It is likely that the practices of the Nayars stem from indigenous traditions with an origin that pre-dates the arrival of the Brahmins into Kerala. The strict orthodoxy and primogeniture of the Namboodri may have developed in this region due to the matrilineal practices of many castes groups. The tali tying ceremony and sambhadham marriage is not an outgrowth of Hindu systems, for the roots of this system pre-dated the arrival of Brahmins into the region. Yalman draws parallels between a Universal Hindu Pollution Concept and the tali tying ceremonies of the Nayar.

While his structural approach, provides insights into the cultural meanings of such ceremonies, Yalman emphasizes only one particular aspect of these rituals. In doing so, he reduces the multi-faceted meaning and manifestations of sexuality into a simple cultural construction relating primarily to the caste system and orthodox Hindu beliefs. Linking many cultural practices of Kerala to Hindu religious beliefs is problematic in Kerala due to the diversity of religions present in this region. Christianity is an important religion of the region, and yet Christian women observe pollution restriction in much the same way as those with Hindu affiliation. The purity/pollution dichotomy is present not only within Hindu castes of the region, but also in the Christian communities. In this way, sexuality and menstruation taboos cannot simply be construed as a Hindu phenomenon, but a more pervasive cultural construction. Conversely, if the purity/pollution dichotomy is universal in South Asian ideology, why did these rituals take place only in Kerala among certain castes?

These rituals are not simply ritual manifestations of a pan-Indian beliefs and ideology, but provide important insight into the way in which sexuality is constructed and ritualised in a manner specific to the Nayars of Kerala. Also demonstrated are cultural attitudes and opinions the sexual nature of the female gender.

The tali tying ceremony employs three main groups of symbols during the ritual: objects used by a married women for adornment symbolising a change of status, symbols of household prosperity and items linked with sexuality (Moore 1988:258). The importance of these symbols implies a correlation between the married state of the girl, household prosperity and sexuality. While, the other rituals focus on the girl as an individual, it is the relationship of the female to the prosperity of the household which is emphasised during this ritual. Bhagavati figured prominently in the celebration of the tali. She was the deity most commonly associated with the Nayar taravad or extended household, as household prosperity is linked with the presence of the Goddess. During the ceremony, the tali is carried to Bhagavati's temple, ritual acts are performed to bring Bhagavati to the taravad, and the girl is linked to objects which represent the goddess. The association of the girl with Bhagavti illustrates the relationship between the girl and household prosperity. The importance and presence of the goddess at the tali tying ritual emphasizes the importance of the girl to the continuation of household prosperity. The ritual is once again linked with household prosperity in its elaborate nature. The tali rite is an occasion to show off the wealth and prestige of the household. The ritual is not only performed for the benefit of the girl, but also has the socioeconomic function of demonstrating the economic power of the household. It is not only the prosperity of the girl that is sought during this ritual, but her prosperity is linked to the prosperity of the household as a whole.

Sexual Overtones

While there is a discernable link between prosperity, and the tali tying ceremony the importance of sexuality within this ritual has yet to be established. The ceremony certainly has sexual overtones embodied within the ritual defloration and marriage of the girl. What was yet to be distinguished is the link between the girl's sexuality and prosperity. Symbols of sexuality are employed such as an arrow, the tool of the god of love and a coconut flower. Also, the marriage ceremony is associated with the start of the agricultural calendar thereby creating a link between the ceremony and fertility. The collusion of these symbols links the sexuality and fertility of the girl to the prosperity of the household.

In light of this symbolic connection, the primary function of this ceremony is not so much to alleviate the threat of pollution through sexual contact, but to emphasize the importance of the girl's sexuality and fertility to the social status of the taravad. Caste status is not a static conditions but is constantly negotiated through a variety of mechanisms. One such mechanism is the hypergamous marriage in Kerala. This marriage arrangement allows women of the Nayar caste to marry men of a higher caste, thereby increasing their taravad and caste status. The hypergamous marriage to a Brahman is not a means to lessen the fear associated with the sexuality of the girl, but more likely a demonstration of her ability to increase the status of the taravad, through hypergamous unions and the bearing of children.

The Nayars construct female sexuality in the tali ceremony not as something that is threatening to the household, but as a source of power and increase. Another important ceremony for women in the Nayar caste was the tirandukalyanam ceremony, or the first menstruation ceremony. The purpose of this ceremony as an informant told Moore was to "let it be known that the girl is mature, so that good proposals will come." This ceremony gives more overt emphasis on the sexualised nature of the girl and well as stressing protection. The protection motif is most prominent during menstruation, when the girl is secluded in the house and measures are taken to ward off possession. The girl is initiated as a sexual being on the fourth-day during a ritual bath. During this ritual, vulgar songs relating to sexual intercourse are sung before the girl and her kinswomen.

This ritual also has a more communal meaning for the Nayars. During this ritual, a reversal occurs in which the women are given the portion of the household typically held by men, and women are permitted to eat before men at a feast. This reversal also takes place at birthday celebrations and is designed to give prominence and importance to the birthday person. In this situation, however, the celebration esteems not an individual but the female gender as a whole. Femaleness is celebrated and the solidarity of women is affirmed through participation in this ritual.

It is significant that women are given prominence during the celebration of a ritual that marks a girl as a sexualised being thereby creating another ritual correlation between female sexuality and female status. It is through the recognition of a woman's sexuality, and its subsequent importance to the household that women are afforded a place of esteem and the female gender is celebrated. Women's fertility and sexuality are a source of power for women in the Nayar caste, therefore, it follows that they would be given a special position during a ritual which initiates a woman as a sexual and fertile person. It is this power and importance that is recognised during the puberty ritual of the Nayars. The onset of the menstrual cycle is not simply a polluting but also an empowering event. It is a time of celebration, not only for the initiate but also for all women.

Accompanied by the importance of sexuality in this ritual, is vulnerability and the need for protection. This shows that while sexual initiation is a time for celebration, there is an element of fear within accompanying this ritual. While a woman's sexuality is a source of power, with increased power comes an increased capacity for destruction, therefore, during her first menstrual period, it follows that the initiate has the capacity to harm herself as well as her household.

Another meaning of this ritual is its position as a rite of passage ritual. During her menstrual period the girl is changing her status from to a woman able to engage in sexual relations. Until she takes the ritual bath she is outside the social order. She is not a child, but neither she is fully a sexualised woman. The girl inhabits a liminal area during this time and is therefore vulnerable to spirit possession and needs to be protected. The need for seclusion is not simply a fear of newly acquired procreative ability, but also the fear of a gray area which stands outside the definable social order.

A third important ritual is the marriage ritual or the sambadham which results in a union between the bride and the groom. This ritual is much less elaborate than the other two rituals. This relationship can occur between Nayars or between a Nayar woman and a man of the Brahman caste. While Brahman men can enter into relationships with Nayar women, women cannot form unions with a lower caste. These unions are rarely permanent and women are afforded a certain amount of autonomy in their choice of partners. These relationships can result from a mutual sense of attraction or through family arrangements which establish suitably matched partners.

Traditionally, women continue to live in their natal taravad, and children of the relationship belonged to the taravad of the mother. Through the establishment of sambadham relationships with higher caste partners, women have the ability to increase the status of their household. The symbolism of the sambadham ritual emphasizes pure eroticism rather than its connection to fertility and emergence as with the previous two rituals. In the sambadham ritual, sexuality is related to hospitality as the household accepts an outsider (Moore 1998:70). Female sexuality is therefore extremely important to the household for it ensures that the lineage will continue as well as connects the taravad to other powerful and influential families.

Female Sexuality

The marriage practices of the Namboodri Brahmans as well as the marriage practices in other areas of India vary a great deal from those of the Nayar in their treatment of female sexuality. Placing these rituals in a pan-Indian context ignores the obvious discrepancies in the construction of sexuality and the position of women with regards to sexual unions and control of their bodies.

Women in the Namboordri Brahman caste of Kerala experience different marriage traditions and possess different sexual meanings in association with these traditions. Only the eldest son of the Brahmans is permitted to marry, and he must marry another Brahman. This rule creates an excess of marriageable women, but few men eligible for marriage. Due to this rule large dowries are expected of the bride's family in order to secure a good marriage. It is considered quite bad to have many unmarried women in the house past the age of puberty for fear of their sexuality, but marriage is difficult and expensive to secure. Due to these marriage practices daughters become more of a burden upon the economic resources of the household than a source of power and social status.

Little good comes from the sexuality of Brahman women, and therefore it is something to be repressed and strictly controlled. If a woman who is not married has sexual liaisons with a man, or worse with a lower caste man, this has negative repercussions on the entire household. For this reason, women are given little autonomy and are strictly confined to the women's quarters of the household. The need for a significant dowry means that many women were never married and spent a lifetime as isolated virgins. Younger sons of the Namboodri are permitted to form sambadham unions with Nayar women, because thesewomen did not claim membership and resources of the household. These relationships also served to form alliances with strong Nayar households.

The marriage patterns of the Namboordri produce different attitudes regarding the women's sexuality. A daughter is not a source of power, but an economic burden upon the resources of the family. Her sexuality has the potential of creating disaster for the family, with little chance of bringing benefit to the family, therefore it is something to be controlled and repressed. Conversely, although the Nayar women have the capacity to bring trouble to the household through frustrated sexuality, but they can also use their sexual nature to form important alliances, have children, and increase the status and prosperity of the household. The Namboodri are believed to be decendants of the first Sanskrit speaking peoples to inhabit Kerala, therefore, their customs exhibit less connection to more ancient Keralan traditions.

Central and Northern India traditions form marriage patterns that more closely resemble the Namboodri Brahmans than the Nayars of Kerala. Unlike the Namboodri, however, all sons and daughters typically marry. While all sons are permitted to marry, hypergamous relationships as performed in Kerala are not permissible within other South Asian traditions, so daughters can rarely increase the status of her natal family. In Central and Northern India, a large dowry must be paid to the groom's family as compensation for the extra burden of another mouth. Marriages are arranged by families, with little chance of a marriage arrangement based upon mutual affection, as is permitted for the Nayar.

A woman's sexuality autonomy is strictly limited, for she does not choose her marriage partner. After marriage, high caste Brahman women and other high caste women are placed in "purdah" or seclusion which limits not only their sexual autonomy, but also their personal autonomy.

The marriage ceremony does not take place in three separate rituals, but is performed all at once. Instead of connecting the girl's sexuality to the home, through the acceptance of a male outsider into the taravad, Northern traditions emphasise the girl's membership into a new family. Upon arrival at her new home, the girl is tied to the groom, and then placed on a mat in the middle of the courtyard, where the female kin of the groom lift her veil and judge the girl's beauty. Such traditions emphasise the groom's family and their control and ownership of the bride as opposed to rituals of the Nayar which venerate the bride.

The girl's ability to engage in sexual relations is regulated by the husband's mother-in-law. She can keep a new bride and groom apart, and not allow them to sleep together thereby controlling the relationship. While Nayar women remain relatively free with regard to their sexual relations, as they are permitted to choose their partners and their behaviour is not so strictly regulated, the same does not hold true for other regions of India. Their sexual autonomy is strictly regulated through familial marriage arrangements, *purdah* restrictions, and the dictates of their mother-in-law. The large dowry requirement insures that instead of being a means for the family to achieve a higher status and form important family links, daughters are perceived as a financial burden to their natal family rather than a benefit.

Matriliny

It is well known that many castes of Kerala are matrilineal, in that they trace descent through the mother's line as opposed to the father. This stands in contrast to the Namboodri Brahmans of Kerala as well as the strict patriarchy and patriliny of Northern and Central India. Matrilineal systems and matrilocal systems in particular generally have a positive affect upon the status of women. In matrilineal systems, daughters are necessary to maintain the family lineage; therefore daughters and women are an important part of the household. This contrasts with the strict patriliny and patrilocality of other regions. Daughters are only a temporary member of their natal household, and upon marriage they join the groom's family. This means that they are never fully integrated into either household. They are considered visitors and alien in the home of their groom, but they are also no longer a member of the natal family. This relationship diminishes the voice that women have and the chance of exerting their own autonomy. Along with the favourable position of women in matrilineal societies in South Asia comes an increased sexual autonomy. The sexuality of women is less regulated by men and the interests of the male householders in matrilineal societies than in patriliny. Female sexuality poses less of a threat to matrilineal systems with more relaxed marriage bonds than a strict patriliny in which female sexual indiscretions can threaten the stability of the lineage.

Food and Sexuality

Throughout South Asia, people's relationship with food is continuously used as a metaphor for sexual meanings. However, the meanings about sexuality that are constructed are different in Kerala than in other regions of India. In the Christian fishing village of Marianad, men and women eat together as an important statement of equality. During a domestic dispute, the worst threat that a husband can direct toward his wife is refusal to eat with her. In Northern India, a husband will not eat with his wife for fear of being polluted by a mixing of fluids. The wife is expected to consume the leftovers of the husband.

In Marianad, men and women eat off the same plate and do not harbour fears about food pollution. Such variations in eating practices correspond to variations in how the sexual act is viewed and interpreted in Marianad as opposed to other regions of Kerala. Men and women are viewed as being of one body, each an oppositely gendered part of a whole. Men and women are believed to be complimentary aspects of a larger whole body. Although men are viewed as possessing stronger sexual desire than women, the sexual union is a union of merger and equal exchange between men and women. If the sexual act is viewed as an equal relationship and pollutions does not result from this equal exchange, then a wife cannot pollute a husband through an exchange of fluids during intercourse. The higher status of men is not expressed through the sexual act or through eating separately during the dinner hours in the fishing village of Kerala. The closeness of husband and wife, shown through their sharing of food and sex is expressed through the notion that they are "one body".

Food as a sexual metaphor exists strongly in other regions of Indian. Food is considered to be permeated with the substances of those who have cooked handled and eaten them. Therefore, people are very careful about whose food they eat and whose substances they digest. Women eat men's leftovers, but men would never touch the food of women. The sexual identity of women is constructed in part through her relationship to food as well as intercourse. Women are thought to possess a stong digestive capacity than men, resulting in their ability to digest more food as well as more sexual activity than men. Intercourse is not perceived as an equal exchange but as women absorbing or digesting the fluids of the man. As exchange of fluids does not occur during the sexual act, exchanging fluids during meals could be seen as problematic for the man, but not the woman who "digests" semen during sexual intercourse.

There is a strong connection between food and sexual meanings, as such the relationships of men and women to food correlates to views of the relationship of men and women during intercourse. In Marianod, intercourse is perceived as a means of equal exchange and merger into one body, similarly there is not an eating hierarchy between men and women. Husbands and wives eat the same food as an expression of their equal and complimentary nature. This stands in contrast to the Northern Indian view of food in which a man can never consume food that contains the substances of his wife, for this would be dangerous and polluting. Similarly during intercourse, there is not an exchange of bodily substance, but women digest the substance from the man, creating an unequal sexual relationship as well as an unequal relationship in eating patterns.

Expressions of Sexuality in Folklore

According to Ann Gold "folk performances instil as well as articulate cultural values". Through hearing and understanding the oral folklore of South Asia it is possible to make assumptions regarding the cultural values of the society. Such performances teach listeners the "right" way to behave, lessons which they internalise into their cultural schema. Similarly, through their construction and presentation these oral epics also reflect important values of the people. While there is a generic version of the tale, an important facet of oral folklore lies in the emphasis and the nuances of the performance. *The Ramayana* is an oral epic that is preformed throughout India exhibiting a certain amount of regional variation. This epic is performed as a shadow puppet theater in hundreds of goddess temples in Kerala. The women in the performance are presented differently in Kerala than in other versions of the story.

Rama in the Keralese performance is not the epitome of male virtue, but has human qualities which make him susceptible to evil. In the story, Rama's brother Laskmama accidentally kills an innocent demon. Surpanakha, the demon's mother, goes looking for her son and finds him dead. In the traditional creation of the story, she is portrayed as a danger ready to strike out against the innocent Rama. However, in the puppet theater she is portrayed as an unfortunate victim of Rama. Supanadkha in the Keralese Theater is portrayed as a demon devotee of the goddess Lakshmi, not an evil incarnate. When she spies Rama, Lakshmi transforms her into a irresistible beautiful woman, and Rama lusts for her. In the Keralese version, Rama, instead of laughing at the woman, is attracted by her charm and feminine beauty. Her beauty and sexuality give her power to use against the God. Despite his might and virtue, he is temporarily dissuaded from his purpose by the mere sight of a beautiful woman.

In a later verse, Supanadkha defends her sexuality and feelings of lust. When Rama condemns her as shameless, instead of being insulted she rises to her own defense against him. She says that she is driven by the God Kamadeva, and to not fulfil her desire would bring pain. Love and desire is not an evil but a neutral force. Love and lust are considered necessary and should not be eliminated. They should be moderated but not denied. Sexuality in this sense is not perceived as something sin and shameful, but as an essential life force. The Keralese performance departs from other tales of the Ramayana in that it is not the demon's sexuality that threatens Rama, but Rama's own vulnerability that make him susceptible to her arguments. She is not a evil force, but a neutral one, and it is Rama's own moral fallibility which causes his attraction to her, not her bad character.

Lust and Sexuality

This tale shows us that sexuality and lust are not viewed as a subversive element in Keralese literature, but as a natural and neutral force. While lust and sexuality of women in excess is a bad thing, in moderation it is part of life's balance. This stands in contrast to other versions of the epic in which lust is a quality of demons which is designed to subvert Rama from his purpose, and is a feeling that ought to be repressed. The contrast in the portrayal of lust and sexuality in these two epics reflect different cultural patterns regarding the acceptability of lust and sexuality. In the Keralese version female sexuality in acceptable and a necessary part of life whereas, in Northern epic performances it is dangerous and ought to be repressed.

Conclusion

Gender constructions in India are not uniform, but show vast regional variation. Academic work which does not consider the regional differences based upon the unique history, geography and cultural patterns of the region, creates inaccurate conceptions of gender within the nation of India. The region of Kerala exhibits different patterns of gender meaning and constructions from the Hindu regions of the north. The history of the region is Dravidian, therefore many beliefs regarding the status of women are derived from eras previous to the influx of Sanskrit culture into the region. Marriage rituals in Kerala show a positive symbolic link between household prosperity and female sexuality. Similarly, these rituals are designed to elevate the female gender rather than subordinate them to their male counterparts. Matrilineal, and Matrilocal patterns provide women with a greater amount of control of their circumstances and autonomy than in more northern reaches of the nation.

Eating practices in portions of Kerala embody values about the relationship between men and women. Male/ female sexual relationships are regard as relationships of exchange which places women on a more equal footing with men, as contrary to northern India in which the sexual act is not a relationship of exchange, but of women absorbing male substance. Such conceptions of sexuality are also manifested as variations in eating practices throughout the different regions of India. Similarly folklore, like the epic *Ramayana*, is told throughout India. The telling of the story, however, embodies the different values of the regions of India.

In the Keralese version of the *Ramayana*, women and sexuality are constructed in a much more positive manner than in the more northern reaches of the nation. The status of women and their relationship to sexuality has developed differently in Kerela creating a different experience for women of this region, than other Indian regions.

Kerala is currently undergoing the process of Sanskritisation, and is increasingly subscribing to Hindu goals. Similarly, economic changes have decreased the importance of the taravad and increased the growth of nuclear households as the economic unit. These changes alter the position of women within Keralese society. Sankritisation places women in a position more in accordance with the prevailing system of Northern India, and the growth of the nuclear family undermines the position of women within the taravad. Despite these changes women in Kerala continue to have a higher literacy rate and life expectancy than elsewhere in India. The meaning of gender and the position of women continues to vary from that of Northern and Central India.

In order to create a true picture of how sexuality becomes integrated into the meaning of gender within Kerala, intensive fieldwork should be undertaken in this region. Such fieldwork should not stem from pre-existing theories regarding and notions about gender and sexuality in other regions of India, but should treat Kerala as a separate entity with its own unique history and gender meanings. As such studies of gender in Kerala should not attempt to fit its unique character into a readymade framework by emphasising only the similarities between gender in Kerala and other regions of India, but should take into account the wide ranging differences.

NOTES AND REFERENCES

Blackburn, Stuart. "Hanging in the Balance: Rama in the Shadow Puppet Theater Kerala. " *Gender Genre and Power in South Asian Expressive Traditions.* Philadelphia:University of Pennsylvania Press 1991. Busby, Cecilia. "Agency, Power, and Personhood." *Critique of Anthropology.* 19 (1999) 227-248.

Dempsey, Corinne. *Kerala Christian Sainthood: Collisons of Culture and Worldview in South India.* Oxford:Oxford University Press 2001.

Den Uyl, Marion. "Kinship and Gender Identity: Some Notes on Marumakkathayam in Kerala." Culture, Creation and Procreation: Concepts of Kinship in South Asian Practive. New York: Berghahn Books 2000.

Dirks, Nicholas. "Homo Hierarchies: Origins of an Idea." Castes of Mind. Princeton: Princeton University Press 2001.

Dube, Leela. "Negotiating Patriliny: Intra-household Consumption and Authority in Northwest India." Shifting Circles of Support: Contexualising Gender and Kinship in South Asia and Sub-Saharan Africa. Walnut Creek: Altat Mira Press, 1996.

Dumont, Louise. *Affinity as Value:Marriage Alliance in South India With Comparative Essays on Australia.* Chicago: University of Chicago Press, 1983.

Goldberg, Helen and Joan Mencher. Kinship and Marriage Regulations Among the Namboodiri Brhamans of Kerala. *Man* 2 (1967), 87-106.

Gold, Anne. "Gender and Illustion in a Rajasthani Yogic Tradition." *Gender, Genre, and Power in South Asian Expressive Traditions.* Philadelphia: University of Pennsylvania Press, 1991.

Gough, E. Katherine. "Female Initiation Rites on the Malabar Coast." *The Journal of the Royal Anthropological Institute of Great Britain and Ireland* 85 (1955:45-80).

Lamb, Sarah. *White Sari's and Sweet Mangoes.* Berkeley: University of California Press 2000.

Marriot, McKim. "Constructing an Indian Ethnosociology." *India Through Hindu Categories.* New Delhi:Sage Publications 1990.

Menon, Sreedhara. *Social and Cultural History of Kerala.* New Delhi: Sterling 1979.

Moore, Melinda. "New Look at the Nayar Taravad." *Man* 20 (1985) 523-41.

Moore, Melinda. "Symbol and Meaning in Nayar Marriage Ritual." *American Ethnologist.* 15 (1998) 254-73.

Mukhopadhyay, Carol and Patricia Higgins. "Anthropological Studies of Women's Status Revistited: 1977-1987." *Annual Review of Anthropology.* 17 (1988) 461-95

Saradomi, K. "Women's Rights and the Decline of Matriliny in Southern India." *Shifting Circles of Support. Contexualising Gender and Kinship in South Asia And Sub-Saharan Africa.* Walnut Creek: Alta Mira Press 1996.

Wadley, Susan. *Struggling With Destiny in Karmipur.* Berkeley:University of California Press 1994.

Yalman, Nur. "On the Purity of Women in the Castes of Ceylon and Malabar." *The Journal of the Royal Anthropologica Institute of Great Britain and Ireland.* 93 (1963) 22-58.

BIBLIOGRAPHY

Agarwal, Gita, 1994. *A Field of One's Own: Gender and Land Rights in South Asia.* Cambridge UK: Cambridge University Press.

Anand, Anita, & Gouri Salvi, eds., 1998. *Beijing: UN Fourth Conference on Women.* New Delhi: Systems Vision for Women's Feature Service.

Angeles, Leonora C. & Rebecca Tarbotton, 2001. "Local transformation through global connection: Women's assets and environmental activism for sustainable agriculture in Lahakh, India." *Women's Studies Quarterly,* special issues on Earthwork" Women and Environments, 29/1&2: 99-115.

Bari, Farzana & Saba Gul Khattak, 2001. "Power configurations in public and private arenas: the women's movement's response," in *Power and Civil Society in Pakistan,* Anita M. Weiss & S. Zulfiqar Gilani, editors. NY: Oxford U. Press. pp. 217-247

Basu, Amrita (ed.), 1995, in Amrita Basu with Elizabeth McGrory, *The Challenge of Local Feminisms.* Boulder, CO: Westview.

Chen, Martha Alter, 1983. *A Quiet Revolution: women in transition in rural Bangladesh.* Cambridge MA: Schenkman Publishing Co.

Crook, Isabel, Lu Dongxiao, Lisa Stearns, 1995. "A conversation with Wu Qing," in *A Rising Public Voice: Women in Politics Worldwide,* Alida Brill (ed.). NY: Feminist Press. pp 41-57.

Currie-Namgyal, Anne, 1999. Preliminary gender study for the World Food Programme in Bhutan. Thimphu, Bhutan, September.

Das Gupta, Monica, & Li Shuzhou, "Gender bias in China, South Korea, and India 1920-1990: effects of war, famine, and fertility decline," in Razavi 2000: 205-38.

Devadas, Rajammal P., 1999. "Role and participation of women in panchayats" in *Role of Democratic Decentralization (Panchayati Raj) in TSP [Tribal Sub Plan] Areas by* Bhupinder Singh & Neeti Mahanti, eds., 1999. New Delhi: InterIndia Publications, Tribal Series of India Series, 187.

Edwards, Louise, 2000. "Women in the People's Republic of China: new challenges to the grand gender narrative." In Edwards and Roces: 59-84.

Edwards, Louise, & Mina Roces, eds., 2000. *Women in Asia: Tradition, Modernity and Globalisation.* Ann Arbor: U. of Michigan Press.

Florini, Ann H. (ed.) 2000. *The Third Force: the Rise of Transnational Civil Society.* Washington, DC: Carnegie Endowment for International Peace.

Fraser, Arvonne & Irene Tinker, editors, forthcoming. *Networking for Change: Women and International Development.* New York: Feminist Press.

Ganguly-Scrase, Ruchira, 2000. "Diversity and the status of women: the Indian experience," in *Women in Asia: Tradition, Modernity and Globalisation,* Louise Edwards and Mina Roces, editors. Ann Arbor: U. of Michigan Press. pp. 85-111.

Hampson, Sasha. 2000. "Rhetoric or reality?: contesting definitions of women in Korea," in Edwards & Roces: 170-186.

Ibrahim, Ruslam (ed.) 1996. *The Indonesian NGO Agenda: Toward the Year 2000.* Jakarta: LP3ES press.

Ireson, Carol, 1996. *Field, Forest, and Family: Women's Work and Power in Rural Laos.* Boulder CO: Westview.

Jahan, Roushan,1995. "Men in seclusion, women in public: Rokeya's dream and women's struggles in Bangladesh," in Amrita Basu with Elizabeth McGrory, *The Challenge of Local Feminisms.* Boulder, CO: Westview. pp. 87-109.

Jain, Devaki, 1995. "Healing the wounds of development," in *The Politics of Women's Education: Perspectives from Asia, Africa, and Latin America,* Jill Conway and Susan Bourque, editors. Ann Arbor: U. of Michigan Press. pp. 45-58.

—, 1980. *Women's Quest for Power.* New Delhi: Vikas.

Jaquette, Jane. 1997. "Women in power: from tokenism to critical mass," in *Foreign Policy* # 108: 23-37.

Jayawardena, Kumari, 1995. *The White Woman's Other Burden.* London: Routledge.

—, 1986. *Feminism and Nationalism in the Third World.*

Kabeer, Naila, 1994. *Reversed Realities: Gender Hierarchies in Development Thought.* London: Verso.

Lazo, Lucita, 1996. "Women's empowerment in the making: the Philippine bid for social protection," in *Homeworkers in Global Perspective: invisible no more,* Eileen Boris & Elizabeth Prugl, eds. London: Routledge. pp. 259-271.

Lee, In-ho. 1995. "Work, education, and women's gains: the Korean experience," in *The Politics of Women's Education: Perspectives from Asia, Africa, and Latin America,* Jill Conway and Susan Bourque, editors. Ann Arbor: U. of Michigan Press. pp. 77-104.

Li, Xiaorong, 1995, "Gender inequality in China and the Cultural revolution," in Nussbaum and Glover. pp. 407-25.

Loutfi, Martha Fetherolf (ed.) 2001. *Women, Gender and Work: What is Equality and How do we get it?* Geneva: ILO.

Molyneux, Maxine. 1985. "Mobilization without emancipation? Women's interest, state and revolution in Nicaragua," *Feminist Studies* 11/2: 227-54.

Moser, Caroline O. N., 1993. *Gender Planning and Development: Theory, Practice and Training.* London: Routledge.

Nussbaum, Martha & Jonathan Glover, eds. 1995. *Women, Culture and Development: A Study of Human Capabilities.* New York: Oxford University, Press.

Oey-Gardiner, Mayling, & Carla Bianpoen, editors, 2000. *Indonesian Women: the journey continues.* Canberra: Australian National University.

Pongsapich, Amara, & Nitaya Kataleeradabhan, 1994. *Philanthropy, NGO Activities, and Corporate Funding in Thailand.* Bangkok: Chulalongkorn University Social Research Institute.

Renken, Lynn, 2001. "Microfinance in Pakistan: perpetuation of power or a viable avenue for empowerment?" in *Power and Civil Society in Pakistan,* Anita M. Weiss & S. Zulfiqar Gilani, editors. New York: Oxford University. Press. pp. 248-76.

Razavi, Shahra, 2000. "Women in Contemporary Democratization, " Occasional paper 4. Geneva: United Nations Research Institution for Social Development (UNRISD).

__, editor, 2000. *Gendered Poverty and Well-being.* Oxford: Blackwell Publishers.

Robinson, Kathryn, 2001. "Gender equity and the transition to democracy in Indonesia." Talk at the Indonesian-American Society, Washington, DC. December 7.

__, 2000. "Indonesian women: form *Orde Baru* to *Reformasi,"* in Edwards & Roces: 139-169.

Roces, Mina, 2000. "Negotiating modernities: Filipino women 190-2000," in Edwards & Roces: 12-138.

Samarasinghe, Vidyamali, 1993. "The last frontier or a new beginning? Women's microenterprises in Sri Lanka," in *Women at the Center: Development issues and practices for the 1990s.* W. Hartford, CN: Kumarian Press.

Santiago, Lilia Quindoza, 1995. " Rebirthing Babaye: the women's movement in the Philippines," in Amrita Basu with Elizabeth McGrory, *The Challenge of Local Feminisms,* Boulder, CO: Westview. pp. 110-28.

Sen, Amartya, 1999. *Development as Freedom.* New York: Anchor Books.

Shiva, Vandana, 2001. "Golden rise and neem: biopatents and the appropriation of women's environmental knowledge," *Women's Studies Quarterly,* special issues on Earthwork" *Women and Environments,* 29/172:12-23.

Silliman, G. Sidney & Lela G. Noble, 1997. *Non-Governmental Organizations in the Philippines: Civil Society and the State.* Honolulu:U of Hawaii Press.

Sizoo, Edith (ed.) 1997. *Women's Lifeworlds: women's narratives on shapting their realities.* London, Routledge.

Sreenivasan, Jyotsna. 2000. *Ela Bhatt, Uniting Women in India.* Feminist Press, NYC.

—, 1980. "Toward Equity for Women in Korea's Development Plans," prepared for the World Bank and published in Korean, Social Science and Policy Research, 2/2.

Tinker, Irene (ed.) 1990. *Persistent Inequalities: Women and World Development.* New York: Oxford University Press.

Tinker, Irene, & Jane Jaquette, 1986. "UN Decade for Women: its impact and legacy." *World Development* 15/3: 419-427.

Tinker, Irene, & Gale Summerfield, eds. 1999. *Women's Rights to House and Land: China, Laos, Vietnam.* Boulder CO: Lynne Rienner.

Todd, Helen. 1996. *Women at the Center: Grameen Bank Borrowers After One Decade.* Boulder CO: Westview.

Torres, Amaryllis Tiglao, 1995. "Women's education as an instrument for change: the case of the Philippines," in *The Politics of Women's Education: Perspectives from Asia, Africa, and Latin America,* Jill Conway and Susan Bourque, editors. Ann Arbor: U. of Michigan Press. pp. 103-19.

UN 2000. *Human Development Report, 2000.* NYC: UNDP.

Under, Esta, 2000. "Re-gendering Vietnam: from militant to market socialism," in Edwards & Roces: 291-317.

Verghese, Jamila, 1997. *Her Gold and Her Body.* New Delhi: Vikas. Revised edition.

Walker, Millidge, 1996. "Non-governmental Organizations in a Corporate State: The Case of Indonesia." Berkeley, CA: Institute for Urban and Regional Development Working Paper # 678.

Weiss, Anita M., & Farzana Bari, 2002. "Struggling for a Political Voice: Women Contesting the System in Pakistan." Paper presented at the Annual Meeting of the Association of Asian Studies, Washington, D€, 4 April.

Weiss, Anita M. & S. Zulfiqar Gilani (eds.) 2001. *Power and Civil Society in Pakistan.* New York: Oxford University Press.

Weiss, Anita, 2002. "Engendering development, engendering rights: women and public space in the Islamic Republic of Pakistan."

Presented on a panel "Ideology, cultural politics, and development" at a conference on *Pakistan " Islam and Civil Society at the Dawn of the 21st Century.* American University, Washington, DC., 8 April, 2002.

—, 1997. "Women, civil society, and politics in Pakistan," discussion paper presented at University of California, Berkeley, November 1997.

—, 1996. "Within the walls: home-based work in Lahore," *Homeworkers in Global Perspective: invisible no more,* Eileen Boris & Elizabeth Prugl, eds. London: Routledge. pp. 81-92.

Wolf, Diane, 1992. *Factory daughters: gender, household dynamics, and rural industrialization in Java.* Berkeley, CA: University of California Press.

INDEX

T

U

V

W

Y